READING HEGEL

READING HEGEL
the introductions

G. W. F. Hegel

Edited and Introduced by
Aakash Singh and Rimina Mohapatra

re.press Melbourne 2008

re.press

PO Box 75, Seddon, 3011, Melbourne, Australia
http://www.re-press.org
© re.press 2008

This work is 'Open Access', published under a creative commons license which means that you are free to copy, distribute, display, and perform the work as long as you clearly attribute the work to the authors, that you do not use this work for any commercial gain in any form whatsoever and that you in no way alter, transform or build on the work outside of its use in normal academic scholarship without express permission of the author (or their executors) *and* the publisher of this volume. For any reuse or distribution, you must make clear to others the license terms of this work. For more information see the details of the creative commons licence at this website:
http://creativecommons.org/licenses/by-nc-nd/2.5/

British Library Cataloguing-in-Publication Data
A catalogue record for this book is available from the British Library

Library of Congress Cataloguing-in-Publication Data
A catalogue record for this book is available from the Library of Congress

National Library of Australia Cataloguing-in-Publication Data
Author: Hegel, Georg Wilhelm Friedrich, 1770-1831.
Title: Reading Hegel : Hegel's introductions / G. W. F. Hegel;
            editor Aakash Singh, Rimina Mohapatra.
ISBN: 9780980544015 (pbk.)
Notes: Includes index.
            Bibliography.
Subjects: Hegel, Georg Wilhelm Friedrich, 1770-1831.
            Philosophy.
Other Authors/Contributors:
            Singh, Aakash.
            Mohapatra, Rimina.

Dewey Number: 193

Designed and Typeset by *A&R*

This book is produced sustainably using plantation timber, and printed in the destination market reducing wastage and excess transport.

CONTENTS

The Texts *page* vii

EDITORS' INTRODUCTION   1

The Circle of Knowledge - 3; The Concretion of Knowledge - 5; The Phenomenology of Spirit - 8; The Science of Logic - 8; The Philosophy of Right - 10; The Philosophy of History - 11; The Philosophy of Fine Art - 12; The Philosophy of Religion - 15; The History of Philosophy - 17; Closing the Circle - 17; References - 19

PHENOMENOLOGY OF SPIRIT   21

Preface: On Scientific Knowledge - 23; The Element of Truth is the Concept/Notion (*Begriff*), And its True Form, the Scientific System - 25; Present Position of the Spirit - 26; The Principle is not the Completion; Against Formalism - 28; The Absolute is Subject, and What this is - 29; The Element of Knowledge - 33; The Ascent into this is the Phenomenology of Spirit - 34; The Transformation of the Familiar into Thought - 35; Transformation into the Concept - 37; In What Way the Phenomenology of the Spirit is Negative - 39; Historical and Mathematical Truth - 40; The Nature of Philosophical Truth and its Method - 42; Against Schematizing Formalism - 43; The Demands of the Study of Philosophy - 46; Argumentative Thinking in its Negative Attitude - 47; In its Positive Attitude; its Subject - 47

SCIENCE OF LOGIC   53

Preface to the First Edition - 55; Preface to the Second Edition - 58; Introduction: General Concept of Logic - 67; General Classification of Logic - 80

PHILOSOPHY OF RIGHT   85

Preface - 87; Introduction - 89

PHILOSOPHY OF HISTORY   111

Introduction - 113; Original History - 113; Reflective History - 114; Philosophical History - 116; Reason Governs the World - 117; Essential Destiny of Reason - 120; The Course of the World's History - 142

PHILOSOPHY OF FINE ART   155

The Limits of Aesthetics - 157; Aesthetics Confined to Beauty of Art - 157; Is Art Unworthy of Scientific Consideration? - 158; Scientific Methods which Apply to the Beautiful and Art - 165; The Empirical Method - 165; Abstract Reflection - 166; The Philosophical Idea of Artistic Beauty - 166;

The Notion of the Beauty of Art - 167; The Art-Work is a Creation of Human Activity - 167; The Art-Work is Addressed to Human Sense - 172; The End or Interest of Art - 178

PHILOSOPHY OF RELIGION — 191

Preliminary - 193; The Severance of Religion from the Free, Worldly Consciousness - 195; The Position of the Philosophy of Religion Relatively to Philosophy and to Religion - 199; Division of the Subject - 206

HISTORY OF PHILOSOPHY — 221

Introduction - 223; The Notion of the History of Philosophy - 225; The Relation of Philosophy to Other Departments of Knowledge - 229; Relation of Philosophy to Religion - 232; Commencement of Philosophy and of Its History - 236; Division of the History of Philosophy - 240

THE END OF INTRODUCTIONS — 247

The End of Introductions - 249; The Phenomenology of Spirit - 250; The Science of Logic - 251; The Philosophy of Right - 253; The Philosophy of History - 254; The Philosophy of Fine Art - 254; The Philosophy of Religion - 255; The History of Philosophy - 256; Conclusion - 257; Further Readings - 257

INDEX — 261

THE TEXTS

Although the translations used in this volume are no longer under copyright and now in the public domain, the editors would like to gratefully acknowledge both the translators and their publishers for the texts that have served as our sources. The present work would not have been possible without them.

All the texts, however, have been slightly altered from the sources: not only have the translations each been modified in part, but also the texts have been abridged for readability and concision. A word on our method of abridgement: we essentially strove to produce a reader-friendly text, one that novices to Hegel could ease into without feeling intimidated; in this effort, we not only excluded what was obviously excludable, such as long digressions or internal repetitions, but also excised text if the idea or argument expressed in a certain chapter had been articulated in another chapter elsewhere in the book. Thus, with the exception of the final chapter (from *The History of Philosophy*), Hegel's recycling of the same examples and metaphors has been curtailed herein. The final chapter, however, weaves together so many threads and themes from all the earlier chapters that it was thought best to permit Hegel to revive all his previously employed images and arguments, such that the overall systematic nature of Hegel's thought would be adequately conveyed. For those who seek the complete, unaltered translations of Hegel's writings, the editors would advert to the following originals:

Phenomenology of Spirit, trans. J. B. Baillie, New York, Macmillan, 1910.
Hegel's Science of Logic, trans. W. H. Johnston and L. G. Struthers, vol. 1, 2 vols. London, George Allen & Unwin, 1929.
Philosophy of Right, trans. S. W. Dyde [1896], New York, Dover, 2005.
Philosophy of History, trans. J. Sibree [1857], New York, Dover, 1956.
The Philosophy of Fine Art, trans. F. P. B. Osmaston, vol. 1, 4 vols., London, G. Bell and Sons, 1920.
Lectures on the Philosophy of Religion, trans. E. B. Speirs and J. B. Sanderson, vol. 1, 3 vols., London, Routledge and Kegan Paul, 1895.
Hegel's Lectures on the History of Philosophy, trans. E. S. Haldane, vol. 1, 3 vols., London, Routledge and Kegan Paul, 1892.

EDITORS' INTRODUCTION

'The life of the ever present Spirit is a circle of progressive embodiments, which looked at in one respect still exist beside each other, and only as looked at from another point of view appear as past'.

THE CIRCLE OF KNOWLEDGE

THE CIRCLE OF KNOWLEDGE

The present collection consists of a string of different 'Introductions' that Hegel wrote for each of his major works, beginning with the famous (and infamous) Preface to his *Phenomenology of Spirit*, which celebrated its second centenary in 2007 (it first appeared in 1807, when Hegel was 37 years old).

After 200 years of thought profoundly influenced by Hegel's *magnum opus*, we seek through these Introductions to cast a fresh look at the sheer creative insight and philosophical brilliance of one of the rather distantly understood great philosophers of modern times. In a crucial sense, his Introductions, seen together in this way, offer a panoramic overview of his grand system, of his conception of philosophy and of his endeavour to bring out an ingenious re-interpretation of many of the classical philosophical ideas. This study, at the same time, foreshadows many popular themes that one associates with contemporary accounts, social narratives and discourses of history, aesthetics, culture and politics.

Hegel's impact on Karl Marx is already well-known and often critically discussed. Through the texts that follow, the reader will become equally aware of the enormous influence that Hegel had on all subsequent European reflection, from Edmund Husserl, Martin Heidegger, Alexandre Kojève, Jean-Paul Sartre and Jacques Lacan to Max Weber, Walter Benjamin, Theodore Adorno and Jürgen Habermas, and indeed, even well beyond Europe, from Japan's great Kyoto-school philosophers like Nishida, America's nemesis of pragmatism Josiah Royce, and an entire neo-Hegelian movement in Britain (R. G. Collingwood is an eminent figure) that in its turn influenced a generation of thought throughout the commonwealth and beyond.

In order that the reader may become cognizant of the full range of Hegel's influence, we have chosen and abridged a representative selection of Hegel's works treating of a wide variety of disciplines, including philosophy, history, art, and religious studies. Our sources include: the *Phenomenology of Spirit*, the *Science of Logic*, the *Philosophy of Right*, the *Philosophy of History*, the *Philosophy of Fine Art*, the *Philosophy of Religion*, and the *History of Philosophy*.

We have specifically chosen the Introductions since they are the most accessible of Hegel's works, and because they lay out the Hegelian project in a concise fashion. This book, therefore, will allow the reader to comprehend the whole of the Hegelian System as it is built up from the parts within it, without having to try to locate and gather together his numerous works or the even greater burden of struggling to fathom their depths in their entirety.

Offering a critical summary of his works, Hegel's Introductions stand complete in themselves, each capturing a logical facet of Hegel's overarching notion of truth. At the same time, seen all together, they present the inter-linkages in Hegel's thought, the dialectical progression of one work to another, one philosophical moment to another. Before moving on to understand Hegel's dialectical System, let us look briefly at the man himself to gain insight into some of the motivations behind his writings.

G. W. F. Hegel was born into a vibrant and rapidly changing Europe at the end of the eighteenth century, with news of the American Revolution igniting people's minds, and the effects of the French Revolution motivating people's deeds. Napoleon would soon spread the ideals of the Revolution through conquest, and indeed, his forces took Hegel's city of Jena just when Hegel had finished writing his *Phenomenology of Spirit*.

In the German areas, the arts and letters were thriving: Beethoven was composing his great Symphonies (his *Ninth* often compared with Hegel's *Phenomenology*), Goethe was composing his masterpiece *Faust* (to which, again, Hegel's *Phenomenology* is often compared), and the effects of Kant's *Critiques* were still reverberating from Prussia throughout the world. Amidst this inspiring cultural milieu, Berlin—where Hegel would ultimately settle—was being developed into a veritable Athens on the Spree (the main river in Berlin), where the vision of the Enlightenment would find concrete expression in the classicist architecture and sculpture adorning the pompous boulevards that Hegel would perambulate daily.

Synthetic thoughts seemed to reign supreme among the 'globalized' intellectuals of the time, whether in their political manifestation as socialism, their aesthetic manifestation as romanticism, their philological manifestation as the search for an *Ursprache* or proto-Indo-European language ultimately linking all great civilizations at a unified cradle or source, or their philosophical manifestation as a quest for absolute knowledge with not merely a universally valid force, but indeed, a universally comprehensive source. It was in this vein that the German Indologists so eagerly explored and promulgated whatever morsels of literature or philosophy were available to them from India.

Hegel was himself willy-nilly immersed in this syncretist mood, albeit vectored by his peculiar genius. He had the personal ambition to collect from all corners every worthwhile sundry piece of human knowledge and cultural achievement and to synthesize it all into one resource, a compendium of complete knowledge, which he would call *The Encyclopaedia of Philosophical Sciences*.

At the centre of the word *encyclopaedia* we observe the term *cyclo*—circle or cycle. Hegel would consciously use the imagery of the circle as symbol of the completeness of his philosophical System. Having come back round to Hegel's System, let us now turn to an exposition of Hegel's works in order to prepare the reader for what to expect in the Introductions of Hegel to follow.

THE CONCRETION OF KNOWLEDGE

Central to Hegel's thought overall is the idea that truth is never abstract; the Hegelian absolute is never a 'lifeless universal' as a bare statement of an aim of philosophical work (p. 24).[1] In effect, Hegel demands that the universal, the general and the abstract must be constantly shaped by a living particular, a rich concretion. For this reason, truth for him is mediation; it cannot be untouched pure abstraction. To put this in another way, activity is the condition of being. Something needs to be stirred *in* action, in thriving reality for it to have meaning and being.

Far from the charges of mechanistic formalism and abstraction, Hegel transforms the notion of a 'pure' knowledge to one which is concrete, historically mediated, derived, evolved, strived for, experienced, lived, and realized. His disdain towards empty schema, skeletal framework of concepts and categories is only indicative of his derision against pure formal abstract universals. The absolute, universal and objective, then, cannot be seen in isolation of the concrete, the particular and the subjective. Our minds are mediated by history; the real, therefore, for him, is the actual. In contrast to the belief that immediacy and a primal encounter with knowledge is superior because it is less distorted in human hands, Hegel brings in the idea of mediation, which is necessary for absolute knowledge. Human manipulation in fact brings forth determinate knowledge. It could be remarked, therefore, that there is a certain humanizing dimension that Hegel injects into philosophy, into ontology and knowledge; and by doing this in its entirety he gives spirit the full potential access to absolute knowledge. At the end of this process, spirit would become fully itself, mediated by its actions in time.

This move in Hegel is, to a large extent, an implication of his phenomenological turn. That this is so is especially clear from his emphasis that the real is the actual; essences are mediated through phenomena, never isolated and abstract. Hegel's conception of concretion, then, is fundamentally connected with his view of phenomenology. A brief examination will make this obvious. Phenomenology asserts that the phenomenon can be the ground of absolute knowledge. The etymology of 'phenomenology' in fact exposes the intrinsic connection between the illumination of self-showing phenomena as such and the idea of uncovering that emerges along the root meaning of 'logos' as 'laying out' or 'to bare'. In Hegel, an

---

1. Unless otherwise stated in-text references refer to Hegel's works in this volume.

exploration is directed at laying bare how consciousness or mind appears to itself. Hegel criticizes, for this reason, Immanuel Kant's conception of phenomenon that seems to act as an obstruction between 'us' and 'truth', between us and the absolute knowledge of things-in-themselves. Instead, for Hegel, truth shines forth, out of the appearance of an object. It is through the concrete appearance that the real is understood. In fact, we mediate truth; truth or the real is actualized through us.

The Hegelian absolute is never static and at rest; rather it is a function of a dynamic, fiery process. Fundamental to the nature of spirit is its rich concretion, the life of passion, activity, force and will. This passionate activity or striving entails that the change which ensues is a product of contradiction, strife, struggle and negativity. This brings to mind his celebrated insight as regards dialectic. Though this method marks its entry already in Kant in the form of antinomies, Hegel's dialectic brings with it, rather, an overcoming of skepticism, not antinomies. Antinomies show that there is a dead-end at the formulation of certain questions. They proscribe absolute knowledge. Instead, the Hegelian dialectic makes absolute knowledge possible. And what then is absolute knowledge? It is the self-reflexive subject asserting that it has knowledge of the subject, the object, and the relation between them.

The fact that Kant claimed that absolute knowledge is not accessible to us, is a standpoint that *itself* was never accommodated in his epistemological frame. For Kant, the thing-in-itself is not accessible to us. But in making Kant's very overarching standpoint succumb to history, Hegel desires to go beyond Kant, in claiming that this precisely is the evidence that absolute knowledge is possible! If absolute knowledge is unbounded knowledge of things-in-themselves, it really comprises an awareness of the subject, object and the awareness itself. While this is something beyond limits; to express this view from nowhere is a peculiar limitation. So, Hegel would argue that in defining the limits of knowledge one is already *beyond* the limits of knowledge.

Further, Hegel is convinced that dialectic is progressive. It exposes contradictions, and yet it lays bare a field on which spirit will make the next move. The seemingly inconceivable balance of apparently contradictory characters, or the projected harmony of what appear as incompatible elements is founded on the idea of sublation. Hegel's use of the richly potent term 'aufheben', translated as 'sublation', connotes simultaneously three entirely different, even conflicting, ideas: picking up, cancelling, and preserving. It indicates that in any development, these three different moments fuel the spirit in its journey. Something is identified—it is grasped at its point of origin; then, something negative strikes, which, in turn, leads it to the next step where something of the earlier moment is retained still. Strikingly, this *is* the description of the way all meaningful things evolve.

Now, history is about the spirit realizing its freedom, about the self coming to realize *that* it is self. This self-conscious freedom is nothing other than truth for the spirit. And in order to discover this, the self needs something other-to-itself. Hegel, therefore, posits further that subjectivity is pure negativity. It is here that contradiction first strikes: a contradiction, however, that is central to all development. The subject turns into an object to be more fully a subject; that is how subjectivity develops. For Hegel, subject must be both in-itself (potential) and for-itself (actual)—it seeks to objectify, project and comprehend itself as freedom, namely, to be self and to be an object, non-self. As an aside, one may ground here Jean-Paul Sartre's thoughts on human freedom and material objects, germane to the distinction between things-in-themselves (*en-soi*) and things-for-themselves (*pour-soi*). In being self-reflexive and in being reflected upon, absolute knowledge is achieved, and that is at the same time, the justification of how absolute knowledge is possible.

Although they deal with distinct themes in themselves, the Introductions of Hegel are rather inextricably linked together. This is simply a function of Hegel's philosophy itself. Hegel's thought comes across as a system where all particulars take their respective places along the circle of knowledge or metaphysics. Analogously, each step develops an element in this edifice. It is the demand of his systematic philosophy that the varieties of particulars—aesthetics, metaphysics, ethics, logic, political philosophy and philosophy of religion—find themselves united into one organic whole.

The pictorial representation of the 'system' in Hegel, though simplified, is therefore best captured as a circle. It is a circle in that it presupposes its ends; yet, its end signals a beginning, for it would present all that which brings it to concretion. In Hegel, although the circle appears as a kind of closure, this closure is rather representative of the infinite, not finality. It is infinite because fundamental to this closure is the concrete progression of the curve, that is, the development, the movement of the life of the spirit. There is a constant forward and backward movement in it. And, for Hegel that is a product of dialectical movement and sublation.[2]

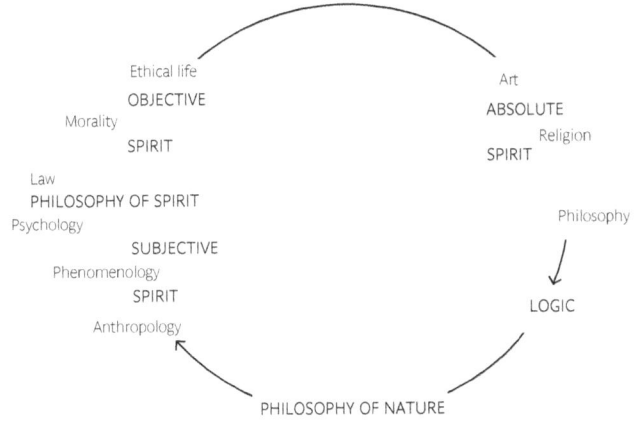

---

2. This representation is from Walter A. Kaufmann, *Hegel: Reinterpretation, Texts and Commentary*, New York, Doubleday & Company, 1965, p. 243.

THE PHENOMENOLOGY OF SPIRIT

The *Phenomenology of Spirit* is founded on the principle that we do indeed have access to absolute knowledge. The life of the spirit, in fact, reflects a progressive development of truth. Truth is therefore the result of a long travail of history, manifested in a number of ways. For the spirit, the core point of this truth is about realizing its inherent freedom. This development, in turn, is impossible without its concrete moments in history. The remarkable analogy that is introduced here is that of the relation between a seed, a bud, a flower and a fruit, indicative of the organic unity and the progressive sublation of different moments involved in the course of any development. In a sense, the plant cancels the seed, and the fruit cancels the flower. But this, Hegel would claim, is best seen as the working out of an inherent contradiction in the positive development of life. Though there is a cancelling involved, there is also a picking up and a preserving at each moment. Truth is the actual that is, in turn, a product of the Hegelian system—his circle—with its moments of sublation.

Just as in Aristotle, 'becoming' falls between 'being' and 'nothing', 'change' in Hegel is between being and negativity. This is functional to any dialectical process, any development. The action of subjectivity applies its 'negative' touch to alter the merely given; positivity is mediated by negativity to reach fuller being. In other words, subjectivity alters, molds—or, negatively destroys—and forms something else out of positive raw givenness. By adding negation to positivity, one *alters* it.

Further, it is Hegel's conviction that substance is to become subject which, in essence, is nothing but pure freedom in-and-for-itself. This brings in the notion of estrangement or alienation, the movement of a thing to what is other-to-itself. The essence of substance is freedom. But substance is fully other to subject. Yet, radically, the point of history is that substance becomes subject (or what is wholly other-to-itself) through a long difficult process at the end of which we realize the absolute.

THE SCIENCE OF LOGIC

For Hegel, logic cannot be a mere schema of empty rules; these rules necessarily need content. The idea of a purely formal logic dissociated from truth is absurd to him. Logic cannot be posed *against* metaphysics, since its content is nothing but, just, metaphysics. This drives Hegel's famous claim that he presents God's thought before creation. Progressive truth is a logical culmination of that which is *actual* in history. No concept, then, is outside time. Truth viewed in this temporal scaffold is what makes Hegel a historicist, for whom the recognition of the contextual value of ideas, events and history would be imperative towards culling out a composite notion of truth. A glance at some of the motivations that impel this truth will express this more fully.

Spirit needs science to reach truth, because, for Hegel, science is related to the being of things; it is that which grasps the essence of 'what is' in a fundamentally systematic, consistent, inherently necessary way through which the free, concrete spirit acquires absolute knowledge. And phenomenology *is* about how the spirit realizes itself. It is a labour that the spirit undertakes through tortuous history.

Given the phenomenology of spirit, ontology must accommodate the temporality of the universal. The philosophical method in Hegel would be science. Now, reason may be negative when it is dialectic, oscillating between being and non-being; and spirit is nothing but reason; so, it is also negativity. When reason is positive, it is universal and it allows thought to be speculative, since it is the contribution of reason that particulars are comprehended under a universal. However, this does not mean that concrete instances of particulars can be isolated away. Reason is spirit because it is reason which understands, and understanding is that which reasons. The development of spirit in Hegel therefore *is* human reason.

Since there is absolute knowledge, as shown in the *Phenomenology*, what is the relation of logic to this? Hegel accepts the Kantian fundamental structure of mind on the whole. But for Hegel, logic is metaphysics. Science of logic *is* the doctrine of being. So, while logic purely exhibits the development of spirit, phenomenology speaks of the spirit; this spirit is one that undergoes historical development. Metaphysics is of 'being', which is, in turn, identical to logic. That the essence of subject is spirit, and spirit is freedom therefore forms the foundation of logic when it comes to trace the journey of the spirit.

Now, for Aristotle, categories are the means through which one has access to beings, or things-in-themselves. Kant, however, posits that although categories may be able to give phenomenal knowledge, they nevertheless block off access to things-in-themselves. Hegel returns to the Greek spirit in claiming that not only are logical categories the only access to absolute knowledge, this logic is identical to reason or spirit; in other words, to being. Moreover, this logic is concretely, historically rooted in the development of spirit. The content of logic is reason, and reason is substance which is nothing but subject or the spirit, which, in turn, is nothing but the object.

In investigating the nature of logic, Hegel would point out that thought has an object, and it is its content which has a truth value. However, formal logic demands that any content lies outside the scope of logic. In contrast, thought for Hegel relies on an object for truth, and reason is the source of truth. What is absolute knowledge, if it was not that truth, certainty and validity would cohere in it? A syllogism in such a scheme would be one where whatever is valid is also true and vice versa, evocative of the Hegelian formulation that the real is the actual and the actual is the real. If validity were separated from reality or truth, then that would not be logic for Hegel. The content of logic, treated substantially, then, would be the thing-in-itself.

If absolute knowledge is reached then logic must have progressed. The essence of spirit thereby captures reason *as* it progresses. If phenomenology is the content of the concrete development of how spirit develops, logic is the form, the laws of reason. Thus, Hegel defines logic as 'spirit's knowledge of its own pure essence' (p. 74). Further, logic must have a systematic, organic arrangement of how its various parts are to relate. It should be modelled on the self-development of spirit, which is found in history, the ground on which spirit's actuality is brought forth. To realize the spirit's essence, its freedom, a moment gives determination. The immanent development of a concept forms, thus, spirit's self-consciousness. For this reason, the sort of knowing involved here is one which is concrete, engrossed in the other's externality. Philosophy brings forth this exhibition of the forward–backward movement of spirit. Religion, philosophy and art have therefore the same content of truth. It is in their form alone that they differ.

Hegel shows the way to go from being-in-itself (metaphysics) through objective logic to being-for-itself (traditional logic) by subjective logic. Being-in-itself is external and immediate. This uses the concept of mediation, and it is here that dialectic becomes important. While the Platonic dialectic is external—arbitrary in a sense—or merely procedural, the Kantian dialectic is a step higher. It is critical, internal to reason but its end is negative, since it results in antinomies. Hegelian dialectic however is speculative; it is internal to reason, but it is the unity of the positive and the negative. Phenomenology of spirit is as much affirmation, as negation and sublation. It does not end with nullity, but rather with absolute knowledge.

Logic comes after phenomenology in the Hegelian circle. Logic must, according to Hegel, also go through a progression, an evolution. This organic logic is the essence of spirit. Essence comes through only with appearance that shines forth; it is meaningful when mediated by appearance. To appear is to appear as qualified, quantified, measured, etc. to someone. This is the reason why the table of categories include Being, Becoming, Nothing, Quality, Quantity, and so on. Appearances are mediated by these categories; and in this manner, logic is integral to phenomenology. Absolute knowledge, then, is precisely this identity of essences and appearances that shows forth in logic. And once more, it is a logic whose 'dead bones' must be 're-vivified' by spirit (p. 75).

THE PHILOSOPHY OF RIGHT

Hegel's *Philosophy of Right* is at the same time a phenomenology of right, which, according to Hegel's view of man and the state, turns out to be—just as in his philosophy of history (about which more will follow)—a phenomenology of freedom. The idea of right is freedom, Hegel argues, and not abstract, theoretical freedom, but concrete ethico-political freedom.

In articulating the nature of concrete freedom, Hegel also delves into its contrary, which he calls the mere freedom of the understanding, or negative freedom. This type of freedom is characterized by an absorption of the would-be citizen (who should be the true locus of real freedom) into some other, such as God (i.e., substance), or else some 'political' ideal or universal. This is what leads to fanaticism in political and religious life.

When speaking of the political and of right, it is essential to delve into the nature of the will. The interrelation of the will and freedom are to be expected in any account of the will; what is unique and fascinating in Hegel's account is the interrelation—at times bordering on equation—of the will and thought or reason. It is the emphasis on rational willing, or willful reason, that serves to fundamentally distinguish Hegel's account of the political from other enlightenment theorists such as Rousseau or Locke.

In addition to an exhaustive account of the will, a necessary propaedeutic to any philosophy of right, of the state, and above all of the citizen, Hegel enters into a fascinating and indeed characteristic discussion of the true scope, sense and meaning—in fact, ambiguity—of the terms *subjective* and *objective*. He intends to reflect on the structure of subjectivity in order to deflect traditional dichotomies between subject and object, creating the necessary space for his own reinterpretation of the form and content of ethical and political freedom vis-à-vis (objective) laws, both moral and civil.

By rethinking the nature of willing, the subject-object dualism, and also by treating the entire content of the political dialectically (which is to say as inherently logical, rather than as the mere external ordering by some subjective agency), Hegel creates a philosophy of right, of law, of the state, that offers us the gloriously optimistic notion that there has been and continues to be a rational development, an inherent progress, in the political domain, and that concrete, actual freedom for all is to be its inevitable result.

THE PHILOSOPHY OF HISTORY

If in *Phenomenology* Hegel shows that absolute knowledge is possible, and that the spirit is the embodiment of that knowledge, then how in fact spirit realizes itself is the account of a philosophy of history. In his outlining of history, we therefore see a characterization of the 'development of Spirit in *Time*' (p. 149). If phenomenology is about the spirit appearing to itself, it does this in tracing the movement from ignorance to absolute knowing—to understand the real through the actual. In fact, reason is the essence of the real and it reveals itself in the world *in* history. History for Hegel, therefore, is a rational process and is a development of a kernel that was there already present.

Clearly, the emphasis on the rationality of history is a much contended idea owing both to the determinism and the tacit epistemic/moral justification that it entails. Hegel seems to view history as a product of dialectics, where the resultant moment is somehow superior to the original. However, he certainly does not appear to be blind to the deep unease associated with the claim that there is reason in history. The fact that he maintains the notion of the rational (and, ultimately, progressive development) despite the apparent incoherence and contingency of human history is, if anything, consistent with his encyclopedic system as a whole.

In recounting the tale of history, Hegel pictures it as an array of events and actions—strange, inspiring, loathsome, glorious, banal—of a 'vast picture of changes and transactions' (p. 149), of a 'motliest throng of events drawing us within the circle of its interest' (p. 150), of the 'ruins of some ancient sovereignty' (p. 150), causing 'sorrow at the decay of a splendid and highly cultured national life' (p. 150), among others. In putting these together, Hegel seems to bring out, once again, his underlying principled intuition about the way life typically evolves itself.

That 'dissolution, involves at the same time the rise of *new life*—that while death is the issue of life, life is also the issue of death' (p. 150) merely recasts Hegel's passionate insight that the evolution of the spirit is dialectical and progressive. The spirit 'makes war upon itself' (p. 150) to create new material out of itself for successive endeavours. If there is a rational necessity about the dialectical life of the spirit, then history by default must express this reason, since history is nothing but development of spirit in time. For this reason, each moment is as integral as another to the development of the spirit.

History is eternally present, and yet it is true only because it is actualized through every determinate moment. This however does not determine us, because the realization of truth was something that was latent; and it is what the spirit sought to realize anyway. The nature of spirit is such that its essence is freedom, a centre that is within itself. A depiction of spirit in terms of its freedom then only reinforces the idea that it actualizes itself in history to arrive at the 'real'. And, this real is mediated; since the 'very essence of Spirit is activity' (p. 150). Hegel's idea that reason guides history therefore is coupled with the view that *passion* is the fuel of history. If this is so, then logically speaking, there is no end of history. Instead, a raging theatre of phenomena confronts us where spirit is working itself out in a constant restless fashion. In Hegel, we see that history is constantly cycled and recycled. Once more, therefore, we return to the circle.

THE PHILOSOPHY OF FINE ART

Hegel turns to spirit's engagement with art in a characteristic phenomenological intervention. While the aesthetics involves perception, the word 'kalos' means the fine, noble and the excellent, as well as skill and moral virtue. The word used in German is 'schöne'. Excellence is, then, both beautiful and virtuous. Perception, on the other hand, is to do with surface and appearance. This comes from the word 'schein' or what merely seems. Now, of course, the point of art is about schöne (the beautiful) coming out of schein (what seems), and this is something that needs to be justified. The justification is a demand that almost the whole of the rationalist tradition since Plato, in particular, places. For Plato, art is *unreal* appearance, because it lies in the realm of perception—changing, disintegrating in the world, like illusions. His claim is, of course, based on a framework of reality; a reality that is ultimately invariant, immutable, eternal, spaceless, timeless, and consisting of absolute essences. The unreality of art comes from the fact of its change, and further, from Plato's view that what is merely *seen* is ultimately unreal. Art for him lies in the realm of the sensible, i.e., in the world of change. In contrast, mathematical truths are ever real because they are unperceived, pure and sublime. Plato's idea comes across, then, as the drive to separate the invisible/intelligible from the visible/sensible, to separate the world of abstract form of Beauty from particular objects that may be beautiful, to separate the original from the copy, and so on.

In some sense, this is perhaps the total antithesis of the Hegelian view. The only way that one can hold on to the view that beauty can come through art, or that schöne can come out of schein, is by arguing that schein itself *is*. That is, appearance itself is the ground of the real. This dramatic move comes forth explicitly in the phenomenology of Edmund Husserl, more radically in Martin Heidegger; but originally in Hegel.

Truth is truth because it shows itself, not because it is hidden. As Heidegger points out in *Being and Time*, phenomenology uncovers that which is in fact shining. The original Greek meaning of phenomena is rephrased as: 'that which shows itself is the Being of entities, its meaning'[3] as opposed to Kant who nurtures the distinction between phenomena (appearance) and noumena (the realm of things-in-themselves). Because, in general, phenomenon is covered, undiscovered, buried or hidden, phenomenology is needed. But in actuality, phenomenon shines, shows itself as itself. That which phenomenology 'lets us see' is 'something that lies hidden'.[4] For Heidegger, like Hegel, the phenomenon is not a mere 'semblance', 'seeming' or 'appearance', as it is for Kant. Heidegger reaffirms this by highlighting that truth or aletheia is nothing but that which is 'uncovered' by phenomenology. It is in fact, that which shows itself as it is in itself. The phenomenon, then, can be the thing-in-itself. Indeed, we even have direct access to it since it simply shines forth. This idea pervades the Hegelian spirit and is reinforced in the insight that there 'could be no such thing as truth if it did not appear, or, rather, let itself appear' (p. 161).

In Hegel, there is a move, in fact, towards a reinterpretation of art, deriving out of this typically phenomenological stance. He overturns Plato's idea of a bad transitory world—where art is deception, where it figures lowest in the 'divided line', having the lowest degree of reality—to something else altogether. For Hegel, rather, the mere physical world is lower than art. In fact, art lifts the spirit away from this bad physical world. Truth is truth only when it appears; and art liberates the true from what is merely physical. Again, to draw a comparison, this too appears at the core of Heidegger's thought, as evident from 'The Origin of the Work of Art' (1950),[5] which posits that art lights up mere 'earth' to disclose a 'world' of truth. For Hegel, the essence of art is that it is the vehicle of the spirit. In contrast to the 'divided line' in Plato, Hegel construes art instead as a kind of

---

3. Martin Heidegger, *Being and Time*, trans. John Macquarrie and Edward Robinson, San Francisco, Harper, 1962, p. 60.

4. Heidegger, *Being and Time*, p. 59.

5. Martin Heidegger, 'The Origin of the Work of Art', in *Off the Beaten Track*, trans. Julian Young and Kenneth Haynes, Cambridge, Cambridge University Press, 2002, pp. 1-56.

bridge for the spirit to move from the physical to the rational; in other words, to freedom.

There is a constant tension in attempting to answer as to whether Hegel is an absolutist or a relativist when it comes to art. While, the particularity of civilization and time certainly dominates the art of a nation—the specific form is a foreignness that art displays—yet somehow all these varied forms have the same universal content, and that is what is essential to them.[6] What is universal about art—its content, namely the Idea—can be found by overcoming its foreignness which is only the aspect of its form, namely 'the configuration of sensuous material'.[7] On the one hand, there is the sensuous which deals with perception or 'aesthesis', and on the other, there is the spirit which indulges in cognition, knowledge and is guided by reason, idea or the concept. There is a kind of conflict here. Art points to the spirit, and yet it has to do with passion, senses, interests, deception, imitation and the sensuous. Existent works have the requirement that they are sensed. This derives out of the constant demand for the concrete in Hegel. The Platonic abstraction is, by definition, outside concretion, so it is insufficient.[8] For Hegel, everything, including art, must be organically tied to spirit. It has to have internal logic. The ideal of beauty must be filled in with the concrete, which is again a product of dialectic, and that *is* the basis of scientific treatment. Though paradoxical, in a way therefore both universality and relativity are found together in Hegel.

Why do we have art in the first place? Hegel claims that the 'universal demand for artistic expression is based on the rational impulse in man's nature to exalt both the world of his soul experience and that of Nature for himself into the conscious embrace of mind as an object in which he rediscovers himself' (pp. 171-2). One can be in-itself and for-itself. In art, one rediscovers oneself, in seeing both the modes of one's being. Moreover, in art, one represents or duplicates. Since man is a free subject, and that is something universal about art, it can be said that art adds the stamp of the human in the act of 're-presentation'. One sees art as duplicate when one contemplates on it, and it is art itself that allows one to contemplate that way. In the *Phenomenology*, it is shown that nature is the anti-thesis of spirit. Man is free by wrestling with nature, by shaping, molding, carving, creating, and refining natural things to bring the spirit to manifest. By this, one also removes their foreignness. A similar situation emerges in art. What is merely sensuous is there as a key to reveal in/for-itself. It turns our attention to how the sensuous is *there* for man (p. 173-4). We can let a work of art be in freedom, even in its sensuousness. It is therefore entirely different from other material objects which are not in freedom.

In Kant's *Critique of Judgment*, natural beauty is seen as art. Further, what is

---

6. See G. W. F. Hegel, *Aesthetics: Lectures on Fine Art*, trans. T. M. Knox, vol. 1, 2 vols., Oxford, Clarendon Press, 1975, p. 20.

7. Hegel, *Aesthetics: Lectures on Fine Art*, p. 70.

8. Hegel, *Aesthetics: Lectures on Fine Art*, p. 22.

the ineffable or the sublime is also beautiful. Hegel rejects both. Fine art is created out of a destruction of nature, it is not nature itself. For Hegel, it is absurd to conceive that the aim of art is imitation. Nature is just too vivid and dynamic in its raw materiality than art, and it is therefore pointless to attempt to imitate it.

Also, for Hegel, art is not ineffable, mystical, and indescribable. The nature of everything according to the phenomenologicasl approach is that it is already all laid out, so ineffability can only be a product of lack of experience and knowledge. Philosophy of Art thus does not quite permit something wholly mysterious. If one knows enough, one knows why art moves us so much. If we understood the history, culture, religion, spirit of a civilization, then we would understand art completely.

To return to the conflict, the problem of art is that it is sensuous. Hegel however reverses the dogma. And this is picked up by Husserl and Heidegger in their phenomenology. To the question of why art is rational, Hegel would answer that it is so because it creates the stamp of the human over nature. The dialectic in art consists in its destruction of the natural in order to lift it to the spiritual. The question of relativity versus universality in Hegel appears in a kind of dialectic again and this universality is achieved in overcoming the foreignness of form (owing to space and time).

Contrary to common opinion, the aim of art also cannot merely be the expression of subjective passions. That is too romantic a notion for Hegel; there is too much turbulence in it. Art can be viewed as analogous to a state which is a product of order and law (p. 179 ff.). Art is liberation because of its representative character. It frees the spirit from the sensuous by means of the sensuous alone. And that is concretion at play once more.

Again, Hegel dismisses the idea that the aim of art is purification/catharsis or moral. We delight in art, and this needs to be recognized. Yet this shows that art needs a higher purpose—that is dialectic. If we say art is for a moral purpose, it amounts to claiming that art has an external reason. However, for Hegel, the aim of art must be internal to it, with an inner dialectic that will ultimately lift spirit to freedom—from the sensuous with the sensuous. This dialectic dissolves differences which are now preserved in objectivity, and not in the subject, as for Kant where subjectivity had no access to absolute knowledge. In the Hegelian conception, instead, there appears a unity of the particular and the universal, of necessity and freedom, of sense and reason. In looking at art, thus, Hegel posits that feeling is *in* reason, idea is *in* the sensuous.

THE PHILOSOPHY OF RELIGION

In conceiving of a philosophy of religion Hegel seeks to accentuate its import for the spirit. An overview of his work suggests: first, that the familiar triadic structure manifests here as well—the universal/objective, the particular/subjective, and the absolute. But given that this dialectic already appears with Kant, the real originality of Hegel consists in the fact that he is able to put these moments together in an order: conceptual and historical. In its universal aspect, religion as such is the object of study; in its particular aspect, a comparative study of various world religions is undertaken. Finally, the absolute is one that Hegel proposes to be most satisfying—it is that which incorporates all that is good in a religion, and which dialectically supersedes all other religions. It is argued that the movement from the one to the other is inherently necessary, and that they are all placed within an integrated philosophical system where each form has its own significance.

Religion, like other things, is a growing organic phenomenon. A particular religion is present somewhere, which is the complex of a specific historical circumstance. And yet particularities are only portions, they are unequal to the whole. The revealed religion is always present, already contained in the particular religions. Religion, therefore, is a product of a philosophy of history, however, its real content—the absolute—is something that was already there, but needed to be manifested through historical time.

If God is truth, Hegel must show that in order that absolute knowledge is possible (that it is, in fact, necessary), God's truth must be conceivable, rationally comprehensible. Hegel rejects the idea that God is something wholly other. God is the spirit, the idea, the reason. Hegel therefore rejects the romanticist's view that truth is in feeling. This would be for him an unscientific way to approach an issue. Again, Hegel rejects the ideas both *(a)* that there is a particular relation, namely god is the 'other'; and *(b)* that god is ineffable and completely mysterious, in which case this relation is not determinate. Just as in art, in his philosophy of religion, too, Hegel attempts to seek the spirit.

The argument relating the ordinary conception of religion—that it is feeling—is a problem for Hegel. If it is feeling, it should be wholly individual. However, we see that the existence of religion is over an entire community, a culture in a given context. In that case, however, the conflicting faiths would confront, and they will have expression in the conflict of states and nations. The expression of the absolute in religion is precisely to overcome individual differences. This, of course, raises the question as to whether for Hegel the whole point of particularities are their syntheses. In response, we may point out that, even so, the fact remains that in Hegel's conception of religion, subjectivity is sought to be fully articulated, and ultimately, God is achieved in reason, not in subjective passion, which is certainly a necessary moment, but not the final one.

The other way of looking at religion is through the mode of worship. In worship, one attempts to make contact with God or absolute spirit. That is, absolute spirit is realized through subjective spirit. But this absolute spirit can never be wholly other. In fact, objective spirit is not different from subjective spirit, and hence, in the act of worship there is a return of the spirit to itself—that which was divided, isolated from itself now returns to itself. Worship, however, is only the operation of reflection; Philosophy, on the other hand, reconciles this chasm by thinking knowledge, for the spirit seeks Being into itself. This being-at-home-with-self, or coming-to-self, is for Hegel, its complete and highest end. Religion is that in which spirit realizes what God is, or absolute spirit; in phenomenology, logic, and history, too, as we have already seen, it is, once more, the absolute spirit that realizes itself.

THE HISTORY OF PHILOSOPHY

For Hegel, philosophy *is* the history of philosophy.[9] The progressive development of history shows that there is a reason underlying every step, every link. It is David Hume's skepticism, for instance, that makes Kant possible in the way we know him; the former is a necessary step for the latter to appear. In fact, each step acts as a catalyst for the spirit to move forward to the next one. History of spirit seeks its liberation, which basically consists in absolute knowledge. And yet in so far as skepticism is necessary to this liberation, the history of the movement from skepticism to absolute knowledge tells us something essential about the spirit. It is through the history of philosophy that the spirit works itself out.

Spirit has potentiality. It is in-itself, and it has the power to become for-itself, by becoming concrete. It has the power to create freedom for-itself. In the beginning, a spirit may be in-itself, in animality; and in the end it could be for-itself, in freedom. Being 'at-home-with-self' is the highest end (p. 227), and this is precisely concrete freedom, in essence.

If spirit is alienated and divided, through the history of philosophy it would work toward uniting itself to itself. This freedom is the aim of spirit. Anything that stands against us, or any object, is recognized because of the value *we* give to it. That is why, for Hegel, history is to be understood in terms of spirit's freedom, which is essentially manifested as political freedom.

In the *Phenomenology*, we see that spirit's nature is negativity; in contrast, nature is characterized as positivity. Though nature is positive—a full solid substantiality—it is ultimately divided because its centre, that is gravity, is outside it. Spirit, though presently described as negativity, is ultimately undivided because its centre of freedom is within itself. In other words, spirit can be free, nature cannot be.

Furthermore, spirit is a function of dialectics. And the process of mediation in the case of spirit is history. Philosophy is, then, the mediating link between the subjective spirit and the absolute. This return to itself is something that the dialectical process facilitates. For Hegel, there is a certain necessity about events in the world, since everything is inherently connected. Moreover, the end is always a result of a process of striving. It is a thriving field of labour.

CLOSING THE CIRCLE

The preoccupation with truth, to conclude, then, is the absolute object of spirit.

---

9. G. W. F. Hegel, *Hegel's Lectures on the History of Philosophy*, trans. E. S. Haldane, vol. 1, 3 vols., London, Routledge and Kegan Paul, 1892, p. 30.

There is a triadic structure that Hegel has across all of his many works: subjective, objective and absolute. This structure allows him to bring in dialectics, sublation, and mediation. We see in Hegel a certain circle of a system, which presupposes its end by this dialectical progress. The concretion has within it both the execution and the end or the aim. It is the peculiar inner necessity of the Hegelian system that there is movement from one step to another. What follows illustrates the direction that the spirit takes:

Logic is in-itself but not for-itself.
It is truth reflecting God's thought before creation.
↓
Nature is finite. It is creation without the presence of man.
↓
Subjective spirit has man in an image.
It is the subject of the *Phenomenology*.
↓
Objective spirit has man in community.
The *Philosophy of History* and the *Philosophy of Right* study this.
↓
Absolute spirit is captured in art, religion and philosophy.
In the moment of religion, it reflects the unity between
God and the individual, reflecting pure freedom.
This liberation is based on the idea, however, that the
identity was something already there in the first place.

In their content, therefore, art, religion, and philosophy stand on the same footing, insofar as they all seek truth. For Hegel, though, art is subordinate to religion, and religion subordinate to philosophy. In art, the sensuous material grasps the concept or idea, namely, its content. The defect of art lies in that it yields a sensuous manipulation of the idea. Although it breathes spirit into matter, the idea or concept itself is not sensuous. The problem with religion, again, is the anchor in pictorial thinking. Like art, it is not entirely free from form, since religious consciousness views God *as* incarnate or in some representative form. In the act of worship, in fact, spirit is back to its subjective character since feeling is indispensable in it.

If religion is higher than art because of the fact that in art concept is not quite suitable to sensuous material, then religion is defective too because man is still the subjective form in this act. Art breathes *out* spirit, making it external; religion breathes *in* spirit, making it internal. In art, spirit has taken itself as objective. In religion, spirit has returned to self, but it turns out that it is not without feeling. So, the limitation of religion emanates out of pictorial thinking and associated feeling. Religion begins as being external and objective and then becomes completely internal. This inwardness is not the highest form of truth for Hegel. It is not fully adequate for the spirit. Philosophy therefore emerges as the field of unmingled thinking, not mixed with subjective feeling, not mingled with pictorial thinking. That is, it displays free thinking; it is pure, perfect, and absolute.

Freedom consists in the fact that what confronts a subject is not alien to it; the subject finds oneself in it, and at home. Thus, when foreignness is overcome, freedom is realized. Art and religion for that reason unite in philosophy, preserving the content of truth while sublating the form, placing it in the realm of the absolute. Since true thought is the most universal, Hegel is able to seek the spirit's abode in the unity of its form (or Idea) and content (or truth) in a fiery existential reality called life.

REFERENCES

Hegel, G. W. F., *Phenomenology of Spirit*, trans. J. B. Baillie, New York, Macmillan, 1910 [1807].

Hegel, G. W. F., *Hegel's Science of Logic*, trans., W. H. Johnston and L. G. Struthers, London, George Allen & Unwin, 1929 [1812].

Hegel, G. W. F., *Philosophy of History*, trans. J. Sibree, New York, Dover, 1956 [1837].

Hegel, G. W. F., *Aesthetics: Lectures on Fine Art*, trans. T. M. Knox, vol. 1, 2 vols., Oxford, Clarendon Press, 1975 [1835].

Hegel, G. W. F., *The Philosophy of Fine Art*, trans. F. P. B. Osmaston, vol. 1, 4 vols., London, G. Bell and Sons, 1920 [1835].

Hegel, G. W. F., *Lectures on the Philosophy of Religion*, trans. E. B. Speirs and J. B. Sanderson, vol. 1, 3 vols., London, Routledge and Kegan Paul, 1895 [1832].

Hegel, G. W. F., *Hegel's Lectures on the History of Philosophy*, trans. E. S. Haldane, vol. 1, 3 vols., London, Routledge and Kegan Paul, 1892 [1837].

Heidegger, Martin, *Being and Time,* trans. John Macquarrie and Edward Robinson, San Francisco, Harper, 1962 [1927].

Heidegger, Martin, 'The Origin of the Work of Art', in *Off the Beaten Track*, trans. Julian Young and Kenneth Haynes, Cambridge, Cambridge University Press, 2002 [1950], pp. 1-56.

Kaufmann, Walter A., *Hegel: Reinterpretation, Texts and Commentary*, New York, Doubleday & Company, 1965.

PHENOMENOLOGY OF SPIRIT

'Appearance is the process of arising into being and passing away again, a process that itself does not arise and does not pass away, but is *per se,* and constitutes reality and the life-movement of truth. The truth is thus the bacchanalian revel, where not a member is sober; and because every member no sooner becomes detached than it *eo ipso* collapses straightway, the revel is just as much a state of transparent unbroken calm'.

1

PHENOMENOLOGY OF SPIRIT

PREFACE: ON SCIENTIFIC KNOWLEDGE

In the case of a philosophical work it seems not only superfluous, but, in view of the nature of philosophy, even inappropriate and misleading to begin, as writers usually do in a preface, by explaining the end the author had in mind, the circumstances which gave rise to the work, and the relation in which the writer takes it to stand to other treatises on the same subject, written by his predecessors or his contemporaries. For whatever it might be suitable to state about philosophy in a preface—say, an historical sketch of the main drift and point of view, the general content and results, a string of desultory assertions and assurances about the truth—this cannot be accepted as the form and manner in which to expound philosophical truth.

Moreover, because philosophy has its being essentially in the element of that universality which encloses the particular within it, the end or final result seems, in the case of philosophy more than in that of other sciences, to have absolutely expressed the complete fact itself in its very nature; contrasted with that the mere process of bringing it to light would seem, properly speaking, to have no essential significance. On the other hand, in the general idea of, e.g., anatomy—the knowledge of the parts of the body regarded as lifeless—we are quite sure we do not possess the objective concrete fact, the actual content of the science, but must, over and above, be concerned with particulars. Further, in the case of such a collection of items of knowledge, which has no real right to the name of science, any talk about purpose and suchlike generalities is not commonly very different from the descriptive and superficial way in which the contents of the science these nerves and muscles, etc. are themselves spoken of. In philosophy, on the other hand, it would at once be felt incongruous were such a method made use of and yet shown by philosophy itself to be incapable of grasping the truth.

In the same way too, by determining the relation which a philosophical work professes to have to other treatises on the same subject, an extraneous interest is introduced, and obscurity is thrown over the point at issue in the knowledge of the truth. The more the ordinary mind takes the opposition between true and false to be fixed, the more is it accustomed to expect either agreement or contradiction with a given philosophical system, and only to see reason for the one or the other in any explanatory statement concerning such a system. It does not conceive the diversity of philosophical systems as the progressive evolution of truth; rather, it sees only contradiction in that variety. The bud disappears when the blossom breaks through, and we might say that the former is refuted by the latter; in the same way when the fruit comes, the blossom may be explained to be a false form of the plant's existence, for the fruit appears as its true nature in place of the blossom. These stages are not merely differentiated; they supplant one another as being incompatible with one another. But the ceaseless activity of their own inherent nature makes them at the same time moments of an organic unity, where they not merely do not contradict one another, but where one is as necessary as the other; and this equal necessity of all moments constitutes alone and thereby the life of the whole. But contradiction as between philosophical systems is not wont to be conceived in this way; on the other hand, the mind perceiving the contradiction does not commonly know how to relieve it or keep it free from its one-sidedness, and to recognize in what seems conflicting and inherently antagonistic the presence of mutually necessary moments.

The demand for such explanations as also the attempts to satisfy this demand, very easily, pass for the essential business philosophy has to undertake. Where could the inmost truth of a philosophical work be found better expressed than in its purposes and results? If, however, such procedure is to pass for more than the beginning of knowledge, if it is to pass for actually knowing, then we must, in point of fact, look on it as a device for avoiding the real business at issue, an attempt to combine the appearance of being in earnest and taking trouble about the subject with an actual neglect of the subject altogether. For the real subject-matter is not exhausted in its purpose, but in working the matter out; nor is the mere result attained the concrete whole itself, but the result along with the process of arriving at it. The purpose of itself is a lifeless universal, just as the general drift is a mere activity in a certain direction, which is still without its concrete realization; and the naked result is the corpse of the system which has left its guiding tendency behind it. Similarly, the distinctive difference of anything is rather the boundary, the limit, of the subject; it is found at that point where the subject-matter stops, or it is what this subject-matter is *not*. To trouble oneself in this fashion with the purpose and results, and again with the differences, the positions taken up and judgments passed by one thinker and another, is therefore an easier task than perhaps it seems. For instead of laying hold of the matter in hand, a procedure of that kind is all the while away from the subject altogether. Instead of dwelling within it and becoming absorbed by it, knowledge of that sort is always grasping at something else; such knowledge, instead keeping to the subject-matter and giving itself up to it, never gets away from itself. The easiest thing of all is to pass judgments on what has a solid substantial content; it is more difficult to grasp it, and most of all difficult to do both together and produce the systematic exposition of it.

The beginning of culture and of the struggle to pass out of the unbroken immediacy of naive Psychical life has always to be made by acquiring knowledge of universal principles and points of view, by striving, in the first instance, to work up simply to the *thought* of the subject-matter in general, not forgetting at the same time to give reasons for supporting it or refuting it, to apprehend the concrete riches and fullness contained in its various determinate qualities, and to know how to furnish a coherent, orderly account of it and a responsible judgment upon it. This beginning of mental cultivation will, however, very soon make way for the earnestness of actual life in all its fullness, which leads to a living experience of the subject-matter itself; and when, in addition, conceptual thought strenuously penetrates to the very depths of its meaning, such knowledge and style of judgment will keep their due place in everyday thought and conversation.

THE ELEMENT OF TRUTH IS THE CONCEPT/NOTION (*BEGRIFF*), AND ITS TRUE FORM, THE SCIENTIFIC SYSTEM

The systematic development of truth in scientific form can alone be the true shape in which truth exists. To help to bring philosophy nearer to the form of science—that goal where it can lay aside the name of *love* of knowledge and be actual knowledge—that *is* what I have set before me. The inner necessity that knowledge should be science lies in its very nature; and the adequate and sufficient explanation for this lies simply and solely in the systematic exposition of philosophy itself. The external necessity, however, so far as this is apprehended in a universal way, and apart from the accident of the personal element and the particular occasioning influences affecting the individual, is the same as the internal: it lies in the form and shape in which the process of time presents the existence of its moments. To show that the time process does raise philosophy to the level of scientific system would, therefore, be the only true justification of the attempts which aim at proving that philosophy must assume this character; because the temporal process would thus bring out and lay bare the necessity of it, nay, more, would at the same time be carrying out that very aim itself.

When we state the true form of truth to be its scientific character—or, what is the same thing, when it is maintained that truth finds the medium of its existence in notions or conceptions alone—I know that this seems to contradict an idea with all its consequences which makes great pretensions and has gained widespread acceptance and conviction at the present time. A word of explanation concerning this contradiction seems, therefore, not out of place, even though at this stage it can amount to no more than a dogmatic assurance exactly like the view we are opposing. If, that is to say, truth exists merely in what, or rather exists merely *as* what, is called at one time intuition, at another immediate knowledge of the Absolute, Religion, Being—not being in the centre of divine love, but the very Being of this centre, of the Absolute itself—from that point of view it is rather the opposite of the notional or conceptual form which would be required for systematic philosophical exposition. The Absolute on this view is not to be grasped in conceptual form, but felt, intuited; it is not its conception, but the feeling of it and intuition of it that are to have the say and find expression.

PRESENT POSITION OF THE SPIRIT

If we consider the appearance of a claim like this in its more general setting, and look at the level which the self-conscious spirit at present occupies, we shall find that self-consciousness has got beyond the substantial fullness of life, which it used to carry on in the element of thought—beyond the state of immediacy of belief, beyond the satisfaction and security arising from the assurance which consciousness possessed of being reconciled with ultimate reality and with its all pervading presence, within as well as without. Self-conscious spirit has not merely passed beyond that to the opposite extreme of insubstantial reflection of self into self, but beyond this too. It has not merely lost its essential and concrete life, it is also conscious of this loss and of the transitory finitude characteristic of its content. Turning away from the husks it has to feed on, and confessing that it lies in wickedness and sin, it reviles itself for so doing, and now desires from philosophy not so much to bring it to a knowledge of what it is, as to obtain once again through philosophy the restoration of that sense of solidity and substantiality of existence it has lost. Philosophy is thus expected not so much to meet this want by opening up the compact solidity of substantial existence, and bringing this to the light and level of self-consciousness—is not so much to bring chaotic conscious life back to the orderly ways of thought, and the simplicity of the notion, as to run together what thought has divided asunder, suppress the notion with its distinctions, and restore the feeling of existence. What it wants from philosophy is not so much insight as edification. The beautiful, the holy, the eternal, religion, love—these are the bait required to awaken the desire to bite: not the notion, but ecstasy, not the march of cold necessity in the subject-matter, but ferment and enthusiasm—these are to be the ways by which the wealth of the concrete substance is to be stored and increasingly extended.

With this demand there goes the strenuous effort, almost perfervidly zealous in its activity, to rescue mankind from being sunken in what is sensuous, vulgar, and of fleeting importance, and to raise men's eyes to the stars; as if men had quite forgotten the divine, and were on the verge of finding satisfaction, like worms, in mud and water. Time was when man had a heaven, decked and fitted out with endless wealth of thoughts and pictures. The significance of all that is, lay in the thread of light by which it was attached to heaven; instead of dwelling in the present as it is here and now, the eye glanced away over the present to the Divine, away, so to say, to a present that lies beyond. Spirit's gaze had to be directed under compulsion to what is earthly, and kept fixed there; and it has needed a long time to introduce that clearness, which only celestial realities had, into the crassness and confusion shrouding the sense of things, earthly, and to make attention to the immediate present as such, which was called Experience, of interest and of value. Now we have apparently the need for the opposite of all this; man's mind and interest are so deeply rooted in the earthly that we require a like power to have them raised above that level. His spirit shows such poverty of nature that it seems to long for the mere pitiful feeling of the divine in the abstract, and to get refreshment from that, like a wanderer in the desert craving for the merest mouthful of water. By the little which can thus satisfy the needs of the human spirit we can measure the extent of its loss.

This easy contentment in receiving, or stinginess in giving, does not suit the character of science. The man who only seeks edification, who wants to envelop in mist the manifold diversity of his earthly existence and thought, and craves after the vague enjoyment of this vague and indeterminate Divinity—he may look where he likes to find this: he will easily find for himself the means to procure something he can rave over and puff himself up with. But philosophy must beware of wishing to be edifying.

Still less must this kind of contentment, which holds science in contempt, take upon itself to claim that raving obscurantism of this sort is something higher than science. Moreover, when this unreflective emotional knowledge makes a pretence of having immersed its own very self in the depths of the absolute Being, and of philosophizing in all holiness and truth, it hides from itself the fact that instead of devotion to God, it rather, by this contempt for all measurable precision and definiteness, simply attests in its own case the fortuitous character of its content, and in the other endows God with its own caprice. When such minds commit themselves to the unrestrained ferment of sheer emotion, they think that, by putting a veil over self-consciousness, and surrendering all understanding, they are thus God's beloved ones to whom He gives His wisdom in sleep. This is the reason, too, that in point of fact, what they do conceive and bring forth in sleep is dreams.

For the rest it is not difficult to see that our epoch is a birth-time, and a period of transition. The spirit of man has broken with the old order of things hitherto prevailing, and with the old ways of thinking, and is in the mind to let them all sink into the depths of the past and to set about its own transformation. It is indeed never at rest, but carried along the stream of progress ever onward. But it is here as in the case of the birth of a child; after a long period of nutrition in silence, the continuity of the gradual growth in size, of quantitative change, is suddenly cut short by the first breath drawn—there is a break in the process, a qualitative change and the child is born. In like manner, the spirit of the time, growing slowly and quietly ripe for the new form it is to assume, disintegrates one fragment after another of the structure of its previous world. That it is tottering to its fall is indicated only by symptoms here and there. Frivolity and again ennui, which are spreading in the established order of things, the undefined foreboding of something unknown—all these betoken that there is something else approaching. This gradual crumbling to pieces, which did not alter the general look and aspect of the whole, is interrupted by the sunrise, which, in a flash and at a single stroke, brings to view the form and structure of the new world.

But this new world is perfectly realized just as little as the new-born child; and it is essential to bear this in mind. It comes on the stage to begin with in its immediacy, in its bare generality. A building is not finished when its foundation is laid; and just as little, is the attainment of a general notion of a whole the whole itself. When we want to see an oak with all its vigour of trunk, its spreading branches, and mass of foliage, we are not satisfied to be shown an acorn instead. In the same way science, the crowning glory of a spiritual world, is not found complete in its initial stages. The beginning of the new spirit is the outcome of a widespread revolution in manifold forms of spiritual culture; it is the reward which comes after a chequered and devious course of development, and after much struggle and effort. It is a whole which, after running its course and laying bare all its content, returns again to itself; it is the resultant abstract notion of the whole. But the actual realization of this abstract whole is only found when those previous shapes and forms, which are now reduced to ideal moments of the whole, are developed anew again, but developed and shaped within this new medium, and with the meaning they have thereby acquired.

THE PRINCIPLE IS NOT THE COMPLETION; AGAINST FORMALISM

While the new world makes its first appearance merely in general outline, merely as a whole lying concealed and hidden within a bare abstraction, the wealth of the bygone life, on the other hand, is still consciously present in recollection. Consciousness misses in the new form the detailed expanse of content; but still more the developed expression of form by which distinctions are definitely determined and arranged in their precise relations. Only what is perfectly determinate in form is at the same time exoteric, comprehensible, and capable of being learned and possessed by everybody. Intelligibility is the form in which science is offered to everyone, and is the open road to it made plain for all. To reach rational knowledge by our intelligence is the just demand of the mind which comes to science. For intelligence, understanding (*Verstand*), is thinking, pure activity of the self in general; and what is intelligible (*Verständige*) is something from the first familiar and common to the scientific and unscientific mind alike, enabling the unscientific mind to enter the domain of science.

Hence everything appears brought within the compass of the Absolute Idea, which seems thus to be recognized in everything, and to have succeeded in becoming a system *in extenso* of scientific knowledge. But if we look more closely at this expanded system we find that it has not been reached by one and the same principle taking shape in diverse ways; it is the shapeless repetition of one and the same idea, which is applied in an external fashion to different material, the wearisome reiteration of it keeping up the semblance of diversity. The Idea, which by itself is no doubt the truth, really never gets any farther than just where it began, as long as the development of it consists in nothing else than such a repetition of the same formula. If the knowing subject carries round everywhere the one inert abstract form, taking up in external fashion whatever material comes his way, and dipping it into this element, then this comes about as near to fulfilling what is wanted—viz. a self-origination of the wealth of detail, and a self-determining distinction of shapes and forms-as any chance fancies about the content in question. It is rather a monochrome formalism, which only arrives at distinction in the matter it has to deal with, because this is already prepared and well known.

This monotonousness and abstract universality are maintained to be the Absolute. This formalism insists that to be dissatisfied therewith argues an incapacity to grasp the standpoint of the Absolute, and keep a firm hold on it. If it was once the case that the bare possibility of thinking of something in some other fashion was sufficient to refute a given idea, and the naked possibility, the bare general thought, possessed and passed for the entire substantive value of actual knowledge; similarly we find here all the value ascribed to the general idea in this bare form without concrete realization; and we see here, too, the style and method of speculative contemplation identified with dissipating and resolving what is determinate and distinct, or rather with hurling it down, without more ado and without any justification, into the abyss of vacuity. To consider any specific fact as it is in the Absolute, consists here in nothing else than saying about it that, while it is now doubtless spoken of as something specific, yet in the Absolute, in the abstract identity A = A, there is no such thing at all, for everything is there all one. To pit this single assertion, that 'in the Absolute all is one', against the organized whole of determinate and complete knowledge, or of knowledge which at least aims at and demands complete development—to give out its Absolute as the night in which, as we say, all cows are black—that is the very *naïveté* of emptiness of knowledge.

The formalism which has been deprecated and despised by recent philosophy, and which has arisen once more in philosophy itself, will not disappear from science, even though its inadequacy is known and felt, till the knowledge of absolute reality has become quite clear as to what its own true nature consists in. Having in mind that the general idea of what is to be done, if it precedes the attempt to carry it out, facilitates the comprehension of this process, it is worthwhile to indicate here some rough idea of it, with the hope at the same time that this will give us the opportunity to set aside certain forms whose habitual presence is a hindrance in the way of speculative knowledge.

THE ABSOLUTE IS SUBJECT, AND WHAT THIS IS

In my view—a view which the developed exposition of the system itself can alone justify—everything depends on grasping and expressing the ultimate truth not as

Substance but as Subject as well. At the same time we must note that concrete substantiality implicates and involves the universal or the immediacy of knowledge itself, as well as that immediacy which is being, or immediacy *qua* object *for* knowledge. If the generation which heard God spoken of as the One Substance was shocked and revolted by such a characterization of his nature, the reason lay partly in the instinctive feeling that in such a conception self-consciousness was simply submerged, and not preserved. But partly, again, the opposite position, which maintains thinking to be merely subjective thinking, abstract universality as such, is exactly the same bare uniformity, is undifferentiated, unmoved substantiality. And even if, in the third place, thought combines with itself the being of substance, and conceives immediacy or intuition (*Anschauung*) as thinking, it is still a question whether this intellectual intuition does not fall back into that inert, abstract simplicity, and exhibit and expound reality itself in an unreal manner.

The living substance, further, is that being which is truly subject, or, what is the same thing, is truly realized and actual (*wirklich*) solely in the process of positing itself, or in mediating with its own self its transitions from one state or position to the opposite. As subject it is pure and simple negativity, and just on that account a process of splitting up what is simple and undifferentiated, a process of duplicating and setting factors in opposition, which [process] in turn is the negation of this indifferent diversity and of the opposition of factors it entails. True reality is merely this process of reinstating self-identity, of reflecting into its own self in and from its other, and is not an original and primal unity as such, not an immediate unity as such. It is the process of its own becoming, the circle which presupposes its end as its purpose, and has its end for its beginning; it becomes concrete and actual only by being carried out, and by the end it involves.

The life of God and divine intelligence, then, can, if we like, be spoken of as love disporting with itself; but this idea falls into edification, and even sinks into insipidity, if it lacks the seriousness, the suffering, the patience, and the labour of the negative. *Per se* the divine life is no doubt undisturbed identity and oneness with itself, which finds no serious obstacle in otherness and estrangement, and none in the surmounting of this estrangement. But this 'per se' is abstract generality, where we abstract from its real nature, which consists in its being objective to itself, conscious of itself on its own account (*für sich zu sein*); and where consequently we neglect altogether the self-movement which is the formal character of its activity. If the form is declared to correspond to the essence, it is just for that reason a misunderstanding to suppose that knowledge can be content with the 'per se', the essence, but can do without the form, that the absolute principle, or absolute intuition, makes the carrying out of the former, or the development of the latter, needless. Precisely because the form is as necessary to the essence as the essence to itself, absolute reality must not be conceived of and expressed as essence alone, i.e., as immediate substance, or as pure self-intuition of the Divine, but as form also, and with the entire wealth of the developed form. Only then is it grasped and expressed as really actual.

The truth is the whole. The whole, however, is merely the essential nature reaching its completeness through the process of its own development. Of the Absolute it must be said that it is essentially a result, that only at the end is it what it is in very truth; and just in that consists its nature, which is to be actual, subject, or self-becoming, self-development. Should it appear contradictory to say that the Absolute has to be conceived essentially as a result, a little consideration will set this appearance of contradiction in its true light. The beginning, the principle, or the Absolute, as at first or immediately expressed, is merely the universal. If we say 'all animals', that does not pass for zoology; for the same reason we see at once that the words absolute, divine, eternal, and so on do not express what is implied in them; and only mere words like these, in point of fact, express intuition as the immediate. Whatever is more than a word like that, even the mere transition to a proposition, is a form of mediation, contains a process towards another state from which we must return once more. It is this process of mediation however that is rejected with horror, as if absolute knowledge were being surrendered when more is made of mediation than merely the assertion that it is nothing absolute, and does not exist in the Absolute.

This horrified rejection of mediation, however, arises as a fact from want of acquaintance with its nature, and with the nature of absolute knowledge itself. For mediating is nothing but self-identity working itself out through an active self-directed process; or, in other words, it is reflection into self, the aspect in which the ego is for itself, objective to itself. It is pure negativity, or, reduced to its utmost abstraction, the process of bare and simple becoming. The ego, or becoming in general, this process of mediating, is, because of its being simple, just immediacy coming to be, and is immediacy itself. We misconceive therefore the nature of reason if we exclude reflection or mediation from ultimate truth, and do not take it to be a positive moment of the Absolute. It is reflection which constitutes truth the final result, and yet at the same time does away with the contrast between result and the process of arriving at it. For this process is likewise simple, and therefore not distinct from the form of truth, which consists in appearing as simple in the result; it is indeed just this restoration and return to simplicity. While the embryo is certainly, in itself, implicitly a human being, it is not so explicitly, it is not by itself a human being (*für sich*); man is explicitly man only in the form of developed and cultivated reason, which has made itself to be what it is implicitly. Its actual reality is first found here. But this result arrived at is itself simple immediacy; for it is self conscious freedom, which is at one with itself, and has not set aside the opposition it involves and left it there, but has made its account with it and become reconciled to it.

What has been said may also be expressed by saying that reason is purposive activity. The exaltation of so-called nature at the expense of thought misconceived, and more especially the rejection of external purposiveness, have brought the idea of purpose in general into disrepute. All the same, in the sense in which Aristotle, too, characterizes nature as purposive activity, purpose is the immediate, the undisturbed, the unmoved which is self-moving; as such it is subject. Its power of moving, taken abstractly, is its existence for itself, or pure negativity. The result is the same as the beginning solely because the beginning is purpose. Stated otherwise, what is actual and concrete is the same as its inner principle or notion simply because the immediate *qua* purpose contains within it the self or pure actuality. The realized purpose, or concrete actuality, is movement and development unfolded. But this very unrest is the self; and it is one and the same with that immediacy and simplicity characteristic of the beginning just for the reason that it is the result, and has returned upon itself—while this latter again is just the self, and the self is self-referring and self-relating identity and simplicity.

The need to think of the Absolute as subject, has led men to make use of statements like 'God is the eternal', the 'moral order of the world', or 'love', etc. In such propositions the truth is just barely stated to be Subject, but not set forth as the process of reflectively mediating itself with itself. In a proposition of that kind we begin with the word 'God'. By itself this is a meaningless sound, a mere name; the predicate says afterwards *what* it is, gives it content and meaning: the empty beginning becomes real knowledge only when we thus get to the end of the statement. So far as that goes, why not speak alone of the eternal, of the moral order of the world, etc., or, like the ancients, of pure conceptions such as being, the one, etc., i.e., of what gives the meaning without adding the meaningless sound at all? But this word just indicates that it is not a being or essence or universal in general that is put forward, but something reflected into self, a subject. Yet at the same time this acceptance of the Absolute as Subject is merely anticipated, not really affirmed. The subject is taken to be a fixed point, and to it as their support the predicates are attached, by a process falling within the individual knowing about it, but not looked upon as belonging to the point of attachment itself; only by such a process, however, could the content be presented as subject. Constituted as it is, this process cannot belong to the subject; but when that point of support is fixed to start with, this process cannot be otherwise constituted, it can only be external. The anticipation that the Absolute is subject is therefore not merely *not* the realization of this conception; it even makes realization impossible. For it makes out the notion to be a static point, while its actual reality is self-movement, self-activity.

Among the many consequences that follow from what has been said, it is of importance to emphasize this, that knowledge is only real and can only be set forth fully in the form of science, in the form of system; and further, that a so-called fundamental proposition or first principle of philosophy, even if it is true, is yet nonetheless false just because and in so far as it is merely a fundamental proposition, merely a first principle. The refutation consists in bringing out its defective character, and it *is* defective because it is merely the universal, merely a principle, the beginning.

That the truth is only realized in the form of system, that substance is essentially subject, is expressed in the idea which represents the Absolute as Spirit

(*Geist*)—the grandest conception of all, and one which is due to modern times and its religion. Spirit is alone Reality. It is the inner being of the world, that which essentially is, and is *per se;* it assumes objective, determinate form, and enters into relations with itself—it is externality (otherness), and exists for self; yet, in this determination, and in its otherness, it is still one with itself—it is self-contained and self-complete, in itself and for itself at once. This self-containedness, however, is first something known by us, it is implicit in its nature (*an sich*); it is Substance spiritual. It has to become self-contained *for itself,* on its own account; it must be knowledge of spirit, and must be consciousness of itself as spirit. This means, it must be presented to itself as an object, but at the same time straightway annul and transcend this objective form; it must be its own object in which it finds itself reflected. In so far as spirit knows itself to be for itself, then this self-production, the pure notion, is the sphere and element in which its objectification takes effect, and where it gets its existential form. In this way it is in its existence aware of itself as an object in which its own self is reflected. Spirit, which, when thus developed, knows itself to be spirit, is science. Science is its realization, and the kingdom it sets up for itself in its own native element.

THE ELEMENT OF KNOWLEDGE

A self having knowledge purely of itself in the absolute antithesis of itself, this pure ether as such, is the very soil where science flourishes, is knowledge in universal form. The beginning of philosophy presupposes or demands from consciousness that it should feel at home in this element. But this element only attains its perfect meaning and acquires transparency through the process of gradually developing it. It is pure spirituality as the universal which assumes the shape of simple immediacy; and this simple element, existing as such, is the field of science, is thinking, which can be only in spirit. Because this medium, this immediacy of spirit, is the spirit's substantial nature in general, it is the transfigured essence, reflection which itself is simple, which is aware of itself as immediacy; it is being, which is reflection into itself. Science on its side requires the individual self-consciousness to have risen into this high ether, in order to be able to live with science, and in science, and really to feel alive there. Conversely the individual has the right to demand that science shall hold the ladder to help him to get at least as far as this position, shall show him that he has in himself this ground to stand on. His right rests on his absolute independence, which he knows he possesses in every type and phase of knowledge; for in every phase, whether recognized by science or not, and whatever be the content, his right as an individual is the absolute and final form, i.e., he is the immediate certainty of self, and thereby is unconditioned being, were this expression preferred. Let science be *per se* what it likes, in its relation to naïve immediate self-conscious life it presents the appearance of being a reversal of the latter; or, again, because naïve self-consciousness finds the principle of its reality in the certainty of itself, science bears the character of unreality, since consciousness 'for itself' is a state quite outside of science. Science has for that reason to combine that other element of self-certainty with its own, or rather to show that the other element belongs to itself, and how it does so. When devoid of that sort of reality, science is merely the content of spirit *qua* something implicit or potential (*an sich*); purpose, which at the start is no more than something internal; not spirit, but at first merely spiritual substance. This implicit moment (*Ansich*) has to find external expression, and become objective on its own account. This means nothing else than that this moment has to establish self-consciousness as one with itself.

THE ASCENT INTO THIS IS THE PHENOMENOLOGY OF SPIRIT

It is this process by which science in general comes about, this gradual development of knowing, that is set forth here in the *Phenomenology of Spirit*. Knowing, as it is found at the start, spirit in its immediate and primitive stage, is without the essential nature of spirit, is sense-consciousness. To reach the stage of genuine knowledge, or produce the element where science is found—the pure conception of science itself—a long and laborious journey must be undertaken. This process towards science, as regards the content it will bring to light and the forms it will assume in the course of its progress, will not be what is primarily imagined by leading the unscientific consciousness up to the level of science: it will be something different, too, from establishing and laying the foundations of science; and anyway something else than the sort of ecstatic enthusiasm which starts straight off with absolute knowledge, as if shot out of a pistol, and makes short work of other points of view simply by explaining that it is to take no notice of them.

The task of conducting the individual spirit from its unscientific standpoint to that of science had to be taken in its general sense; we had to contemplate the formative development (*Bildung*) of the universal [or general] individual, of self-conscious spirit. As to the relation between these two [the particular and general individual], every moment, as it gains concrete form and its own proper shape and appearance, finds a place in the life of the universal individual. The particular individual is incomplete spirit, a concrete shape in whose existence, taken as a whole, one determinate characteristic predominates, while the others are found only in blurred outline. In that spirit which stands higher than another the lower concrete form of existence has sunk into an obscure moment; what was formerly an objective fact (*die Sache selbst*) is now only a single trace: its definite shape has been veiled, and become simply a piece of shading. The individual, whose substance is spirit at the higher level, passes through these past forms, much in the way that one who takes up a higher science goes through those preparatory forms of knowledge, which he has long made his own, in order to call up their content before him; he brings back the recollection of them without stopping to fix his interest upon them. The particular individual, so far as content is concerned, has also to go through the stages through which the general spirit has passed, but as shapes once assumed by spirit and now laid aside, as stages of a road which has been worked over and levelled out. In this respect culture or development of spirit

(*Bildung*), regarded from the side of the individual, consists in his acquiring what lies at his hand ready for him, in making its inorganic nature organic to himself, and taking possession of it for himself. Looked at, however, from the side of universal spirit *qua* general spiritual substance, culture means nothing else than that this substance gives itself its own self-consciousness, brings about its own inherent process and its own reflection into self.

Science lays before us the morphogenetic process of this cultural development in all its detailed fullness and necessity, and at the same time shows it to be something that has already sunk into the spirit as a moment of its being and become a possession of spirit. The goal to be reached is spirit's insight into what knowing is. The length of the journey has to be borne with, for every moment is necessary; and again we must halt at every stage, for each is itself a complete individual form, and is fully and finally considered only so far as its determinate character is taken and dealt with as a rounded and concrete whole, or only so far as the whole is looked at in the light of the special and peculiar character which this determination gives it. Because the substance of individual spirit, nay, more, because the universal spirit at work in the world *(Weltgeist)*, has had the patience to go through these forms in the long stretch of time's extent, and to take upon itself the prodigious labour of the world's history, where it bodied forth in each form the entire content of itself, as each is capable of presenting it; and because by nothing less could that all-pervading spirit ever manage to become conscious of what itself is—for that reason, the individual spirit, in the nature of the case, cannot expect by less toil to grasp what its own substance contains. All the same, its task has meanwhile been made much lighter, because this has historically been implicitly (*an sich*) accomplished, the content is one where reality is already cancelled for spiritual possibilities, where immediacy has been overcome and brought under the control of reflection, the various forms and shapes have been already reduced to their intellectual abbreviations, to determinations of thought (*Gedankenbestimmung*) pure and simple. Being now a thought, the content is the property of the substance of spirit; existence has no more to be changed into the form of what is inherent and implicit (*Ansichseins*), but only the implicit—no longer merely something primitive, nor lying hidden within existence, but already present as a recollection—into the form of what is explicit, of what is objective to self (*Fürsichseins*).

THE TRANSFORMATION OF THE FAMILIAR INTO THOUGHT

We have to state more exactly the way this is done. At the point at which we here take up this movement, we are spared, in connection with the whole, the process of cancelling and transcending the stage of mere existence. This process has already taken place. What is still to be done and needs a higher kind of transformation, is to transcend the forms as ideally presented and made familiar to our minds. By that previous negative process, existence, having been withdrawn into spirit's substance, is, in the first instance, transferred to the life of self only in an immediate way. The property the self has thereby acquired has still the same character of uncomprehended immediacy, of passive indifference, which existence itself had; existence has in this way merely passed into the form of an ideal presentation. At the same time, by so doing, it is something familiar to us, something 'well-known', something which the existent spirit has finished and done with, and hence takes no more to do with and no further interest in. While the activity that is done with the existent is itself merely the process of the particular spirit, of spirit which is not comprehending itself, on the other hand, *knowledge* is directed against this ideal presentation which has hereby arisen, against this 'being-familiar' and 'well-known;' it is an action of *universal self*, the concern of *thought*.

What is 'familiarly known' is not properly known, just for the reason that it is 'familiar'. When engaged in the process of knowing, it is the commonest form of self-deception, and a deception of other people as well, to assume something to be familiar, and give assent to it on that very account. Knowledge of that sort, with all its talk, never gets from the spot, but has no idea that this is the case. Subject and object, and so on, God, nature, understanding, sensibility, etc., are uncritically presupposed as familiar and something valid, and become fixed points from which to start and to which to return. The process of knowing flits between these secure points, and in consequence goes on merely along the surface.

Analysis of an idea, as it used to be carried out, did in fact consist in nothing else than doing away with its character of familiarity. To break up an idea into its ultimate elements means returning upon its moments, which at least do not have the form of the given idea when found, but are the immediate property of the self. Doubtless, this analysis only arrives at thoughts which are themselves familiar elements, fixed inert determinations. But what is thus separated, and in a sense is unreal, is itself an essential moment; for just because the concrete fact is self-divided, and turns into unreality, it is something self-moving, self-active. The action of separating the elements is the exercise of the force of Understanding, the most astonishing and greatest of all powers, or rather the absolute power. The circle, which is self-enclosed and at rest, and, *qua* substance, holds its own moments, is an immediate relation, the immediate, continuous relation of elements with their unity, and hence arouses no sense of wonderment. But that an accident as such, when out loose from its containing circumference,—that what is bound and held by something else and actual only by being connected with it,—should obtain an existence all its own, gain freedom and independence on its own account—this is the portentous power of the negative; it is the energy of thought, of pure ego. Death, as we may call that unreality, is the most terrible thing, and to keep and hold fast what is dead demands the greatest force of all. Beauty, powerless and helpless, hates understanding, because the latter exacts from it what it cannot perform. But the life of spirit is not one that shuns death, and keeps clear of destruction; it endures death and in death maintains its being. It only wins to its truth when it finds itself utterly torn asunder. It is this mighty power, not by being a positive which turns away from the negative, as when we say of anything it is nothing or it is false, and, being then done with it, pass off to something else:

on the contrary, spirit is this power only by looking the negative in the face, and dwelling with it. This dwelling beside it is the magic power that converts the negative into being. That power is just what we spoke of above as subject, which by giving determinateness a place in its substance, cancels abstract immediacy, i.e., immediacy which merely *is*, and, by so doing, becomes the true substance, becomes being or immediacy that does not have mediation outside it, but is this mediation itself.

TRANSFORMATION INTO THE CONCEPT

This process of making what is objectively presented a possession of pure self-consciousness, of raising it to the level of universality in general, is merely one aspect of mental development; spiritual evolution is not yet completed. The manner of study in ancient times is distinct from that of the modern world, in that the former consisted in the cultivation and perfecting of the natural mind. Testing life carefully at all points, philosophizing about everything it came across, the former created an experience permeated through and through by universals. In modern times, however, an individual finds the abstract form ready made. In straining to grasp it and make it his own, he rather strives to bring forward the inner meaning alone, without any process of mediation; the production of the universal is abridged, instead of the universal arising out of the manifold detail of concrete existence. Hence nowadays the task before us consists not so much in getting the individual clear of the stage of sensuous immediacy, and making him a substance that thinks and is grasped in terms of thought, but rather the very opposite: it consists in actualizing the universal, and giving it spiritual vitality, by the process of breaking down and superseding fixed and determinate thoughts. But it is much more difficult to make fixed and definite thoughts fuse with one another and form a continuous whole than to bring sensuous existence into this state. The reason lies in what was said before. Thought determinations get their substance and the element of their existence from the ego, the power of the negative, or pure reality; while determinations of sense find this in impotent abstract immediacy, in mere being as such. Thoughts become fluent and inter-fuse, when thinking pure and simple, this inner immediacy, knows itself as a moment, when pure certainty of self abstracts from itself. It does not 'abstract' in the sense of getting away from itself and setting itself on one side, but of surrendering the fixed quality of its self-affirmation, and giving up both the fixity of the purely concrete—which is the ego as contrasted with the variety of its content—and the fixity of all those distinctions [the various thought-functions, principles, etc.] which are present in the element of pure thought and share that absoluteness of the ego. In virtue of this process pure thoughts become notions, concepts, and are then what they are in truth, self-moving functions, circles, are what their substance consists in, are spiritual entities.

This movement of the spiritual entities constitutes the nature of scientific procedure in general. Looked at as the concatenation of their content, this movement is the necessitated development and expansion of that content into an organic systematic whole. By this movement, too, the road, which leads to the notion of knowledge, becomes itself likewise a necessary and complete evolving process (*Werden*). This preparatory stage thus ceases to consist of casual philosophical reflections, referring to objects here and there, to processes and thoughts of the undeveloped mind as chance may direct; and it does not try to establish the truth by miscellaneous ratiocinations, inferences, and consequences drawn from circumscribed thoughts. The road to science, by the very movement of the notion itself, will compass the entire objective world of conscious life in its rational necessity.

Further, a systematic exposition like this constitutes the first part of science, because the positive existence of spirit, *qua* primary and ultimate, is nothing but the immediate aspect of spirit, the beginning; the beginning, but not yet its return to itself. The characteristic feature distinguishing this part of science [Phenomenology] from the others is the element of positive immediate existence.

Spirit's immediate existence, conscious life, has two aspects—cognition and objectivity which is opposed to or negative of the subjective function of knowing. Since it is in the medium of consciousness that spirit is developed and brings out its various moments, this opposition between the factors of conscious life is found at each stage in the evolution of spirit, and all the various moments appear as modes or forms (*Gestalten*) of consciousness. The scientific statement of the course of this development is a science of the experience through which consciousness passes; the substance and its process are considered as the object of consciousness. Consciousness knows and comprehends nothing but what falls within its experience; for what is found in experience is merely spiritual substance, and, moreover, object of its self. Spirit, however, becomes object, for it consists in the process of becoming an other to itself, i.e., an object for its own self, and in transcending this otherness. And experience is called this very process by which the element that is immediate, unexperienced, i.e., abstract—whether it be in the form of sense or of a bare thought—externalizes itself, and then comes back to itself from this state of estrangement, and by so doing is at length set forth in its concrete nature and real truth, and becomes too a possession of consciousness.

The dissimilarity which obtains in consciousness between the ego and the substance constituting its object, is their inner distinction, the factor of negativity in general. We may regard it as the defect of both opposites, but it is their very soul, their moving spirit. It was on this account that certain thinkers long ago took the void to be the principle of movement, when they conceived the moving principle to be the negative element, though they had not as yet thought of it as self. While this negative factor appears in the first instance as a dissimilarity, as an inequality, between ego and object, it is just as much the inequality of the substance with itself. What seems to take place outside it, to be an activity directed against it, is its own doing, its own activity; and substance shows that it is in reality subject. When it has brought out this completely, spirit has made its existence adequate to and one with its essential nature. Spirit is object to itself just as it *is*, and the abstract element of immediacy, of the separation between knowing and the truth, is overcome. Being is entirely mediated; it is a substantial content, that is likewise directly in the possession of the ego, has the character of self, is notion. With the attainment of this the *Phenomenology of Spirit* concludes. What spirit prepares for itself in the course of its phenomenology is the element of true knowledge. In this element the moments of spirit are now set out in the form of thought pure and simple, which knows its object to be itself. They no longer involve the opposition between being and knowing; they remain within the undivided simplicity of the knowing function; they are the truth in the form of truth, and their diversity is merely diversity of the content of truth. The process by which they are developed into an organically connected whole is Logic or Speculative Philosophy.

IN WHAT WAY THE PHENOMENOLOGY OF THE SPIRIT IS NEGATIVE

Now, because the systematic statement of spirit's experience embraces merely its ways of appearing, it may well seem that the advance from that to the science of ultimate truth in the form of truth is merely negative; and we might readily be content to dispense with the negative process as something altogether false, and might ask to be taken straight to the truth at once: why meddle with what is false at all? The point formerly raised, that we should have begun with science at once, may be answered here by considering the character of negativity in general regarded as something false. The usual ideas on this subject particularly obstruct the approach to the truth. The consideration of this point will give us an opportunity to speak about mathematical knowledge, which non-philosophical knowledge looks upon as the ideal which philosophy ought to try to attain, but has so far striven in vain to reach.

    Truth and falsehood as commonly understood belong to those sharply defined ideas which claim a completely fixed nature of their own, one standing in solid isolation on this side, the other on that, without any community between them. Against that view it must be pointed out, that truth is not like stamped coin that is issued ready from the mint and so can be taken up and used. Nor, again, is there something false, any more than there is something evil. Evil and falsehood are indeed not so bad as the devil, for in the form of the devil they get the length of being particular subjects; *qua* false and evil they are merely universals, though they have a nature of their own with reference to one another. Falsity (that is what we are dealing with here) would be *otherness,* the negative aspect of the substance, which [substance], *qua* content of knowledge, is truth. But the substance is itself essentially the negative element, partly as involving distinction and determination of content, partly as being a process of distinguishing pure and simple, i.e., as being self and knowledge in general. Doubtless we can know in a way that is false.

To know something falsely means that knowledge is not adequate to, is not on equal terms with, its substance. Yet this very dissimilarity is the process of distinction in general, the essential moment in knowing. It is, in fact, out of this active distinction that its harmonious unity arises, and this identity, when arrived at, is truth. But it is not truth in a sense which would involve the rejection of the discordance, the diversity, like dross from pure metal; nor, again, does truth remain detached from diversity, like a finished article from the instrument that shapes it. Difference itself continues to be an immediate element within truth as such, in the form of the principle of negation, in the form of the activity of Self. All the same, we cannot for that reason say that falsehood is a moment or forms even a constituent part of truth. That 'in every case of falsity there is something true' is an expression in which they are taken to be like oil and water, which do not mix and are merely united externally. Just in the interest of their real meaning, precisely because we want to designate the aspect or moment of complete otherness, the terms true and false must no longer be used where their otherness has been cancelled and superseded. Just as the expressions 'unity of subject and object', of 'finite and infinite', of 'being and thought', etc., are clumsy when subject and object, etc., are taken to mean what they are *outside* their unity, and are thus in that unity not meant to be what its very expression conveys; in the same way falsehood is not, *qua* false, any longer a moment of truth.

Dogmatism as a way of thinking, whether in ordinary knowledge or in the study of philosophy, is nothing else but the view that truth consists in a proposition, which is a fixed and final result, or again which is directly known. To questions like, 'When was Caesar born', 'How many feet make a furlongs', etc., a straight answer ought to be given; just as it is absolutely true that the square of the hypotenuse is equal to the sum of the squares of the other two sides of a right-angled triangle. But the nature of a so-called truth of that sort is different from the nature of philosophical truth.

HISTORICAL AND MATHEMATICAL TRUTH

As regards truth in matters of historical fact—to deal briefly with this subject—so far as we consider the purely historical element, it will be readily granted that they have to do with the sphere of particular existence, with a content in its contingent and arbitrary aspects, features that have no necessity. But even bare truths of the kind, say, like those mentioned, are impossible without the activity of self-consciousness.

All the same, while proof is essential in the case of mathematical knowledge, it still does not have the significance and nature of being a moment in the result itself; the proof is over when we get the result, and has disappeared. *Qua* result the theorem is, no doubt, one that is seen to be true. But this eventuality has nothing to do with its content, but only with its relation to the knowing subject. The process of mathematical proof does not belong to the object; it is a function that takes place outside the matter in hand. Thus, the nature of a right-angled triangle does not break itself up into factors in the manner set forth in the mathematical construction which is required to prove the proposition expressing the relation of its parts. The entire process of producing the result is an affair of knowledge which takes its own way of going about it. In philosophical knowledge, too, the way existence, *qua* existence, comes about (*Werden*) is different from that whereby the essence or inner nature of the fact comes into being. But philosophical knowledge, for one thing, contains both, while mathematical knowledge sets forth merely the way an existence comes about, i.e., the way the nature of the fact gets to be in the sphere of knowledge as such. For another thing, too, philosophical knowledge unites both these particular movements.

In mathematical knowledge the insight required is an external function so far as the subject-matter dealt with is concerned. It follows that the actual fact is thereby altered. The means taken, construction and proof, contain, no doubt, true propositions; but all the same we are bound to say that the content is false.

The real defect of this kind of knowledge, however, affects its process of knowing as much as its material. As to that process, in the first place we do not see any necessity in the construction. The necessity does not arise from the nature of the theorem: it is imposed; and the injunction to draw just these lines, an infinite number of others being equally possible, is blindly acquiesced in, without our knowing anything further, except that, as we fondly believe, this will serve our purpose in producing the proof. Later on this design then comes out too, and is therefore merely external in character, just because it is only after the proof is found that it comes to be known. In the same way, again, the proof takes a direction that begins anywhere we like, without our knowing as yet what relation this beginning has to the result to be brought out. In its course, it takes up certain specific elements and relations and lets others alone, without its being directly obvious what necessity there is in the matter. An external purpose controls this process.

Its purpose or principle is quantity. This is precisely the relationship that is non-essential, alien to the character of the notion. The process of knowledge goes on, therefore, on the surface, does not affect the concrete fact itself, does not touch its inner nature or notion, and is hence not a conceptual way of comprehending. The material which provides mathematics with these welcome treasures of truth consists of space and numerical units (*das Eins*). Space is that kind of existence wherein the concrete notion inscribes the diversity it contains, as in an empty, lifeless element in which its differences likewise subsist in passive, lifeless form. What is concretely actual is not something spatial, such as is treated of in mathematics.

As to time, which, it is to be presumed, would, by way of the counterpart to space, constitute the object-matter of the other division of pure mathematics, this is the notion itself in the form of existence. The principle of quantity, of difference which is not determined by the notion, and the principle of equality, of abstract, lifeless unity, are incapable of dealing with that sheer restlessness of life and its absolute and inherent process of differentiation. It is therefore only in an arrested, paralysed form, only in the form of the quantitative unit, that this essentially negative activity becomes the second object-matter of this way of knowing, which, itself an external operation, degrades what is self-moving to the level of mere matter, in order thus to get an indifferent, external, lifeless content.

THE NATURE OF PHILOSOPHICAL TRUTH AND ITS METHOD

Philosophy, on the contrary, does not deal with a determination that is non-essential, but with a determination so far as it is an essential factor. The abstract or unreal is not its element and content, but the real, what is self-establishing, has life within itself, existence in its very notion. It is the process that creates its own moments in its course, and goes through them all; and the whole of this movement constitutes its positive content and its truth. This movement includes, therefore, within it the negative factor as well, the element which would be named falsity if it could be considered one from which we had to abstract. The element that disappears has rather to be looked at as itself essential, not in the sense of being something fixed, that has to be cut off from truth and allowed to lie outside it, heaven knows where; just as similarly the truth is not to be held to stand on the other side as an immovable lifeless positive element. Appearance is the process of arising into being and passing away again, a process that itself does not arise and does not pass away, but is *per se,* and constitutes reality and the life-movement of truth. The truth is thus the bacchanalian revel, where not a member is sober; and because every member no sooner becomes detached than it *eo ipso* collapses straightway, the revel is just as much a state of transparent unbroken calm. Judged by that movement, the particular shapes which spirit assumes do not indeed subsist any more than do determinate thoughts or ideas; but they are, all the same, as much positive and necessary moments, as negative and transitory. In the entirety of the movement, taken as an unbroken quiescent whole, that which obtains distinctness in the course of its process and secures specific existence, is preserved in the form of a self-recollection, in which existence is self-knowledge, and self-knowledge, again, is immediate existence.

It might well seem necessary to state at the outset the chief points in connection with the method of this process, the way in which science operates. Its nature, however, is to be found in what has already been said, while the proper systematic exposition of it is the special business of Logic, or rather is Logic itself. For the method is nothing else than the structure of the whole in its pure and essential form. But it is not difficult to see that the method of propounding a proposition, producing reasons for it and then refuting its opposite by reasons too, is not the form in which truth can appear. Truth moves itself by its very nature; but the method just mentioned is a form of knowledge external to its material. Hence it is peculiar to mathematics and must be left to mathematics, which, as already indicated, takes for its principle the relation of quantity, a relation alien to the notion, and gets its material from lifeless space, and the equally lifeless numerical unit.

AGAINST SCHEMATIZING FORMALISM

Now that the triplicity, adopted in the system of Kant—a method rediscovered, to begin with, by instinctive insight, but left lifeless and uncomprehended—has been raised to its significance as an absolute method, true form is thereby set up in its true content, and the conception of science has come to light. But the use this form has been put to in certain quarters has no right to the name of science. For we see it there reduced to a lifeless schema, to nothing better than a mere shadow, and scientific organization to a synoptic table. This formalism—about which we spoke before in general terms, and whose procedure we wish here to state more fully—thinks it has comprehended and expressed the nature and life of a given form when it proclaims a determination of the schema to be its predicate. The predicate may be subjectivity or objectivity, or again magnetism, electricity, and so on, contraction or expansion, East or West, and such like—a form of predication that can be multiplied indefinitely, because according to this way of working each determination, each mode, can be applied as a form or schematic element in the case of every other, and each will thankfully perform the same service for any other.

Instead of the inner activity and self-movement of its own actual life, such a simple determination of direct intuition (*Anschauung*)—which means here sense-knowledge—is predicated in accordance with a superficial analogy, and this external and empty application of the formula is called 'construction'. The same thing happens here, however, as in the case of every kind of formalism. Formalism in the case of speculative Philosophy of Nature (*Naturphilosophie*) takes the shape of teaching that understanding is electricity, animals are nitrogen, or equivalent to South or North and so on. When it does this, whether as badly as it is here expressed or even concocted with more terminology, such forceful procedure brings and holds together elements to all appearance far removed from one another; the violence done to stable inert sense-elements by connecting them in this way, confers on them merely the semblance of a conceptual unity, and spares itself the trouble of doing what is after all the important thing—expressing the notion itself, the meaning that underlies sense-ideas. The instrument for producing this monotonous formalism is no more difficult to handle than the palette of a painter, on which lie only two colours, say red and green, the former for colouring the surface when we want a historical piece, the latter when we want a bit of landscape. It would be difficult to settle which is greater in all this, the agreeable ease with which everything in heaven and earth and under the earth is plastered with that botch of colour. What results from the use of this method of sticking on to everything in heaven and earth, to every kind of shape and form, natural and spiritual, the pair of determinations from the general schema, and filing everything in this manner, is no less than an 'account as clear as noonday' of the organized whole of the universe. It is, that is to say, a synoptic index, like a skeleton with tickets stuck all over it, or like the rows of boxes kept shut and labelled in a grocer's stall; and is as intelligible as either the one or the other. It has lost hold of the living nature of concrete fact; just as in the former case we have merely dry bones with flesh and blood all gone, and in the latter, there is shut away in those boxes something equally lifeless too. We have already remarked that the final outcome of this style of thinking is, at the same time, to paint entirely in one kind of colour; for it turns with contempt from the distinctions in the schematic table, looks on them as belonging to the activity of mere reflection, and lets them drop out of sight in the void of the Absolute, and there reinstates pure identity, pure formless whiteness. Such uniformity of colouring in the schema with its lifeless determinations, this absolute identity, and the transition from one to the other—these are the one as well as the other, the expression of inert lifeless understanding, and equally an external process of knowledge.

Not only can what is excellent not escape the fate of being thus devitalized and despiritualized and excoriated of seeing its skin paraded about by lifeless knowledge and the conceit such knowledge engenders; but rather, such a fate lets us realize the power the 'excellent' exercises over the heart (*Gemüth*), if not over the spirit (*Geist*). Moreover, we recognize thereby, too, the constructive unfolding into universality and determinateness of form which marks the complete attainment of excellence, and which alone makes it possible that this universality can be turned to superficial uses.

Science can become an organic system only by the inherent life of the notion. In science the determinateness, which was taken from the schema and stuck on to existing facts in external fashion, is the self directing inner soul of the concrete content. The movement of what is partly consists in becoming another to itself, and thus developing explicitly into its own immanent content; partly, again, it takes this evolved content, this existence it assumes, back into itself, i.e., makes itself into a moment, and reduces itself to simple determinateness. In the first stage of the process negativity lies in the function of distinguishing and establishing existence; in this latter return into self, negativity consists in the bringing about of determinate simplicity. It is in this way that the content shows its specific characteristic not to be received from something else, and stuck on externally; the content gives itself this determinate characteristic, appoints itself of its own initiative to the rank of a moment and to a place in the whole. The pigeon-holing process of understanding retains for itself the necessity and the notion controlling the content, that which constitutes the concrete element, the actuality and living process of the subject-matter which it labels: or rather, understanding does not retain this for itself, on the contrary, understanding fails to know it. For if it had as much insight as that, it would surely show that it had. It is not even aware of the need for such insight; if it were, it would drop its schematizing process, or at least would no longer be satisfied to know by way of a mere table of contents. A table of contents is all that understanding gives, the content itself it does not furnish at all.

Instead of making its way into the inherent content of the matter in hand, understanding always takes a survey of the whole, assumes a position above the particular existence about which it is speaking, i.e., it does not see it at all. True scientific knowledge, on the contrary, demands abandonment to the very life of the object, or, which means the same thing, claims to have before it the inner necessity controlling the object, and to express this only. Steeping itself in its object, it forgets to take that general survey, which is merely a turning of knowledge away from the content back into itself. But being sunk into the material in hand, and following the course that such material takes, true knowledge returns back into itself, yet not before the content in its fullness is taken into itself, is reduced to the simplicity of being a determinate characteristic, drops to the level of being one aspect of an existing entity, and passes over into its higher truth. By this process the whole as such, surveying its entire content, itself emerges out of the wealth wherein its process of reflection seemed to be lost.

In general, in virtue of the principle that, as we expressed it before, substance is implicitly and in itself subject, all content makes its reflection into itself in its own special way. The subsistence or substance of anything that exists is its self-identity; for its want of identity, or oneness with itself, would be its dissolution. But self-identity is pure abstraction; and this is just thinking. When I say Quality, I state simple determinateness; by means of its quality one existence is distinguished from another or is an 'existence;' it is for itself, something on its own account, or subsists with itself because of this simple characteristic. But by doing so it is essentially Thought.

Here we find contained the principle that Being is Thought: here is exercised that insight which usually tends to deviate from the ordinary non-conceptual way of speaking of the identity of thought and being. In virtue, further, of the fact that subsistence on the part of what exists is self-identity or pure abstraction, it is the abstraction of itself from itself, in other words, is itself its own want of identity with itself and dissolution—its own proper inwardness and retraction into self—its process of becoming.

Owing, to the nature which being thus has, and so far as what is has this nature from the point of view of knowledge, this thinking is not an activity which treats the content as something alien and external; it is not reflection into self away from the content. Rather, since knowledge sees the content go back into its own proper inner nature, the activity of knowledge is absorbed in that content—for it (the activity) is the immanent self of the content—and is also at the same time returned into itself, for this activity is pure self-identity in otherness. In this way the knowing activity is the artful device which, while seeming to refrain from activity, looks on and watches how specific determinateness with its concrete life, just where it believes it is working out its own self-preservation and its own private interest, is, in point of fact, doing the very opposite, is doing what brings about its own dissolution and makes itself a moment in the whole.

While, in the foregoing, the significance of Understanding was stated from the point of view of the self-consciousness of substance; by what has been here stated we can see clearly its significance from the point of view of substance *qua* being. Existence is Quality, self-identical determinateness, or determinate simplicity, determinate thought: this is existence from the point of view of Understanding. On this account it is *nous*, as Anaxagoras first thought reality to be. Those who succeeded him grasped the nature of existence in a more determinate way, i.e., as determinate or specific universality, kind or species. The term species or kind seems indeed too ordinary and inadequate for Ideas, for beauty, holiness, eternal, which are the vogue in these days. As a matter of fact, however, idea means neither more nor less than kind, species.

Precisely for the reason that existence is designated a species or kind, it is naked simple thought: *Nous,* simplicity, is substance. It is on account of its simplicity, its self-identity, that it appears steady, fixed, and permanent. But this self-identity is likewise negativity; hence that fixed and stable existence carries the process of its own dissolution within itself. The determinateness appears at first to be so solely through its relation to something else; and its process seems imposed and forced upon it externally. But its having its own otherness within itself, and the fact of its being a self-initiated process—these are implied in the very simplicity of thought itself. For this is self-moving thought, thought that distinguishes, is inherent inwardness, the pure notion. Thus, then, it is the very nature of understanding to be a process; and being a process it is Rationality.

In the nature of existence as thus described—to be its own notion and being in one—consists logical necessity in general. This alone is what is rational, the rhythm of the organic whole: it is as much knowledge of content as that content is notion and essential nature. In other words, this alone is the sphere and element of speculative thought. The concrete shape of the content is resolved by its own inherent process into a simple determinate quality. Thereby it is raised to logical form, and its being and essence coincide; its concrete existence is merely this process that takes place, and is *eo ipso* logical existence. It is therefore needless to apply a formal scheme to the concrete content in an external fashion; the content is in its very nature a transition into a formal shape, which, however, ceases to be formalism of an external kind, because the form is the indwelling process of the concrete content itself.

This nature of scientific method, which consists partly in being inseparable from the content, and partly in determining the rhythm of its movement by its own agency, finds, as we mentioned before, its peculiar systematic expression in speculative philosophy.

THE DEMANDS OF THE STUDY OF PHILOSOPHY

Hence the important thing for the student of science is to make himself undergo the strenuous toil of conceptual reflection, of thinking in the form of the notion. This demands concentrated attention on the notion as such, on simple and ultimate determinations like being-in-itself, being-for-itself, self-identity, and so on; for these are elemental, pure, self-determined functions of a kind we might call souls, were it not that their conceptual nature denotes something higher than that term contains. The interruption by conceptual thought of the habit of always thinking in figurative ideas (*Vorstellungen*) is as annoying and troublesome to this way of thinking as to that process of formal intelligence which in its reasoning rambles about with no real thoughts to reason with. The former, the habit, may be called materialized thinking, a fortuitous mental state, one that is absorbed in what is material, and hence finds it very distasteful at once to lift its self clear of this matter and be with itself alone. The latter, the process of *raisonnement*, is, on the other hand, detachment from all content, and conceited superiority to it. What is wanted here is the effort and struggle to give up this kind of freedom, and instead of being a merely arbitrary principle directing the content anyhow, this freedom should sink into and pervade the content, should let it be directed and controlled by its own proper nature, i.e., by the self as its own self and should observe this process taking place. We must abstain from interrupting the immanent rhythm of the movement of conceptual thought; we must refrain from arbitrarily interfering with it, and introducing ideas and reflections that have been obtained elsewhere. Restraint of this sort is itself an essential condition of attending to and getting at the real nature of the notion.

ARGUMENTATIVE THINKING IN ITS NEGATIVE ATTITUDE

There are two aspects in the case of that ratiocinative procedure which mark its contrast from conceptual thinking and call for further notice. *Raisonnement*, in the first place, adopts a negative attitude towards the content apprehended; knows how to refute it and reduce it to nothingness. To see what the content is *not* is merely a negative process; it is a dead halt, which does not of itself go beyond itself, and proceed to a new content; it has to get hold of something else from somewhere or other in order to have once more a content. In that this reflection does not even have its own negativity as its content, it is not inside actual fact at all, but for ever away outside it. On the other hand, in the case of conceptual thinking, as was above indicated, the negative aspect falls within the content itself, and is the positive substance of that content, as well as being its inherent character and moving principle as by being the entirety of what these are. Looked at as a result, it is determinate specific negation, the negative which is the outcome of this process, and consequently is a positive content as well.

IN ITS POSITIVE ATTITUDE; ITS SUBJECT

In view of the fact that ratiocinative thinking has a content, whether of images or thoughts or a mixture of both, there is another side to its process which makes conceptual comprehension difficult for it. For just as ratiocinative thinking in its negative reference, which we have been describing, is nothing but the self into which the content returns; in the same way, on the other hand, in its positive cognitive process the self is an ideally presented subject to which the content is related as an accident and predicate. Conceptual thinking goes on in quite a different way. Since the concept or notion is the very self of the object, manifesting itself as the development of the object, it is not a quiescent subject, passively supporting accidents: it is a self-determining active concept which takes up its determinations and makes them its own. In the course of this process that inert passive subject really disappears; it enters into the different constituents and pervades the content; instead of remaining in inert antithesis to determinateness of content, it constitutes, in fact, that very specificity, i.e., the content as differentiated along with the process of bringing this about. Thus the solid basis, which ratiocination found in an inert subject, is shaken to its foundations, and the only object is this very movement of the subject. The subject supplying the concrete filling to its own content ceases to be something transcending this content, and cannot have further predicates or accidents. Conversely, again, the scattered diversity of the content is brought under the control of the self, and so bound together; the content is not a universal that can be detached from the subject, and adapted to several indifferently. Consequently the content is in truth no longer predicate of the subject; it is the very substance, is the inmost reality, and the very principle of what is being considered. Ideational thinking (*vorstellen*), since its nature consists in dealing with accidents or predicates, and in exercising the right to transcend them because they are nothing more than predicates and accidents—this way of thinking is checked in its course, since that which has in the proposition the form of a predicate is itself the substance of the statement. It is met by a counter-thrust, as we may say. Starting from the subject, as if this were a permanent base on which to proceed, it discovers, by the predicate being in reality the substance, that the subject has passed into the predicate, and has thereby ceased to be subject: and since in this way what seems to be predicate has become the entire mass of the content, whole and complete, thinking cannot wander and ramble about at will, but is restrained and controlled by this weight of content.

Usually the subject is first set down as the fixed and objective self; from this fixed position the necessary process passes on to the multiplicity of determinations or predicates. Here the knowing ego takes the place of that subject and is the function of knitting or combining the predicates one with another, and is the subject holding them fast. But since the former subject enters into the determinate constituents themselves, and is their very life, the subject in the second case—viz. the knowing subject—finds that the former, which it is supposed to be done with and which it wants to transcend, in order to return into itself,—is still there in the predicate: and instead of being able to be the determining agency in the process of resolving the predicate—reflectively deciding whether this or that predicate should be attached to the former subject—it has really to deal with the self of the content, is not allowed to be something on its own account (*für sich*), but has to exist along with this content.

What has been said can be expressed in a formal manner by saying that the nature of judgment or the proposition in general, which involves the distinction of subject and predicate, is subverted and destroyed by the speculative judgment; and the identical proposition, which the former becomes [by uniting subject and predicate], implies the rejection and repudiation of the above relation between subject and predicate. This conflict between the form of a proposition in general and the unity of the notion which destroys that form, is similar to what we find between meter and accent in the case of rhythm. Rhythm is the result of what hovers between and unites both. So in the case of the speculative or philosophical judgment; the identity of subject and predicate is not intended to destroy their distinction, as expressed in propositional form; their unity is to arise as a harmony of the elements. The form of the judgment is the way the specific sense appears, or is made manifest, the accent which differentiates the meaning it contains: that the predicate expresses the substance, and the subject itself falls within the universal, is however the unity wherein that accent dies away.

To explain what has been said by examples let us take the proposition God is Being. The predicate is 'being': it has substantive significance, and thus absorbs the meaning of the subject within it. Being is meant to be here not predicate but the essential nature. Thereby, God seems to cease to be what he was when the proposition was put forward, viz. a fixed subject. Thinking [i.e., ordinary reflection], instead of getting any farther with the transition from subject to predicate, in reality finds its activity checked through the loss of the subject, and it is thrown back on the thought of the subject because it misses this subject. Or again, since the predicate has itself been pronounced to be a subject, to be the being, to be the essential reality, which exhausts the nature of the subject, thinking finds the subject directly present in the predicate too: and now, instead of having, in the predicate, gone into *itself*, and preserved the freedom characteristic of ratiocination, it is absorbed in the content all the while, or, at any rate is required to be so.

Similarly when it is said: 'the real is the universal', the real, *qua* subject, passes away in its predicate. The universal is not only meant to have the significance of a predicate, as if the proposition stated that the real is universal: the universal is meant to express the essential nature of the real. Thinking therefore loses that fixed objective basis which it had in the subject, just as much as in the predicate it is thrown back on the subject, and therein returns not into itself but into the subject underlying the content.

There is a difficulty which might well be avoided. It consists in mixing up the methods of procedure followed by speculation and ratiocination, when what is said of the subject has at one time the significance of its conceptual principle, and at another time the meaning of its predicate or accidental quality. The one mode of thinking invalidates the other; and only that philosophical exposition can manage to become plastic in character which resolutely sets aside and has nothing to do with the ordinary way of relating the parts of a proposition.

As a matter of fact, non-speculative thinking has its rights too, which are justifiable, but are disregarded in the speculative way of stating a proposition. Abolishing the form of the proposition must not take place only in an immediate manner, through the mere content of the proposition. On the contrary, we must give explicit expression to this cancelling process; it must be not only that internal restraining and confining of thought within its own substance; this turning of the conception back into itself has to be expressly brought out and stated. This process, which constitutes what formerly had to be accomplished by proof, is the internal dialectical movement of the proposition itself. This alone is the concrete speculative element, and only the explicit expression of this is a speculative systematic exposition. *Qua* proposition, the speculative aspect is merely the internal restriction of thought within its own substance where the return of the essential principle into itself is not yet brought out. Hence we often find philosophical expositions referring us to the inner intuition, and thus dispensing with the systematic statement of the dialectical movement of the proposition, which is what we wanted all the while. The proposition ought to express what the truth is: in its essential nature the truth is subject: being so, it is merely the dialectical movement, this self-producing course of activity, maintaining, its advance by returning back into itself. In the case of knowledge in other spheres this aspect of expressly stating the internal nature of the content is constituted by proof. When dialectic, however, has been separated from proof, the idea of philosophical demonstration as a matter of fact has vanished altogether.

On this point it may be mentioned that the dialectical process likewise consists of parts or elements which are propositions. The difficulty indicated seems therefore to recur continually, and seems to be a difficulty inherent in the nature of the case. This is like what happens in the ordinary process of proving anything; the grounds it makes use of need themselves to be based on other grounds again, and so on, *ad infinitum*. This manner of furnishing grounds and conditions, however, concerns that type of proof from which the dialectical movement is distinct and hence belongs to the process of external knowledge. As to what this movement is, its element is the bare concept; this furnishes a content which is through and through subject *impliciter* and *per se*. There is to be found, therefore, no sort of content standing in a relation, as it were, to an underlying subject, and getting its significance by being attached to this as a predicate. The proposition as it appears is a mere empty form.

Apart from the sensuously apprehended or ideally presented (*vorgestellten*) self, it is in the main the mere name *qua* name which denotes the subject pure and simple, the empty unit without any conceptual character. For this reason it would, e.g., be expedient to avoid the name 'God', because this word is not in its primary use a conception as well, but the special name of an underlying subject, its fixed resting-place; while, on the other hand, being or the one, singleness, subject, etc., themselves directly indicate conceptions. Furthermore, if speculative truths are stated about that subject [God], even then their content is devoid of the immanent notion, because that content is merely present in the form of a passive subject, and owing to this the speculative truths easily take on the character of mere edification. From this side, too, the obstacle, arising from the habit of putting the speculative predicate in the form of a proposition, instead of taking it as an inherent essential conception, is capable of being made greater or less by the mere way philosophical truths are put forward. Philosophical exposition, faithfully following its insight into the nature of speculative truth, must retain the dialectical form, and exclude everything which is not grasped conceptually and is conception.

SCIENCE OF LOGIC

'If Logic has undergone no change since Aristotle—and in fact when one looks at modern compendiums of Logic the changes consist to a large extent merely in omissions—what is rather to be inferred from this is, that Logic is all the more in need of a thorough overhaul; for when Spirit has worked on for two thousand years, it must have reached a better reflective consciousness of its own thought and its own unadulterated essence'.

2

SCIENCE OF LOGIC

PREFACE TO THE FIRST EDITION

The complete transformation which philosophical thought has undergone in Germany during the last twenty-five years and the loftier outlook upon thought which self-conscious spirit has attained in this period, have hitherto had but little influence on the structure of Logic.

That which before this period was called Metaphysics, has been, so to speak, extirpated root and branch, and has disappeared from the ranks of the Sciences. Where could one now catch an echo—where would any echo venture to linger—of the Ontology, the Rational Psychology, the Cosmology, or even the Natural Theology, of former times? Where, for instance, would investigations concerning the Immateriality of the Soul, or Efficient and Final Causes—where would these now arouse any interest? And the other proofs of the existence of God are now brought forward only from an historical standpoint, or with a view to edification and spiritual uplifting. It is the fact that men have lost interest partly in the content of the old Metaphysics, partly in its form—and partly in both content and form. If it is a remarkable thing when a nation finds that its Constitutional Theory, its customary ways of thinking and feeling, its ethical habits and traditional virtues, have become inapplicable, it is certainly not less remarkable when a nation loses its Metaphysics, when the intellect occupying itself with its own pure essence, has no longer any real existence in the thought of the nation.

The exoteric doctrine of Kantian Philosophy that Understanding cannot go beyond Experience, because if so the faculty of cognition would be a merely theoretical intelligence which could by itself produce nothing but idle fancies of the brain—this doctrine has given a scientific justification to the renunciation of Speculative Thought. This popular doctrine was supported by the cry of modern educationalists, voicing the needs of the hard times, which draw men's attention to immediate requirements; it was clamoured that as for knowledge experience is the starting point, so for ability in public and in private life, theoretical insight is actually injurious, while it is practice and technical education which are above all essential, and alone lead to better things. *Philosophy* and crude *Common Sense* playing thus into each other's hands for the downfall of Metaphysics, there was presented the strange spectacle of a cultured people having no Metaphysics—as it were a temple, in all other respects richly ornamented, but lacking its Holy of Holies.—Theology, which in earlier times had been the guardian of speculative mysteries, and of a Metaphysics subordinate to itself, had given up this science in exchange for emotions, for popular practicality, and learned historicity. On the other hand, in correspondence with this change, those lonely souls who were sacrificed by their fellows, and isolated from the world, to the end that contemplation of the eternal and a life dedicated thereto should be maintained—the life and the contemplation being for the sake of an ideal and not of a practical Good—these devotees passed out of existence;—and their passing away may, from another point of view, be regarded as essentially one with the phenomenon of which we have already spoken. And so, when such metaphysical shadows, and such colourless self-concentration of the introspective spirit, had been brushed aside, existence seemed to be transformed into the sunny land of flowers—and, as we know, no flowers are black.

It did not fare quite so ill with Logic as with Metaphysics. The view that by Logic one would learn how to think (the usefulness and hence the purpose of Logic being supposed to consist in this)—which was just as though one were to expect to learn how to digest and how to move, by the study of anatomy and physiology—this prejudice has long ago been exploded, and the spirit of practicality probably intended for Logic a fate no better than that which had fallen to the lot of the sister Science. In spite of this, however, and probably on account of some formal utility, a place among the Sciences was left to Logic, and it was even retained as a subject of public instruction. But this better fate concerned only externals, for the form and content of Logic had remained the same that it had inherited by long tradition—a tradition which in being handed down had become ever more meager and attenuated; there are no traces in Logic of the new spirit which has arisen both in Learning and in Life. It is, however (let us say it once for all), quite vain to try to retain the forms of an earlier stage of development when the inner structure of spirit has become transformed; these earlier forms are like withered leaves which are pushed off by the new buds already being generated at the roots.

But even in the scientific sphere this ignoring of the universal change is beginning to fail. Imperceptibly the new ideas became familiar even to their opposers, who appropriated them and—though persistently slighting and gainsaying the sources and principles of these ideas—yet had to accept their results, and were unable to evade their influence. The only way in which opposers could give content and positive value to their negative attitude (which was getting to be of ever less and less importance) was by giving in their adherence to the new ways of thinking.

On the other hand, the period of fermentation with which a new creation begins seems to be past. At its first appearance such a period generally wears an aspect of fanatical hostility towards the prevalent systematization of the older principle; it is also, partly, fearful of losing itself in the wilderness of particulars while it shuns the labour required for scientific development, and in its need of such a development grasps, at first, at an empty formalism. The demand for the digestion and development of the material now becomes so much the more pressing. This is a period in the development of an age, as in the development of an individual, when the chief business is to acquire and maintain the principle in its undeveloped intensity. But the higher requirement is that the principle should be elaborated into systematized knowledge.

Still, whatever may have been already done for the cause and for the form of philosophy in other respects, the logical science which is the true content of genuine Metaphysics or pure speculative philosophy has heretofore been very much neglected. What I more exactly understand by this Logic and its standpoint I have set forth provisionally in the Introduction. The necessity of once more beginning this science from the very beginning, the nature of the subject itself, and the absence of previous work which could be used in the projected transformation, should all be taken into account by fair and reasonable judges—even though the labour of many ears has not been able to secure for this attempt a nearer approach to perfection. The essential point of view is, that we have to do, altogether, with a new concept of philosophical method. As I have elsewhere recalled, Philosophy, since it is to be Ordered Knowledge, cannot borrow its Method from a subordinate science, such as Mathematics, any more than it can rest satisfied with categorical assertions of pure intuition, or use reasonings based on external reflection. But it is the nature of the content and that alone which lives and stirs in philosophic cognition, while it is this very reflection of the content which itself originates and determines the nature of philosophy.

Understanding makes determinations and maintains them. Reason is negative and dialectical because it dissolves into nothing the determinations of Understanding; Reason is positive because it is the source of the Universal in which the Particular is comprehended. Just as Understanding is commonly held to be something separate from Reason regarded generally, so dialectical Reason is held to be something separate from positive Reason. But in its real truth Reason is Spirit— Spirit which is higher than either Reason which understands, or Understanding which reasons. Spirit is the negative, it is that which constitutes the quality alike of dialectical Reason and of Understanding; it negates the simple and thus posits that determinate distinction which is the work of Understanding, and just as truly it resolves this distinction, and is thus dialectical. Yet it does not abide in the negation which thus results, but is therein just as much positive,—thus it has thereby established the first Simple, but so that the Simple is also a Universal which is in itself concrete; under this universal a given Particular is not subsumed; but, in that determination, and in the solution thereof, the Particular has already been coincidently determined. This movement of Spirit, which in its simplicity gives itself its determinateness and hence self-equality, and which thus is the immanent development of the Notion—this movement is the Absolute Method of knowledge, and at the same time the immanent soul of the Content of knowledge.— It is, I maintain, along this path of self-construction alone that Philosophy can become objective and demonstrated science.—It is after this fashion that I have tried to present consciousness in the *Phenomenology of Spirit*. Consciousness is Spirit as knowing which is concrete and engrossed in externality; but the schema of movement of this concrete knowing (like the development of all physical and intellectual life) depends entirely on the nature of the pure essentialities which make up the content of Logic. Consciousness, as manifested Spirit which as it develops frees itself from its immediacy and external concretions, becomes Pure Knowing, which takes as object of its knowing those pure essentialities as they are in and for themselves. They are pure thought, Spirit thinking its own essence. Their spontaneous movement is their spiritual life: by this movement philosophy constitutes itself; and philosophy is just the exhibition of this movement.

I have thus indicated the relation to Logic of the science which I call *Phenomenology of Spirit*. With regard to the external arrangement, it was intended that the first part of the *System of Knowledge* which contains the *Phenomenology*, should be followed by a second part which should contain Logic and the two concrete Philosophical Sciences, the Philosophy of Nature and the Philosophy of Spirit, thus completing the System of Knowledge. But the extensive elaboration demanded by *Logic* has caused me to allow this portion to be published separately; thus, in an enlarged scheme, Logic constitutes the first sequel to the *Phenomenology of Spirit*. I shall work out later the two concrete Philosophical Sciences already spoken of.—The First Book of this first volume of the Logic is *The Doctrine of Being*; the Second Book contains *The Doctrine of Essence*, which is the second division of the first volume, the second volume will contain *Subjective Logic*, or *The Doctrine of the Notion*.

PREFACE TO THE SECOND EDITION

I have embarked upon the new elaboration of the *Science of Logic* of which this is the first volume, with full consciousness both of the difficulties of the subject in itself and of its exposition, and also of the imperfection of the elaboration contained in the first edition; earnestly as I have striven, after many years' further occupation with the subject, to remedy this imperfection, I still feel that I have good reason to bespeak the indulgence of my readers. The title to such a claim for indulgence may well be based in the first instance upon the circumstance that for the content of the science hardly anything but merely external material was to be found in the earlier Metaphysics and Logic. Though both of these subjects have been universally and assiduously cultivated, the latter even up to our own day, the speculative aspect has met with but slight attention; on the contrary, we have, for the most part, the same things repeated again and again—sometimes thinned down to shallow triviality, while sometimes the old ballast is unloaded afresh and dragged about in ever greater bulk after such a fashion that the efforts expended—to a large extent merely mechanical—could bring no gain to the philosophic content. Hence it had come to pass that to present the realm of thought in its philosophical aspect—that is, in its own immanent activity, or (which comes to the same thing) in its necessary development—this had to be a new undertaking, and to be begun from the very beginning; but the traditional material—the well-known forms of thought—must be regarded as a highly important pattern—in fact a necessary condition, a presupposition to be thankfully acknowledged, even if only providing here and there a barren clue or, as it were, the lifeless bones of a skeleton, sometimes even flung together in disorder.

It is in human Language that the Forms of Thought are manifested and laid down in the first instance. In our day it cannot be too often recalled, that what distinguishes man from the beasts is *the faculty of Thought*. Language has penetrated into whatever becomes for man *something inner*—becomes, that is, an idea, something which he makes his very own;—and what man transforms to Language contains—concealed, or mixed up with other things, or worked out to clearness—a Category; so natural to man is Logic—indeed, Logic itself is just man's peculiar nature. But if Nature in general is opposed, as *physical*, to what is *mental*, then it must be said that Logic is rather that something Super-natural which enters into all the natural behaviour of man—Feeling, Intuition, Desire, Need, Impulse—and thereby alone transforms it all to something human—to ideas and purposes—though, perhaps, only formally human. It is a great advantage to a language when it has a wealth of logical expressions—that is, expressions characteristic and set apart—for the determinations of thought; of prepositions and articles many belong to those relationships which depend upon thinking; the Chinese language is said not to have developed so far, or only in a very small degree; these particles in fact perform an entirely subordinate office, the same as prefixes and suffixes, and in an only slightly more independent form. It is much more important that in a language the determinations of thought should be manifested in Substantives and Verbs and thus receive the stamp of objective form; the German language has here many advantages over other modern languages; indeed, many of its words have the further peculiarity that they have not only various, but even opposed, meanings, so that we must recognize here a speculative spirit in the language; it is a joy to thought to stumble upon such words, and to meet with the union of opposites (a result of Speculative Thought which to Human Understanding seems senseless) in the naïve shape of one word with opposite meanings registered in a dictionary. For this reason, in German, Philosophy for the most part requires no peculiar terminology. Of course some words from foreign languages (which indeed have already acquired by prescription the right of citizenship in the philosophic realm) have to be adopted in German, and an affected purism would be least in place where it is the thing and not the word that is of capital importance. The progress of culture generally, and of the sciences in particular, gradually brings to light higher relations of thought, or at any rate raises these relations to greater generality, and thereby attracts to them more attentive consideration. This is true even of those sciences which relate to what is empirical and sensuous, since they use in general the most familiar categories (for example, Whole and Parts, a Thing and its Properties, and the like). For instance, though in Physics the idea of Force had become supreme, in more modern times the most important part here has been played by the Category of Polarity—which indeed has been too much dragged in everywhere at random, and even into the theory of Light. In this determination of thought a distinction is drawn, while the things distinguished are inseparably bound up together. It is of infinite importance that in this way the abstract form (Identity) by which a thought-determinateness is endowed with independence (as, for example, Force) has been abandoned, and the form of the determination, of a distinction which remains all the while in identity because it is inseparable, is emphasized and becomes a current idea. Owing to the reality which appertains to natural objects, the observation of nature compels us to establish those natural Categories which we cannot ignore even when they may be thoroughly incoherent with others to which also validity is allowed, and does not permit here that passage from opposites to abstracts and universals, which more easily takes place in the case of ideational objects.

But whilst logical objects and the expression of them are thus something that is everywhere familiar in cultivated thought, still, as I have elsewhere observed, what is familiar is not on that account necessarily understood. It even rouses one's impatience to have to go on merely busying oneself about what is thus familiar— and what is more familiar than just those determinations of thought of which we make use at every turn, which proceed out of our mouths with every sentence that we speak? This foreword is intended to give the fundamental points in that course of the progress of Cognition which starts from what is thus *known and familiar*, and in the relation of Scientific thinking to Natural thinking; this, together with what is contained in the earlier *Introduction*, will suffice to furnish that general notion of the meaning of logical Cognition which one is accustomed to demand in the case of any Science, as a preliminary to the presentation of the Science itself.

In the first place, it is to be regarded as an immense advance that the Forms of Thought should be disengaged from the *Matter of Thought* in which they are imbedded in self-conscious Intuition and Ideation as well as in Desire and Will— or rather (since there is no human Desire nor Will without Ideas) in ideating Desire and Will; it is an immense advance that these Universals should be drawn forth and set up as objects of contemplation on their own account, as was done by Plato and then more especially by Aristotle; we have in this the beginning of knowledge. 'It was only', says Aristotle, 'after nearly everything that was necessary, and that pertained to the convenience and intercourse of life, had been obtained, that people began to trouble themselves about philosophic knowledge'. 'In Egypt', he had previously remarked, 'the mathematical sciences were early developed, because there the priestly caste at an early period was in such a position as to make leisure possible'.

In truth the need to busy oneself with pure thought presupposes a long stretch of road already traversed by the human spirit. It is, one may say, the need of a need already satisfied as regards necessaries, the need of an attained absence of need, of abstraction from the matter of intuition, imagination, and so forth—from the concrete interests of Desire, Impulse, and Will, in which the determinations of thought are wrapped up and concealed. In the still spaces of Thought which has come to itself and is purely self-existent, those interests are hushed which move the lives of peoples and of individuals. 'In so many directions', says Aristotle in the same connection, 'the nature of man is dependent; but this science, which is not sought for the sake of utility, this alone, in itself and for itself, is free, and seems therefore to be a possession not wholly human'. Philosophy generally still has in its thinking to deal with concrete objects—God, Nature, Spirit—but Logic is concerned with such thought wholly and solely on account of the thought itself, in complete abstraction from its objects. It is customary to assign to Logic a place among the studies of youth, because the young have not yet entered upon the interests of concrete life. Youth lives at leisure in respect of these interests; its business is to acquire the means and power of entering actively upon the objects of these interests, and even these objects are considered in a merely theoretic manner. In opposition to the view of Aristotle already quoted, logical science is reckoned as part of this equipment; occupation with Logic is a preliminary business, its place is said to be the school, which ought to precede the seriousness of life and action for solid ends. In Life, categories are used—they are degraded from the honour of being contemplated on their own account to serve in intellectual exercise upon living content by production and interchange of the ideas appropriate thereto. They serve, first, as abbreviations, in virtue of their generality; for what an endless multitude of particulars of external existence and of action do ideas comprise, for example, Battle, War, Nation, or Sea, Animal, and so forth;—how in the Idea of God, or of Love, and so on, in the simplicity of such ideating, we have an endless multitude of ideas, activities, conditions, and so on, epitomized! Secondly, Categories serve for the closer determination and discovery of objective relations, in which, however, content and purpose, the validity and truth of the thought which enters into this process, are made entirely dependent on the material presented, and no efficacy in determining the content is ascribed to the determinations of thought in themselves. Such use of the Categories, which has above been called Natural Logic, is unconscious, and when in scientific contemplation the mind assigns to the Categories the function of serving as means, then Thinking in general is turned into something subordinate to other mental functions. We do not say of our Feelings, Impulses and Interests that they serve us—rather, they are regarded as independent faculties and powers, the fact being that so to feel, thus to desire and will, to take interest in this or that—all this is just what we are. On the other hand again, we are likely to become conscious that we are at the disposal of our Feelings, Impulses, Passions, and Interests, let alone Habits, rather than that we are the owners of these or (still less) that they serve us as means, seeing how intimately they are incorporated in us. Such determinations of disposition and intellect soon show themselves as *Particulars* in contradistinction to that Universality of which we are conscious in ourselves and in which we find our Freedom; and indeed we think that we are entangled in these Particularities, and that they tyrannize over us. Consequently we are much less able to hold that the Forms of Thought serve us than that we serve them—that we are their masters and not much rather that they are our masters—those Forms of Thought which permeate all our ideas, whether those ideas are just theories or have a content of Sensation, of Impulse, or of Will. What surplus have *we* as against them, how shall we—how shall I—set myself up as more universal than they—they who are the Universal itself? When we give ourselves up to a sensation, a purpose, an interest, and then feel ourselves to be limited and unfree, the place into which we can withdraw therefrom and get back into freedom is the place where we are certain of ourselves, the region of pure abstraction, the region of Thought. So, when we mean to speak of things, we call the Nature or Essence of them their Concept—and this exists only for thought: but of the concepts of things we cannot say that we govern them, or that the thought-determinations of which they are the complexes serve us; on the contrary, our thought has to limit itself in accordance with them, and our arbitrary choice or Freedom ought not to try to frame them after its own fancy. In so far, then, as subjective Thinking is our own-est and inner most act, and the objective concept of things constitutes their own reality, we cannot get beyond that own act of ours, we cannot stand above it, and just as little can we get beyond the nature of things. We can, however, disregard the latter determination; it coincides in so far with the former, since it would furnish a relation of our thoughts to the thing, giving, however, only an empty result, the real thing being set up as a standard for our concepts, while that thing can for us be nothing else than our concepts of it. When the Critical Philosophy understands the relation of these three Terms so as to make *Thoughts* intermediary between *Us* and *Things* in such a sense that this intermediary rather excludes us from things than connects us with them, this view may be met by the simple observation that these very things which are supposed to stand beyond ourselves, and beyond the thoughts referring to them, at the opposite extreme, are themselves things of thought, and, as being quite undetermined, are just one such thing (the so-called Thing-in-itself), the product of empty abstraction.

Enough said, however, of that point of view at which the relation vanishes away, according to which determinations of thought are regarded merely as means and instrument; more important is the further point connected therewith, according to which it is customary to regard these determinations as external Forms.—That activity of Thinking which works in all our ideas, purposes, interests, and deeds is, as has been already remarked, un-self-consciously active (Natural Logic); what is present to consciousness is the content, the objects of our ideas, that in which we are *interested*; in this connection the determinations of Thought are regarded as *Forms*, which are not the content itself but only *attached to the content*. But if it is true, as was asserted above and is generally admitted, that in an object the nature, the peculiar essence, the truly permanent and substantial among the multiplicity and contingency of its appearance and fleeting manifestation, consists in the concept of the thing, in the Universal immanent in it; as every human individual, though infinitely unique, is so only *because* it belongs to the class of man, every animal only *because* it belongs to the class of animal: if this be true, what remains of such an individual if this basis (i.e. the universal) be removed, however many other predicates it have, and although the universal be only one among them? The indispensable basis, the Concept, the Universal, which is Thought itself—in so far, that is, as in using the word *Thought* one can abstract from the idea—this cannot be regarded as a *merely* indifferent form which is attached to some content. But these thoughts of all natural and spiritual things, even the substantial content, are yet such as to possess manifold determinations and to contain the distinction between Soul and Body, between a concept and its respective reality; the deeper basis is the soul in itself, the pure concept, which is the very core of objects, their very life-pulse, as it is the core and pulse of subjective thinking itself. To bring into clear consciousness this logical character which gives soul to mind and stirs and works in it, this is our problem. Instinctive action is distinguished from intelligent and free action broadly by this, that the latter is accompanied by clear consciousness; when the content of that which stirs the spirit is drawn out of its immediate unity with the Subject, and made an Object for it, then there begins Freedom for the spirt, which while caught in the workings of instinctive mental activity is broken up within the meshes of its Categories into an infinitely various material. In this web strong knots are formed now and then, which are foci of arrest and direction in mental life and consciousness: they owe their firmness and strength to the fact that, brought before consciousness, they are found to be independent concepts of the latter's essentiality. The most important point for the nature of spirit is not merely the relation of that which it is *in itself,* but furthermore of that as which it *knows itself,* to that which it is in actuality; this self-knowledge, because it is essentially consciousness, is the fundamental determination of spirit's actuality. These Categories function only instinctively and as impulses—they are at first introduced into consciousness piecemeal, and therefore are mutable and mutually confusing, and thus yield to mind only a piecemeal and insecure actuality. To purify these Categories and to raise the mind through them to Freedom and Truth, this it is which is the loftier task of Logic.

What we have laid down as the first step in Philosophy (a step the high value of which both on its own account and also as a condition of genuine cognition we have already recognized)—namely, that concepts in general and the moments of concepts (that is, the determinations of thought) should be treated at first as Forms which are distinct from Matter, and merely attached to it,—this procedure advertises itself at once as inadequate for the attainment of truth—truth, which is announced as the subject-matter and goal of Logic. For, taken thus as bare forms, as distinct from the content, they are taken to be standing in a determination which stamps them as finite, and makes them incapable of comprehending the truth, which is in itself infinite. If the true can, in whatever reference, be elsewhere associated with limitation and finitude, this is its aspect of negation, of untruth and unreality—in fact of its end—not its aspect of affirmation, which it is by virtue of being truth. Against the baldness of the merely formal categories, the instinct of common sense has at last felt itself so confirmed as contemptuously to abandon the knowledge of them to the domain of School Logic and School Metaphysics, with a want of appreciation of the intrinsic value that this clue possesses, and completely unaware that it (that is, common sense) is itself held captive when it adopts the instinctive activities of Natural Logic, and still more when it deliberately rejects both cognition and recognition of thought-determinations,—captive by a mode of thinking that is unpurged and therefore unfree. The simple basic or common determination of all these forms is Identity, which as the Law of Identity as A = A, and as the maxim of contradiction, is maintained in the Logic of this collection of forms. Common sense has so thoroughly lost its reverence for the school which is in possession of these laws of truth and still fosters them, that is derides the school on account of the laws, and would regard anyone as insufferable who, in accordance with these laws, made true statements such as, 'The plant is—a plant', 'Science is—Science', and so *ad infinitum*. And as to the formulas which constitute the rules of syllogizing (which, in fact, is one of the principal employments of Understanding)—mistaken as it would be not to recognize their place and validity in cognition and the fact that they are essential material for rational thought, yet the equally just view has been established that these laws are, quite as much, impartial instruments of error and sophistry, and—however Truth may be determined—that they are unserviceable for higher Truth—for instance, for religious Truth;—that, broadly, they are merely a matter of epistemological correctness and not of Truth itself.

The inadequacy of this way of regarding thought, which leaves Truth on one side, can only be supplemented when in the contemplation of Thought, Content is included as well as that which is habitually reckoned as belonging to external form. It very soon appears that what at first is to ordinary reflection, as Content, separated from Form, cannot in fact be formless, cannot be without internal determination; if it were so, it would be only emptiness, the abstraction of the Thing-in-itself. It appears that, on the contrary, Content has in itself Form, indeed it is only through Form that it has Soul and subsistence, and that it is Form itself which changes only into the show of a Content, as also into the show of a something external to this show. With this introduction of Content into logical consideration, the concrete concepts of things become the object of thought, instead of the mere things. And in this connection we may recall that there *is* a multitude of Concepts, a multitude of concrete Things. The way, however, in which this multitude is limited and confined is (as has already been pointed out) partly this, that the Concept as Thought in general, as Universal, immeasurably abbreviates the endless Particularity of mere Things, which in their multitudinousness hover before the eye of indeterminate intuition and ideation; partly, however, *a* Concept is, to start with, *the* Concept in itself, and the Concept is One, and is the substantial basis; and secondly though it is a definite Concept, and this definiteness in it is what appears as Content, yet on the other hand the definiteness of the Concept is a Form-determination of that substantial One-ness, a phase of Form as Totality, of *the Concept itself*, which is the basis of determinate Concepts. This is not sensuously intuited nor ideated; it is only the object, product and content of Thinking, and the Real Thing which exists in and for itself, the Logos, the reason of that which is, the Truth of what we call *a mere thing* (Ding); and it is Logos which should least of all be left outside logical science. We cannot therefore include it in the science, or leave it outside, at our discretion. When the thought-determinations which are only external forms are truly considered in themselves, only their finitude, and the untruth of attempts to make them exist for themselves, show up, and what shows up as their truth is the concept. Hence logical science, since it deals with the determinations of thought (which generally run through our mind instinctively and unreflectively, and—even though they enter into language—remain unidentified and unregarded)—logical science, I say, will be the re-construction of those thought-determinations which are thrown into relief by reflection, and by reflection are fixed as subjective forms, forms external to matter and content.

No unfolding of any subject-matter of Thought is in itself capable of such strictly immanent plasticity as is that of the development of Thinking in accordance with its own necessary Laws; no other carries with it this demand in such a degree of intensity; in this respect the science of Logic must surpass even Mathematics, for no subject-matter of thought has in itself this freedom and independence. By such a free and independent exposition—which after its fashion is present in the process of mathematical thought—it is demanded that there should not appear at any stage of the development, any thought-determination, any reflection, that does not immediately arise at this stage, and that has not passed into it from the stage preceding. However, such abstract perfection of exposition must, I confess, be generally given up; since the Science must begin with the absolutely simple, that is, with what is most general and most empty, the exposition would permit only quite simple expression of that simplicity, without the addition of a single word;—what would be admissible in accordance with the conditions of the case would be negative considerations, the objects of which were to ward off and to banish elements which might otherwise be introduced by imagination or unregulated thinking. Such invasions of the simple immanent process of development are, however, in themselves contingent, and consequently the effort to ward them off is itself tainted with contingency; besides which just because such occurrences lie outside the subject-matter it is vain to try to meet them all, and the systematic completeness demanded would itself be something imperfect. But the peculiar unrest and distraction of our modern consciousness force us to take into account reflections and fancies that lie more or less near at hand. And an explanation which lends itself to the subject calls for a corresponding docility of temper in those who would apprehend and comprehend; but youths and men thus docile, with such tranquil self-denial in the matter of reflections and fancies of *their own*, in which 'original' thought is so impatient to manifest itself—listeners (such as Plato feigns) who only want to follow the argument—such could hardly be set up as interlocutors in a modern dialogue; still less could we reckon upon readers of such a temper of mind. Quite the reverse—I have been only too often and too fiercely attacked by opponents who are incapable of the simple reflection that their onslaughts and objections contain categories which are themselves assumptions and themselves need to be criticized before being employed. Want of knowledge in this matter goes incredibly far; it is guilty of the fundamental misunderstanding, the uninstructed and barbarous procedure of taking a category which is under consideration for *something else* and not for what it is. This ignorance is the less to be justified because this something else consists of other thought-determinations and concepts, and in a system of Logic these other categories themselves must likewise have found their place, and be themselves awaiting consideration in their place in the system. Where this is most surprising is in the great majority of the objections and attacks which are directed against the primary concepts or starting-points of Logic, Being and Nothing, and Becoming, as that which contains the two previous determinations (Being and Nothing) as Moments;—Becoming, which is itself without question a simple determination, as appears on the simplest analysis. Thoroughness seems to demand that the beginning—as the foundation upon which everything is to be built—should be examined before anything else, in fact that we should not proceed further until it has proved itself solid, and on the other hand, if it does not prove so, that everything that follows should be rejected. This thoroughness of procedure has at the same time the advantage that it guarantees a vast easing of the work of thought; it has before it, enclosed in this germ, the whole development of the science, and regards itself as having done the whole of its business when it has done the first part of it. This piece of the work is the easiest to dispatch, for it is the simplest, it deals with simplicity itself; it is the trifling labour that is here required that really recommends this 'thoroughness' of procedure, which is so well satisfied with itself. This restriction to what is simple gives full scope to the free play of thought—thought which cannot go on being simple, but must bring in its reflections on the subject. Having good right to be busied at first *only* with the fundamental principle and, at that stage, not to allow itself to enter upon what is *beyond*, this thoroughness, even when employed on its own business, works in a contrary sense, and brings in what goes beyond the fundamental principle—it brings in, that is, other categories and other presuppositions and prejudices. Such presuppositions as that Infinity is different from Finitude, that Content is other than Form, that the Inner is other than the Outer, that Mediacy is not Immediacy—as though anybody did not know such things—are brought forward by way of information, and related and insisted upon rather than proved. A habit of such instruction is a childish procedure—we can call it nothing else; technically it is unjustifiable, because it presupposes and immediately assumes such things; and it is even more guilty of ignorance of the fact that it is the need and business of logical thought to investigate just this—whether a Finite without Infinity is something true, whether such abstract Infinity, and moreover a Content without Form and a Form without Content, similarly an Inner by itself that has no Outer, an Externality without Inwardness, and so forth—whether these can be *something true*, or *something actual*. But this education and discipline of thought, by which an adaptable attitude of thought is brought about, and the impatience of intrusive reflection overcome—all this can be procured only by going further, only by study, and by actualization of the whole course of development.

Anyone who works at building up anew an independent structure of philosophical science in modern times, may, when referring to the Platonic exposition, be reminded of the story of how Plato revised his *Republic* seven times over. The remembrance of this, the comparison in as far as such may seem to be implied here, should only urge one all the more to the desire, that for a work which, as pertaining to the modern world, has to deal with a deeper principle, a more difficult subject, and material of wider scope—for such a work leisure might have been vouchsafed, to go through it seventy times and seven. The author however, in face of the greatness of the task, has had to content himself with what it has been possible to accomplish under pressure of external necessity, inevitable distractions due to the greatness and many-sidedness of the interests of the time, and under a doubt whether the noisy clamour of everyday affairs, and the bewildering volubility of undisciplined fancy (which takes a pride in limiting its interests to such affairs)—whether these leave any room for sympathy with the passionless calm of purely speculative knowledge.

INTRODUCTION: GENERAL CONCEPT OF LOGIC

The need to begin with the subject itself, without preliminary observations, is felt nowhere more strongly than in the Science of Logic. In every other science, the Subject dealt with, and the Method of the Science, are distinguished from one another; and further the subject is not absolutely original, but depends upon other concepts, and is connected in all directions with other material. It is therefore granted to these other sciences to regard both their Principles (with the connections of these) and also their Method, as starting from assumptions—to begin with applying forms of Definition and so on, which are presupposed as known and accepted, and to make use of familiar forms of reasoning for the establishment of their general concepts and fundamental determinations.

Logic on the other hand cannot take for granted any of these forms of reflection or rules and laws of thought, for these are a part of the very fabric of Logic, and must be demonstrated within the boundaries of the science itself. But not only the scheme of philosophic method, but also the very concept of philosophy in general belongs to the content of Logic and in fact constitutes its final result; what Logic is, cannot be set out beforehand—on the contrary this knowledge of what Logic is can only be reached as the end and consummation of the whole treatment of the subject. Moreover the subject of Logic (Thinking, or more precisely Conceptual Thinking) is really treated of within the boundaries of the science itself; the Concept of this Thinking is engendered in the course of development of the Science, and therefore cannot precede it. Therefore what is set forth in a preliminary way in this Introduction does not aim at establishing the concept of Logic at all, or at justifying beforehand its substance and method scientifically, but—by help of some reasoned and historical explanations and reflections—at bringing more clearly before the mind the point of view from which this science is to be regarded.

When Logic is taken as the science of Thinking in general, it is understood that this Thinking constitutes the *bare form* of cognition, that Logic abstracts from all *content*, and that the (so-called) other constituent of a cognition,—that is, its *Matter*,—must come from a different source; that thus Logic—as something of which this Matter is wholly and entirely independent—can provide only the formal conditions of true knowledge, and cannot, in and by itself, contain real truth, nor even be the path to real truth, because just that which is the essence of truth,—that is, its content—lies outside Logic.

But in the first place it is most inept to say that Logic abstracts from all *Content*, that it teaches only the rules of Thinking without going into what is thought or being able to consider its nature. For since Thinking and the Rules of Thinking are the subject of Logic, Logic has directly in them its own peculiar content;—has in them that second constituent of cognition—its Matter—about the structure of which it concerns itself.

But secondly, the ideas upon which the concept of Logic has hitherto rested have partly died out already, and, for the rest, it is time that they should disappear altogether, and that this science should be taken from a higher point of view, and should receive an entirely different structure.

The hitherto accepted concept of Logic rests upon the assumed separation of the *Content* of knowledge and the *Form* of knowledge (or *Truth* and *Certainty*)—a separation that is assumed once for all in ordinary consciousness. First, it is assumed that the material of knowledge is present in and for itself in the shape of a finished world apart from Thinking, that Thinking is in itself empty, and comes to that world from outside as Form to Matter, fills itself therewith, and only thus gets a content, and thereby becomes real knowing.

Next, these two constituents—for it is supposed that they have the reciprocal relation of constituents, and Cognition is constructed out of them in a mechanical or at best a chemical fashion—these constituents are placed in an order of merit in which the object is regarded as something in itself finished and complete, something which, as far as its reality is concerned, could entirely dispense with thought, while on the other hand, Thought is something incomplete which has to seek completion by means of some material, and indeed has to adapt itself to its material as if it were a form in itself pliable and undetermined. Truth is supposed to be the agreement of Thought with its object, and in order to bring about this agreement (for the agreement is not there by itself) thinking must accommodate and adapt itself to its object.

Thirdly, when the difference of Matter and Form, of Object and Thought, is not left thus nebulous and undetermined, but is taken more definitely, each is regarded as a sphere separated from the other. Thus Thought in its reception and formation of material is supposed not to go beyond itself—its reception of material and accommodation thereto is still regarded as a modification of self by which Thought is not transformed into its Other; moreover, self-conscious determination is held to belong to Thought alone; thus Thought in its relation to the Object of Thought does not go out of itself to the Object, while the Object, as a thing-in-itself, simply remains a something beyond Thought.

These views concerning the relation to one another of Subject and Object express the determinations which constitute the nature of our ordinary consciousness just as it appears; but these prejudices, translated into the sphere of Reason—as if the same relationship held there or had any truth by itself—are errors, the refutation of which throughout all departments of the spiritual and physical world is Philosophy itself; or rather, since these errors bar the way, they must be renounced at the very threshold of Philosophy.

The older Metaphysics had in this respect a loftier conception of Thought than that which has become current in more modern times. For the older Metaphysics laid down as fundamental that which by thinking is known of and in things, that alone is what is really true in them; that what is really true is not things in their immediacy, but only things when they have been taken up into the Form of Thought, as conceptions. Thus this older Metaphysics stands for the view that thinking and the determinations of thinking are not something foreign to the objects of thought, but are rather of the very essence of those objects; in other words that *Things* and the *Thinking* of them are in harmony in and for themselves,—indeed language itself expresses an affinity between them,—that thought in its immanent determinations, and the true nature of things, are one and the same content.

But *reflective* Understanding assumed possession of Philosophy. We must learn precisely what is meant by this expression, which indeed is frequently used as a catch-word; by it is to be understood generally the abstracting and separating intelligence which clings tenaciously to the separations which it has made. Directed against Reason, this intelligence behaves as *crude Common Sense* and maintains the view that Truth rests upon sense-reality, that thoughts are *only* thoughts, meaning that it is sense-perception that first endows them with substance and reality, that Reason—in as far as it is merely Reason—can spin nothing but ideal fancies. In this renunciation of Reason by itself, the concept of Truth is lost; it is restricted to the cognition of merely subjective Truth, of mere appearance, of something to which the nature of the thing itself does not correspond; *knowing* falls back into *opinion*.

But this turn which Cognition takes, and which has the air of being a loss and a retrogression, has something deeper behind it—something upon which the uplifting of Reason to the loftier spirit of the newer Philosophy chiefly depends. That is, the ground of this now everywhere prevalent idea is to be sought in a perception of the *necessary conflict* with each other of the determinations of Understanding. The reflection already mentioned is this, that the immediate concrete must be transcended, and must undergo determination and abstraction. But reflection must, just as much, transcend these its own separative determinations, and forthwith relate them to each other. Then at the standpoint of this relating, the conflict emerges. This relating activity of reflection belongs in itself to Reason; that transcending of these determinations which attains to a perception of their conflict, is the great negative step towards the true concept of Reason. But this perception, being merely partial, falls into the error of fancying that it is Reason which is in contradiction with itself, and does not recognize that the contradiction is just the lifting of Reason above the limitations of Understanding, and the dissolution of these. Instead of starting from this point to make the final step upwards, knowledge, recognizing the unsatisfactory nature of the determinations of Understanding, flies straight back to sensible existence, thinking to find therein stability and unity. But on the other hand, since this knowledge knows itself to be knowledge only of appearances, its insufficiency is confessed, yet at the same time it is supposed that things, though not rightly known in themselves, still are rightly known within the sphere of appearances; as though only the *kinds of objects* were different, and the one kind, namely Things in themselves, did not fall within knowledge, and the other kind, namely Appearances, did so fall. It is as though accurate perception were attributed to a man, with the proviso that he yet could not perceive Truth but only untruth. Absurd as this would be, a true knowledge which did not know the object of knowledge as it is in itself, would be equally absurd.

The *criticism of the Forms of Common Understanding* has had the result (mentioned above) that these Forms have no *applicability to things in themselves*. This can have no other meaning than that the Forms are in themselves something untrue. But if they are allowed to remain as valid for subjective Reason and for experience, then criticism has made no change in them, but leaves them in the same attitude towards the Subject of knowledge, as they formerly had towards the Object of knowledge. But if they do not suffice for the Thing in itself, then still less should common understanding, to which they are supposed to belong, put up with them and be content with them. If they cannot be determinations of the *Thing in itself,* they can still less be determinations of Understanding, to which we must allow at the very least the dignity of a Thing in itself. The determinations of Finite and Infinite are similarly in conflict—whether they are applied to the world, to time and space, or are determinations within the mind; just as black and white produce grey whether they are mixed on a canvas or on the palette; so if our World-representation is dissolved by having the determinations of Finite and Infinite transferred to it, still more must the Spirit itself, which contains them both, be something self-contradictory and self-dissolving. It is not the constitution of the Matter or Object to which they are applied or in which they occur, that can make the difference, for the Object contains the contradiction only through these determinations and in accordance with them.

Thus this Criticism has only separated the forms of objective Thinking from the Thing, and left them, as it found them, in the Subject of Thought. For in doing so, it has not regarded these Forms in and for themselves, according to their characteristic content, but has simply taken them up as a corollary from subjective Logic; so that it was not a question of the deduction of them in themselves, nor of a deduction of them as subjective-logical Forms, and still less a question of the dialectical consideration of them.

Transcendental Idealism, carried more consistently to its logical conclusion, has recognized the emptiness of that spectre of the *Thing-in-itself* which the critical philosophy left over—an abstract shadow, detached from all content—and had it in view to demolish it altogether. Also this philosophy made a beginning of letting Reason produce its own determinations out of itself. But the subjective attitude of this attempt did not admit of its being carried to completion. Henceforth this attitude—and with it that beginning, and the development of pure philosophy—was given up.

But that which has commonly been understood by Logic is considered without any reference to metaphysical import. In its present condition, this Science has indeed no Content of such a kind that it can be regarded by ordinary consciousness as reality and truth. But Logic is not on this account a mere formal science, destitute of significant truth. In any case, the province of truth is not to be looked for in that subject-matter which is lacking in Logic, and to the want of which the inadequacy of the Science is commonly attributed: the emptiness and worthlessness of the logical forms reside solely in the way in which they have been considered and treated. Whilst as fixed determinations they fall apart and cannot be held together in organic unity, they are mere dead forms, and have not dwelling in them the spirit which is their living concrete unity. Thus they are destitute of solid content and substantial filling. The content which we miss in the logical forms, is nothing other than a solid foundation and concreting of those abstract forms, and it is customary to seek this substantial essence for them, from outside. But it is just logical Reason which is that substantial or real, which holds together in itself all abstract determinations, and is their solid absolutely concrete unity. Thus we do not need to seek far afield for what is usually regarded as a filling or content; it is not the fault of the subject-matter of Logic if it is supposed to be without content or filling, but of the way in which Logic is conceived.

This reflection leads us nearer to the problem of the point of view from which Logic is to be regarded; how it is distinguished from the mode of treatment which this science has hitherto received, and to what extent it is the only true point of view upon which Logic is in the future to be permanently based.

In the *Phenomenology of Spirit* (Bamberg and Wurzburg, 1807) I have set forth the movement of consciousness, from the first crude opposition between itself and the Object, up to absolute knowledge. This process goes through all the forms of the *relation of thought to its object*, and reaches the *Concept of Science* as its result. Thus this concept (apart from the fact that it arises within the boundaries of Logic) needs here no justification, having already received its justification in that place; the concept is incapable of any other justification than just this production by consciousness; for to consciousness, all its forms are resolved into this concept, as into the truth. A reasoned deduction or elucidation of the concept of science can at best render this service, that by it the concept is presented to the mind, and a historical knowledge of it is produced; but a definition of science, or—more precisely—of logic, has its evidence solely in the inevitableness (already referred to) of its origin. The definition with which any science makes an absolute beginning can contain nothing other than the precise and correct expression of that which is presented to one's mind *as the accepted and recognized* subject-matter and purpose of the science. That exactly this or that is thus presented is a historical asseveration, in respect of which one may indeed appeal to certain facts as commonly accepted; or rather the request can be made that certain facts may be granted as accepted. And still we find that one man here and another there will bring forward, here a case and there an instance, according to which something more and other is to be understood by various expressions, into the definition of which therefore a narrower or more general determination is to be admitted, and in accordance with which the science is to be arranged. It further depends upon argument *what* should be admitted or excluded, and within what limit and scope; and there stand open to argument the most manifold and varied opinions, among which only arbitrary choice can make a fixed and final decision. In this mode of procedure, of beginning a science with its definition, nothing is said of the need that the *inevitableness* of the *subject-matter,* and therefore of the Science itself, should be demonstrated.

The concept of pure Science, and the Deduction of it, are assumed in the present treatise so far as this, that the *Phenomenology of Spirit* is nothing other than the Deduction of this concept. Absolute Knowledge is the *Truth* of all modes of Consciousness, because according to the process of knowledge, it is only when absolute knowledge has been reached that the separation of the *Object of Knowledge* from *Subjective Certainty* is completely resolved, and Truth equated to this Certainty, and this Certainty equated to Truth.

So pure Science presupposes deliverance from the opposition of Consciousness. Pure Science includes *Thought in so far as it is just as much the Thing in itself as it is Thought*, or *the Thing in itself in so far as it is just as much pure Thought as it is the Thing in itself.* Truth, as *Science*, is pure Self-Consciousness unfolding itself, and it has the form of Self in that what exists in and for itself is the known concept, while the Concept as such is that which exists in and for itself.

This objective thinking is then the content of the pure science. Hence Logic is so little merely formal, so little destitute of the matter necessary for real and true knowledge, that on the contrary its Content is the only Absolutely True, or (if we wish still to employ the word *matter*) is the true genuine matter—a Matter, however, to which Form is not external, since this Matter is in fact Pure Thought, and thus Absolute Form itself. Logic is consequently to be understood as the System of Pure Reason, as the Realm of Pure Thought. *This realm is the Truth as it is, without husk in and for itself.* One may therefore express it thus: that this content *shows forth God as he is in his eternal essence before the creation of Nature and of a Finite Spirit.*

Anaxagoras is praised as the man who first gave voice to the idea that we ought to lay down, as the World-principle, Nous, that is Thought, and Thought as the World-essence. He thus laid the foundation of an intellectualist view of the Universe, and of this view Logic must be the pure form. In it we are not concerned with thinking *about* something lying outside thought, as the basis of thought, nor with Forms which serve merely as *signs* of Truth; on the contrary, the necessary Forms and characteristic determinations of thought are the Content and the Supreme Truth itself.

In order that we may at least envisage this we must put aside the opinion that Truth is something tangible. Such tangibility has for example been imported even into the Platonic Ideas, which are in the thought of God, as though they were things existing, but existing in a world or region outside the world of Reality, a world other than that of those Ideas, and only having real Substantiality in virtue of this otherness. The Platonic Idea is nothing other than the Universal, or more precisely the Concept of an Object of Thought; it is only in its concept that anything has actuality; in so far as it is other than its concept, it ceases to be actual and is a non-entity; the aspect of tangibility and of sensuous externality to self belongs to that non-entical aspect.—From the other side, however, one can refer to the characteristic ideas of ordinary Logic; for it is assumed that, for instance, Definitions comprise not determinations which belong only to the cognizing Subject, but determinations which belong to the Object, and constitute its most essential and inmost nature. Again, when from given determinations we conclude to others, it is assumed that what is concluded is not something external to the Object and foreign to it, but that it belongs to the object,—that Being corresponds to Thought.—Speaking generally, it lies at the very basis of our use of the Forms of Concept, Judgment, Inference, Definition, Division, and so on, that they are Forms not merely of self-conscious Thinking but also of the objective understanding.—*To think* is an expression which attributes specially to Consciousness the determination which it contains. But in as far as it is allowed that

Understanding, and Reason, are of the World of Objects, that Spirit and Nature have General Laws in accordance with which their life and their mutations are governed, in so far is it admitted that the determinations of Thought also have objective validity and existence.

The Critical Philosophy has indeed turned Metaphysics into Logic, but—as already mentioned—like the later idealism it shied at the Object, and gave to logical determinations an essentially subjective signification; thus both the Critical Philosophy and the later idealism remained saddled with the Object which they shunned, and for Kant a 'Thing-in-itself', for Fichte an abiding 'Resistance-principle', was left over as an unconquerable Other. But that freedom from the opposition of consciousness which Logic must be able to assume, lifts these thought-determinations above such a timid and incomplete point of view, and requires that those determinations should be considered not with any such limitation and reference, but as they are in and for themselves, as Logic, as Pure Reason.

Kant considers that Logic—that is, the aggregate of Definitions and Propositions which are called Logic in the ordinary sense—is fortunate in that it has fallen to its lot to attain so early to completion, before the other sciences; for Logic has not taken any step backwards since Aristotle,—but also it has taken no step forwards—the latter because to all appearance it was already finished and complete. If Logic has undergone no change since Aristotle—and in fact when one looks at modern compendiums of Logic the changes consist to a large extent merely in omissions—what is rather to be inferred from this is, that Logic is all the more in need of a thorough overhaul; for when Spirit has worked on for two thousand years, it must have reached a better reflective consciousness of its own thought and its own unadulterated essence. A comparison of the forms to which Spirit has risen in the worlds of Practice and Religion, and of Science in every department of knowledge Positive and Speculative,—a comparison of these with the form which Logic—that is, Spirit's knowledge of its own pure essence—has attained, shows such a glaring discrepancy that it cannot fail to strike the most superficial observer that the latter is inadequate to the lofty development of the former, and unworthy of it.

As a matter of fact the need of a transformation of Logic has long been felt. It may be said that, both in Form and in Content, as exhibited in text-books, Logic has become contemptible. It is still trailed along rather with a feeling that one cannot do without Logic altogether, and from a surviving adherence to the tradition of its importance, than from any conviction that familiar content, and occupation with those empty forms, can be valuable and useful.

The additions—psychological, educational, even physiological—which Logic received during a certain period were, later, almost universally recognized as disfigurements. In themselves, a great part of these psychological, educational, and physiological observations, laws, and rules, must appear very trivial and futile, whether they occur in Logic or anywhere else. Besides, such rules as for instance that one should think out and test what one reads in books or hears by word of mouth, that when one does not see well, one should use spectacles to help one's eyes—rules which in text-books on so-called Applied Logic are put forward with great seriousness and formality to help us to attain to truth—these must appear to all the world to be superfluous—except indeed to the writer or teacher who is at his wits' end to know how to piece out the inadequate lifeless content of his Logic.

As to this content, we have given above the reason why it is so empty and lifeless. Its determinations are assumed to stand immovably rigid and are brought into a merely external relation with one another. Because in the operations of judgment and syllogism it is chiefly their quantitative element that is referred to and built upon, everything rests on an external difference, on mere comparison, and becomes a wholly analytic procedure, a matter of merely mechanical calculation. The deduction of the so-called rules and laws (especially of Syllogism) is not much better than a manipulation of rods of unequal length in order to sort and arrange them according to size—like the child's game of trying of fit into their right places the various pieces of a picture-puzzle. Not without reason, therefore, has this Thinking been identified with Reckoning, and Reckoning with this Thinking. In Arithmetic the numbers are taken as non-significant, as something that, except for equality or inequality—that is, except for quite external relations—has no significance,—that contains no Thought, either in itself or in its relations. When it is worked out in a mechanical way that three-fourths multiplied by two-thirds make a half, this operation involves about as much or as little thought as the calculation whether in any Figure of Syllogism this or that Mood is admissible.

In order that these dead bones of Logic may be re-vivified by Spirit, and endowed with content and coherence, its Method must be that by means of which alone Logic is capable of becoming a Pure Science. In the present condition of Logic, hardly a suspicion of scientific Method is to be recognized. It has very nearly the structure of merely Empirical Science. For attaining their purpose, empirical sciences have hit upon a characteristic Method of defining and classifying their material as best they can. Pure Mathematics again has its own Method, which suits its abstract objects and the quantitative determinations with which alone it is concerned. I have in the Preface to the *Phenomenology of Spirit* said what is essential concerning this Method and especially concerning the subordinate nature of such Science as can find a place in Mathematics; but it will also be more closely considered within the bounds of Logic itself. Spinoza, Wolf, and others, have allowed themselves to be misled into applying this method in Philosophy, and identifying the external process of concept-less quantity with the conceptual process, which is self-contradictory. Hitherto Philosophy had not discovered its own method; it regarded with an envious eye the systematic structure of Mathematics and, as already remarked, borrowed this, or sought help in the method of Sciences which are only a medley of given material and empirical maxims and ideas—or took refuge in a crude rejection of all Method. But the exposition of that which alone is capable of being the true Method of philosophic Science belongs to Logic itself; since method is the consciousness of the form taken by the inner spontaneous movement of the content of Logic. In the *Phenomenology of Spirit* I have set out an example of this Method as applied to a more concrete object, namely to Consciousness. We have here modes of consciousness each of which in realizing itself abolishes itself, has its own negation as its result,—and thus passes over into a higher mode. The one and only thing *for securing scientific progress* (and for quite *simple* insight into which, it is essential to strive)—is knowledge of the logical precept that Negation is just as much Affirmation as negation, or that what is self-contradictory resolves itself not into nullity, into abstract Nothingness, but essentially only into the negation of its *particular* content, that such negation is not an all-embracing Negation, but is *the negation of a definite somewhat* which abolishes itself, and thus is a definite negation; and that thus the result contains in essence that from which it results—which is indeed a tautology, for otherwise it would be something immediate and not a result. Since what results, the negation, is a *definite* negation, it has a *content*. It is a new concept, but a higher, richer concept than that which preceded; for it has been enriched by the negation or opposite of that preceding concept, and thus contains it, but contains also more than it, and is the unity of it and its opposite. On these lines the system of Concepts has broadly to be constructed, and to go on to completion in a resistless course, free from all foreign elements, admitting nothing from outside.

I could not of course imagine that the Method which in this System of Logic I have followed—or rather which this System follows of itself—is not capable of much improvement, of much elaboration in detail, but at the same time I know that it is the only true Method. This is already evident from the fact that the Method is no-ways different from its object and content;—for it is the content in itself, *the Dialectic which it has in itself*, that moves it on. It is clear that no expositions can be regarded as scientific which do not follow the course of this Method, and which are not conformable to its simple rhythm, for that is the course of the thing itself.

In accordance with this Method I would observe that the divisions and headings of the Books, Sections and Chapters which are given in the work, as well as to some extent the explanations connected with them, were made for the purposes of a preliminary survey, and that in fact they have only a *historical* value. They do not belong to the content and body of the Science, but are compiled by external reflection, which has already run through the whole of the scheme, and hence knows and indicates in advance the sequence of its phases, before these introduce themselves in the subject itself.

In the other Sciences too, such preliminary Definitions and Divisions are in themselves no other than such external specifications; but even within each science they are not raised above this status. Even in Logic, for example, we may be told that 'Logic has two principal parts, *(1)* the Doctrine of Elements and *(2)* Methodology;'—then under the first head we forthwith find, perhaps, the superscription: *Laws of Thought*;—and then: *Chapter I—Concepts. First Section: Of the Clearness of Concepts*—and so on.—These Determinations and Divisions, made without any deduction or justification, furnish the systematic framework and the whole bond of connection of such sciences. Such a Logic regards it as its business to say that Concepts and Truths must be *derived* from Principles; but in what this Logic calls Method, derivation is the last thing that is thought of. The procedure consists, it may be, in grouping together what is similar, in putting what is simpler before what is compound, and other external considerations. But as for any inner necessary connection, this goes no further than the list of Sections, and the transition consists merely in saying *Chapter II*; or *We now come to Judgment*, and the like.

The headings and divisions which occur in this system too are designed in themselves to have no other significance than that of a Table of Contents. But in addition to this the *necessity of connection* and *the immanent origination* of distinctions must show themselves in the discussion of the subject-matter, for they are part of the self-development of the concept.

That by means of which the Concept forges ahead is the above-mentioned Negative which it carries within itself; it is this that constitutes the genuine dialectical procedure. *Dialectic*—which has been regarded as an isolated part of Logic, and which as regards its purpose and standpoint has, one may aver, been entirely misunderstood—is thus put in quite a different position.—The Platonic Dialectic too, even in the *Parmenides* (and still more directly in other places), is sometimes intended merely to dispose of and to refute through themselves limited assertions, and sometimes again has nullity for its result. Dialectic is generally regarded as an external and negative procedure, that does not pertain to the subject-matter, that is based on a mere idle subjective craving to disturb and unsettle what is fixed and true, or that at best leads to nothing except the futility of the dialectically treated matter.

Kant set Dialectic higher, and this part of his work is among the greatest of his merits,—for he freed Dialectic from the semblance of arbitrariness attributed to it in ordinary thought, and set it forth as a *necessary procedure of Reason*. Since Dialectic was regarded merely as the art of producing deceptions and bringing about illusions, it was straightway assumed that it played a cheating game, and that its whole power depended solely on concealment of the fraud; that its results were reached surreptitiously, and were a more subjective illusion. When Kant's dialectical expositions in the *Antinomies of Pure Reason* are looked at closely (as they will be more at large in the course of this work) it will be seen that they are not indeed deserving of any great praise; but the general idea upon which he builds and which he has vindicated, is the *Objectivity of Appearance* and the *Necessity of Contradiction* which belong to the very nature of thought-determinations; primarily indeed in so far as these determinations are applied by Reason to *Things in themselves*; but further, just what these determinations are *in Reason* and *in respect of that which is self-existent*,—just this it is which is their own nature. This result, *grasped on its positive side*, is nothing other than the inherent *Negativity* of these thought-determinations, their self-moving soul, the principle of all physical and spiritual life. But if people stop short at the abstract-negative aspect of the Dialectic, they reach only the familiar result that Reason is incapable of cognition of the Infinite;—a strange result, for—since the Infinite is the Reasonable—it amounts to saying that Reason is incapable of cognizing that which is Reasonable.

It is in this Dialectic (as here understood) and in the comprehension of the Unity of Opposites, or of the Positive in the Negative, that *Speculative knowledge* consists. This is the most important aspect of the Dialectic, but for thought that is as yet unpracticed and unfree, it is the most difficult. If thought is still in the process of cutting itself loose from concrete sense-presentation and from syllogizing (*Räsonnieren*), it must first practice abstract thinking, and learn to hold fast concepts in their definiteness and to recognize by means of them. An exposition of Logic with this in view must, in its Method, follow the division above mentioned, and with regard to the more detailed content must hold to the determinations of the particular concepts without embarking upon the Dialectic. As far as external structure is concerned, this Logic would be similar to the usual presentation of the science, but as regards content would be distinct from it, and still would serve for practice in abstract thinking, though not in speculative thinking (a purpose which could not be in any degree fulfilled by the Logic which has become popular by means of psychological and anthropological trappings). It would present to the mind the picture of a methodically ordered whole, although the soul of the structure, the Method itself (which lives in Dialectic), would not be apparent in it.

As regards *education and the relation of the individual to Logic*, I observe in conclusion that this Science, like grammar, has two different aspects or values. It is one thing to him who approaches Logic and the Sciences in general for the first time, and another thing to him who comes back from the Sciences to Logic. He who begins to learn grammar, finds in its Forms and Laws dry abstractions, contingent rules, briefly an isolated multitude of determinations which only indicate the worth and significance of their face-value. At first, knowledge recognizes in them nothing whatever but barely themselves. On the other hand, if anyone has mastered a language, and has also a comparative knowledge of other languages, he and he only is capable of discerning the spirit and the culture of a people in the grammar of their language. Those same dry Rules and Forms have now for him a full and living value. Through grammar he can recognize the expression of mind in general—that is, Logic. Thus he who approaches Logic finds in the science at first an isolated system of abstractions that is self-contained and does not reach out to other knowledges and sciences. On the contrary, contrasted with the wealth of our world-presentations and the apparently real content of the other sciences, and compared with the promise of absolute Science to unfold the essential character of this wealth, the *inner nature* of Spirit and of the world, and to unveil *the Truth*, this science—in its abstract form, in the colourless cold simplicity of its purely formal determinations—looks, rather, as if the last thing to be expected from it were the fulfilment of such a promise, and as if it would stand empty in face of that wealth. On a first acquaintance, the significance of Logic is limited to itself; its content is regarded as only an isolated occupation with thought-determinations, *alongside of* which other scientific activities have their own material and their own intrinsic worth, upon which Logic may perhaps have some formal influence which it seems to exercise spontaneously, and for which logical structure and logical study can certainly be dispensed with, at need. The other Sciences have mostly rejected the regular Method, of a connected series of Definitions, Axioms, Theorems and their Proofs, and so forth; while so-called Natural Logic plays its part automatically in such series, and works of its own motion, without any special knowledge having Thought itself for its object. Above all the matter and content of these sciences keeps entirely independent of Logic, and altogether makes its appeal more to our senses, feeling, impressions, and practical interests.

Thus then Logic must certainly be learnt, at first, as something of which one has indeed perception and understanding, but which seems at the beginning to lack scope, profundity, and wider significance. It is only through a profounder acquaintance with other sciences that Logic discovers itself to subjective thought as not a mere abstract Universal, but as a Universal which comprises in itself the full wealth of Particulars;—just as a proverb, in the mouth of a youth who understands it quite accurately, yet fails of the significance and scope which it has in the mind of a man of years and experience, for whom it expresses the full force of its content. Thus the value of Logic only receives due appreciation when it is seen to result from knowledge of the particular sciences; so regarded, it presents itself to the mind as Universal Truth, not as a *particular* department of knowledge *alongside of* other departments and other realities, but as the very essence of all these other Contents.

Now though when one begins to study it, Logic is not present to the mind in all this recognized power, yet none the less the mind of the student conceives from it a power which will lead him into all truth. The System of Logic is the realm of shades, a world of simple essentialities freed from all concretion of sense. To study this Science, to dwell and labour in this shadow-realm, is a perfect training and discipline of consciousness. In this realm the mind carries on a business which is far removed from the intuitions and aims of sense, from emotions, from ideas which are a mere matter of opinion. Regarded on its negative side, the work consists in holding at bay the accidentals of syllogizing thought and the arbitrary preference and acceptance from among opposing arguments.

But above all, Thought wins thus self-reliance and independence. It becomes at home in the region of the abstract and in progression by means of concepts which have no substratum of sensation, it develops an unconscious power of taking up into the forms of Reason the multiplicity of all other knowledge and science, comprehending and holding fast what is essential therein, stripping off externalities and in this way extracting what is logical,—or, which is the same thing, filling with the content of all truth the abstract outline of Logic acquired by study, and giving it the value of a Universal, which no longer appears as a Particular side by side with other Particulars, but reaches out beyond all this, and is the essential nature thereof,—that is, the Absolute Truth.

GENERAL CLASSIFICATION OF LOGIC

In what has been said to the concept of this Science, and the direction which its justification must take, it is implied that a general classification can at this point be only provisional, and hence can be indicated only so far as the author already knows the Science and is thus in a position to present here, historically and in a preliminary fashion, the principal forms in which the concept will manifest itself in the course of its development.

A provisional attempt can, however, be made to render generally intelligible what is required for such a classification, although in doing so one must employ a method that will only receive its full elucidation and justification within the precincts of the Science itself. First, then, it is to be remembered that we here presuppose that the classification must harmonize with the concept, or rather must be immanent in it. The concept is not indeterminate; it is determinate in itself; and the classification is the developed expression of this its determinateness. It is the fundamental and significant classification of the concept; not of anything taken from without, but the fundamental classification, that is, the determination of the concept by itself. The quality of being right-angled, acute-angled, or equilateral, the determinations according to which triangles are classified, are not contained in the determinateness of the triangle itself; that is, they are not contained in what we are accustomed to call the concept of the triangle, any more than the commonly admitted concept of Animal in general, or of Mammal, Bird, and so forth contains the determinations by which animals are classified into mammals, birds, and so on, and these classes are subdivided into further genera. Such determinations are obtained otherwise, that is, from empirical contemplation; they come to these so-called concepts from without; but in the philosophical treatment of classification, it must be shown that the classification has its origin in the concept itself.

But in the Introduction the concept of Logic itself is stated to be the result of a Science which lies outside Logic, and thus this concept too is here presupposed. Logic was there found to determine itself as the science of pure thought, having pure knowledge as its principle, which is not abstract, but a concrete living unity; for in it the opposition in consciousness between a subjective entity existing for itself, and another similar objective entity, is known to be overcome and existence is known as pure concept in itself, and the pure concept known as true existence. These are then the two *Moments* which are contained in Logic. But they are now known as existing inseparably, and not as in consciousness each existing for itself; it is only because they are known as distinct and yet not merely self-existent that their unity is not abstract, dead, and immobile, but concrete.

This unity constitutes an element of the logical principle, so that the development of the distinction which is immediately latent within it takes place only within this element. We have said that the classification is the fundamental classification of the concept, the positing of the determination immanent in it and thus of its distinction; hence this positing is not to be understood as resolving that concrete unity back into its determinations regarded as self-existent, entities, which here would be mere retrogression to the former position, namely the opposition of consciousness. This opposition, on the contrary, has vanished, and that unity remains the element, beyond which the distinctions which occur in the classification and the development generally, do not pass. And thus determinations (such as the subjective and the objective, thought and being, concept and reality, whatever the respect in which they were determined)—determinations which, at an earlier point on the road to truth, were self-existing, are now, in their unity (which constitutes their truth), degraded to the rank of forms. In their distinctions they therefore remain, in themselves, the whole concept, and this is placed under its own determinations in the classification.

Thus the whole concept is to be considered, first as existent concept, secondly merely as concept; in the former case it is merely the concept in itself, the concept of reality or being; in the latter, it is the concept as such existing for itself (as it is found, to give a concrete example, in thinking man, and even in the sentient animal and in organic individuality in general, though there it is not conscious, still less known; concept *in itself* it is only in inorganic nature).—Logic is accordingly to be divided into the Logic of the Concept as Being, and of the Concept as Concept; or, to employ terms more habitual though least definite and therefore most ambiguous, into *Objective* and *Subjective* Logic.

The basic element, then, is the unity of the concept in itself, and the inseparable nature of its determinations; these, therefore, in so far as they are distinct, and the concept is posited in their distinctness, must at least be somehow related. There results a sphere of mediation—the concept as a system of *determinations of reflection*, that is, of Being in transition to the being in-self of the concept; thus the concept is not yet posited as such for itself; immediate being, as something external, still cleaves to it. This is the Doctrine of Essence which is intermediate between the Doctrine of Being and that of the Notion. In the general classification of this logical work it has been placed under Objective Logic, since, though Essence already is the Inward, the character of Subject has been expressly reserved for the Notion.

In recent times Kant has opposed to what is commonly called Logic yet another, namely *Transcendental Logic*. What has here been called Objective Logic would partly correspond to what is Transcendental Logic with him. He distinguishes it from what he calls General Logic because *(a)* it considers concepts which refer *a priori* to objects and thus does not abstract from the entire content of objective cognition,—in other words it contains the rules of pure thinking about an object; and *(b)* because it further considers the origin of our cognition, so far as this cannot be ascribed to the objects.—It is on the second of these two aspects that the philosophic interest of Kant is exclusively directed. His chief aim is to claim the Categories for Self-consciousness, for the Subjective Ego. By virtue of this determination, his point of view remains within the boundaries of consciousness and its opposition, and there is a surplus, beyond the data of sensation and intuition, which is not posited and determined by thinking self-consciousness and is foreign and external to thought, namely the thing-in-itself; though it is easy to perceive that such an abstraction as the thing-in-itself is itself only a product of thought, namely, of purely abstracting thought. Other disciples of Kant have expressed themselves concerning the determination of the object through the ego in this sense, that the objectifying of the ego is to be considered as an original and necessary activity of consciousness, so that this original activity does not yet contain the idea of the ego itself; this latter being the consciousness, or even the objectifying, *of* such consciousness. On such a view, this objectifying activity, freed from the opposition of consciousness, is just that which can, generally, be called *Thought* as such. But this activity should no longer be called consciousness: consciousness comprehends within it that opposition of ego and object which does not exist in this original activity. The name of consciousness gives a greater appearance of subjectivity to it than the expression 'thought', which, however, is here to be taken in the absolute sense as Thought *infinite* and untainted by the finitude of consciousness: briefly, as Thought as such.

Kant's philosophy then directing its interest on the so-called transcendental element of the determinations of thought, the treatment of these received no attention: it was not considered what they are in themselves apart from the abstract relation to the ego common to all, or what are their reciprocal determinations and relations. Hence this philosophy has in no way contributed to knowledge of their natures. The only interesting matter bearing upon the point occurs in the Critique of Ideas. But for the real progress of philosophy it was necessary that the interest of thought should be directed upon the formal side, the ego, consciousness as such, that is, the abstract relation of subjective knowledge to an object; and that the cognition of infinite form, that is, of the concept, should be introduced in this manner. But in order that this cognition may be reached, that finite determination, in which the form still is ego, or consciousness, has still to be cast off. The form, thus developed into purity by thought, will then have in itself the capacity of self-determination, that is, of giving itself content, and that a necessary content, in the shape of a system of determinations of thought.

Objective Logic then takes the place of the former metaphysics considered as the scientific reconstruction of the world, which was to be built of thoughts alone. If we refer to the last stage in the evolution of this science, we find, first and immediately, that it is Ontology whose place is taken by Objective Logic—that part of this metaphysics which is to investigate the nature of *Ens* in general;— Ens comprehending both Being and Essence, a distinction for which the German language has fortunately preserved different terms.—Secondly, Objective Logic also comprises the rest of metaphysics, in so far as the latter attempted to comprehend with the pure forms of thought certain substrata primarily taken from sensuous representation, such as Soul, World, God; and the determinations of thought constituted what was essential in the method of contemplation. Logic, however, considers these forms detached from such substrata, which are the subjects of sensuous representation; it considers their nature and value in themselves. The old metaphysics neglected this, and thus earned the just reproach of having used these forms uncritically, without a preliminary investigation as to whether and how far they were capable of being determinations of the thing-in-itself, to use the Kantian expression, or, to put it better, determinations of the Rational.— Objective Logic thus is their true critique, a critique which considers the forms of thought not under the abstract form of apriority as opposed to the *a posteriori*, but considers each according to its particular content.

Subjective Logic is the Logic of the Notion,—of Essence which has transcended its relation to any mere being, real or apparent, and in its determination is no longer external, but is the free, independent, and self-determining Subjective, or rather the Subject itself.—Since the subject involves the misconception of the contingent and arbitrary, and, more generally, of determinations belonging to the form of consciousness, no special weight is to be attached to the distinction between the Subjective and the Objective, which will develop itself more clearly within the body of the Logic.

Thus Logic is divided broadly into Objective and Subjective Logic; more definitely, it has three parts, namely—

1 The Logic of Being,
2. The Logic of Essence, and
3. The Logic of the Notion.

PHILOSOPHY OF RIGHT

᷂

'Hence man is by nature good. But natural characteristics, since they are opposed to freedom and the conception of the spirit, and are, hence, negative, must be eradicated. Thus man is by nature evil'.

3

PHILOSOPHY OF RIGHT

PREFACE

It is for science a piece of good fortune that that kind of philosophizing, which might, like scholasticism, have continued to spin its notions within itself, has been brought into contact with reality. Indeed, such contact was inevitable. The real world is in earnest with the principles of right and duty, and in the full light of a consciousness of these principles it lives. With this world of reality philosophic cob-web spinning has come into open rupture. Now, as to genuine philosophy it is precisely its attitude to reality which has been misapprehended. Philosophy is an inquisition into the rational, and therefore the apprehension of the real and present. Hence it cannot be the exposition of a world beyond, which is merely a castle in the air, having no existence except in the terror of a one-sided and empty formalism of thought. In the following treatise I have remarked that even Plato's *Republic*, now regarded as the bye-word for an empty ideal, has grasped the essential nature of the ethical life of the Greeks. He knew that there was breaking in upon Greek life a deeper principle, which could directly manifest itself only as an unsatisfied longing and therefore as ruin. Moved by the same longing Plato had to seek help against it, but had to conceive of the help as coming down from above, and hoped at last to have found it in an external special form of Greek ethical life. He exhausted himself in contriving, how by means of this new society to stem the tide of ruin, but succeeded only in injuring more fatally its deeper motive, the free infinite personality. Yet he has proved himself to be a great mind because the very principle and central distinguishing feature of his idea is the pivot upon which the world-wide revolution then in process turned:

>What is rational is real;
>And what is real is rational.

Upon this conviction stand not philosophy only but even every unsophisticated consciousness. From it also proceeds the view now under contemplation that the spiritual universe is the natural. When reflection, feeling or whatever other form the subjective consciousness may assume, regards the present as vanity, and thinks itself to be beyond it and wiser, it finds itself in emptiness, and, as it has actuality only in the present, it is vanity throughout. Against the doctrine that the idea is a mere idea, figment or opinion, philosophy preserves the more profound view that nothing is real except the idea. Hence arises the effort to recognize in the temporal and transient the substance, which is immanent, and the eternal, which is present. The rational is synonymous with the idea, because in realizing itself it passes into external existence. It thus appears in an endless wealth of forms, figures and phenomena. It wraps its kernel round with a robe of many colours, in which consciousness finds itself at home.

This treatise, in so far as it contains a political science, is nothing more than an attempt to conceive of and present the state as in itself rational. As a philosophic writing, it must be on its guard against constructing a state as it ought to be. Philosophy cannot teach the state what it should be, but only how it, the ethical universe, is to be known.

Ἰδοὺ Ῥόδος, ἰδοὺ καὶ τὸ πήδημα.
Hic Rhodus, *hic* saltus.

To apprehend what is, is the task of philosophy, because what is, is reason. As for the individual, every one is a son of his time; so philosophy also is its time apprehended in thought. It is just as foolish to fancy that any philosophy can transcend its present world, as that an individual could leap out of his time or jump over Rhodes. If a theory transgresses its time, and builds up a world as it ought to be, it has an existence merely in the unstable element of opinion, which gives room to every wandering fancy.

With little change the above saying would read:

Here is the rose, here dance

The barrier which stands between reason, as self-conscious Spirit, and reason as present reality, and does not permit spirit to find satisfaction in reality, is some abstraction, which is not free to be conceived. To recognize reason as the rose in the cross of the present, and to find delight in it, is a rational insight which implies reconciliation with reality. This reconciliation philosophy grants to those who have felt the inward demand to conceive clearly, to preserve subjective freedom while present in substantive reality, and yet thought possessing this freedom to stand not upon the particular and contingent, but upon what is and self-completed.

This also is the more concrete meaning of what was more abstractly called the unity of form and content. Form in its most concrete significance is reason, as an intellectual apprehension which conceives its object. Content, again, is reason as the substantive essence of social order and nature. The conscious identity of form and content is the philosophical idea.

It is a self-assertion, which does honour to man, to recognize nothing in sentiment which is not justified by thought. This self-will is a feature of modern times, being indeed the peculiar principle of Protestantism. What was initiated by Luther as faith in feeling and the witness of the spirit, the more mature mind strives to apprehend in conception. In that way it seeks to free itself in the present, and so find there itself. It is a celebrated saying that a half philosophy leads away from God, while a true philosophy leads to God. This saying is applicable to the science of the state. Reason cannot content itself with a mere approximation, something which is neither cold nor hot, and must be spewed out of the mouth. As little can it be contented with the cold skepticism that in this world of time things go badly, or at best only moderately well, and that we must keep the peace with reality, merely because there is nothing better to be had. Knowledge creates a much more vital peace.

Only one word more concerning the desire to teach the world what it ought to be. For such a purpose philosophy at least always comes too late. Philosophy, as the thought of the world, does not appear until reality has completed its formative process, and made itself ready. History thus corroborates the teaching of the conception that only in the maturity of reality does the ideal appear as counterpart to the real, apprehends the real world in its substance, and shapes it into an intellectual kingdom. When philosophy paints its grey in grey, one form of life has become old, and by means of grey it cannot be rejuvenated, but only known. The owl of Minerva takes its flight only when the shades of night are gathering.

INTRODUCTION

The philosophic science of right has as its object the idea of right, i.e., the conception of right and the realization of the conception.

Philosophy has to do with ideas or realized thoughts, and hence not with what we have been accustomed to call mere conceptions. It has indeed to exhibit the one-sidedness and untruth of these mere conceptions, and to show that, while that which commonly bears the name 'conception' is only an abstract product of the understanding, the true conception alone has reality and gives this reality to itself. Everything, other than the reality which is established by the conception, is transient surface existence, external attribute, opinion, appearance void of essence, untruth, delusion, and so forth. Through the actual shape, which it takes upon itself in actuality, is the conception itself understood. This shape is the other essential element of the idea, and is to be distinguished from the form, which exists only as conception.

The conception and its existence are two sides, distinct yet united, like soul and body. The body is the same life as the soul, and yet the two can be named independently. A soul without a body would not be a living thing, and vice versa. Thus the visible existence of the conception is its body, just as the body obeys the soul which produced it. Seeds contain the tree and its whole power, though they are not the tree itself; the tree corresponds accurately to the simple structure of the seed. If the body does not correspond to the soul, it is defective. The unity of visible existence and conception, of body and soul, is the idea. It is not a mere harmony of the two, but their complete interpenetration. There lives nothing, which is not in some way idea. The idea of right is freedom, which, if it is to be apprehended truly, must be known both in its conception and in the embodiment of the conception.

The science of right is a part of philosophy. Hence it must develop the idea, which is the reason of an object, out of the conception. It is the same thing to say that it must regard the peculiar internal development of the thing itself. Since it is a part, it has a definite beginning, which is the result and truth of what goes before, and this, that goes before, constitutes its so-called proof. Hence the origin of the conception of right falls outside of the science of right. The deduction of the conception is presupposed in this treatise, and is to be considered as already given.

Philosophy forms a circle. It has, since it must somehow make a beginning, a primary, directly given matter, which is not proved and is not a result. But this starting-point is simply relative, since, from another point of view it appears as a result. Philosophy is a consequence, which does not hang in the air or form a directly new beginning, but is self-enclosed.

According to the formal unphilosophic method of the sciences, definition is the first desideratum, as regards, at least, the external scientific form. The positive science of right, however, is little concerned with definition, since its special aim is to give what it is that is right, and also the particular phases of the laws. For this reason it has been said as a warning, *Omnis definitio in jure civili periculosa*; and in fact the more disconnected and contradictory the phases of a right are, the less possible is a definition of it.

A definition should contain only universal features; but these forthwith bring to light contradictions, which in the case of law are injustice, in all their nakedness. Thus in Roman law, for instance, no definition of man was possible, because it excluded the slave. The conception of man was destroyed by the fact of slavery. In the same way to have defined property and owner would have appeared to be perilous to many relations. But definitions may perhaps be derived from etymology, for the reason, principally, that in this way special cases are avoided, and a basis is found in the feeling and imaginative thought of men. The correctness of a definition would thus consist in its agreement with existing ideas. By such a method everything essentially scientific is cast aside. As regards the content there is cast aside the necessity of the self-contained and self-developed object, and as regards the form there is discarded the nature of the conception. In philosophic knowledge the necessity of a conception is the main thing, and the process by which it, as a result, has come into being is the proof and deduction. After the content is seen to be necessary independently, the second point is to look about for that which corresponds to it in existing ideas and modes of speech. But the way in which a conception exists in its truth, and the way it presents itself in random ideas not only are but must be different both in form and structure. If a notion is not in its content false, the conception can be shown to be contained in it and to be already there in its essential traits.

A notion may thus be raised to the form of a conception. But so little is any notion the measure and criterion of an independently necessary and true conception, that it must accept truth from the conception, be justified by it, and know itself through it. If the method of knowing, which proceeds by formal definition, inference and proof, has more or less disappeared, a worse one has come to take its place. This new method maintains that ideas, as, e.g., the idea of right in all its aspects, are to be directly apprehended as mere facts of consciousness, and that natural feeling or that heightened form of it which is known as the inspiration of one's own breast, is the source of right. This method may be the most convenient of all, but it is also the most unphilosophic. Other features of this view, referring not merely to knowledge but directly to action, need not detain us here. While the first or formal method went so far as to require in definition the form of the conception, and in proof the form of a necessity of knowledge, the method of the intuitive consciousness and feeling takes for its principle the arbitrary contingent consciousness of the subject. In this treatise we take for granted the scientific procedure of philosophy, which has been set forth in the philosophic logic.

Right is positive in general *(a)* in its form, since it has validity in a state; and this established authority is the principle for the knowledge of right. Hence we have the positive science of right. *(b)* On the side of content this right receives a positive element *(i)* through the particular character of a nation, the stage of its historical development, and the interconnection of all the relations which are necessitated by nature. Also *(ii)* through the necessity that a system of legalized right must contain the application of the universal conception to objects and cases whose qualities are given externally. Such an application is not the speculative thought or the development of the conception, but a subsumption made by the understanding. And finally *(iii)* through the ultimate nature of a decision which has become a reality.

Philosophy at least cannot recognize the authority of feeling, inclination and caprice, when they are set in opposition to positive right and the laws. It is an accident, external to the nature of positive right, when force or tyranny becomes an element of it. It will be shown later at what point right must become positive. The general phases which are there deduced, are here only mentioned, in order to indicate the limit of philosophic right, and also to forestall the idea or indeed the demand that by a systematic development of right should be produced a law-book, such as would be needed by an actual state. To convert the differences between right of nature and positive right, or those between philosophic right and positive right, into open antagonism would be a complete misunderstanding.

Natural right or philosophic right stands to positive right as institutions to pandects. With regard to the historical element in positive right, it may be said that the true historical view and genuine philosophic standpoint have been presented by Montesquieu. He regards legislation and its specific traits not in an isolated and abstract way, but rather as a dependent element of one totality, connecting it with all the other elements which form the character of a nation and an epoch. In this interrelation the various elements receive their meaning and justification. The purely historical treatment of the phases of right, as they develop in time, and a comparison of their results with existing relations of right have their own value; but they are out of place in a philosophic treatise, except in so far as the development out of historic grounds coincides with the development out of the conception, and the historical exposition and justification can be made to cover a justification which is valid in itself and independently.

This distinction is as manifest as it is weighty. A phase of right may be shown to rest upon and follow from the circumstances and existing institutions of right, and yet may be absolutely unreasonable and void of right. This is the case in Roman law with many aspects of private right, which were the logical results of its interpretation of paternal power and of marriage. Further, if the aspects of right are really right and reasonable, it is one thing to point out what with regard to them can truly take place through the conception, and quite another thing to portray the manner of their appearance in history, along with the circumstances, cases, wants and events, which they have called forth. Such a demonstration and deduction from nearer or more remote historic causes, which is the occupation of pragmatic history, is frequently called exposition, or preferably conception, under the opinion that in such an indication of the historic elements is found all that is essential to a conception of law and institutions of right. In point of fact that which is truly essential, the conception of the matter, has not been so much as mentioned. So also we are accustomed to hear of Roman or German conceptions of right, and of conceptions of right as they are laid down in this or that statute-book, when indeed nothing about conceptions can be found in them, but only general phases of right, propositions derived from the understanding, general maxims, and laws.

By neglect of the distinction, just alluded to, the true standpoint is obscured and the question of a valid justification is shifted into a justification based upon circumstances; results are founded on presuppositions, which in themselves are of little value; and in general the relative is put in place of the absolute, and external appearance in place of the nature of the thing. When the historical vindication substitutes the external origin for the origin from the conception, it unconsciously does the opposite of what it intends. Suppose that an institution, originating under definite circumstances, is shown to be necessary and to answer its purpose, and that it accomplishes all that is required of it by the historical standpoint. When such a proof is made to stand for a justification of the thing itself, it follows that, when the circumstances are removed, the institution has lost its meaning and its right. When, e.g., it is sought to support and defend cloisters on the grounds that they have served to clear and people the wilderness and by teaching and transcribing to preserve scholarship, it follows that just in so far as the circumstances are changed, cloisters have become aimless and superfluous.

The territory of right is in general the spiritual, and its more definite place and origin is the will, which is free. Thus freedom constitutes the substance and essential character of the will, and the system of right is the kingdom of actualized freedom. It is the world of spirit, which is produced out of itself, and is a second nature.

Freedom of will is best explained by reference to physical nature. Freedom is a fundamental phase of will, as weight is of bodies. When it is said that matter is heavy, it might be meant that the predicate is an attribute; but such is not the case, for in matter there is nothing which has not weight; in fact, matter is weight. That which is heavy constitutes the body, and is the body. Just so is it with freedom and the will; that which is free is the will. Will without freedom is an empty word, and freedom becomes actual only as will, as subject. A remark may also be made as to the connection of willing and thinking. Spirit, in general, is thought, and by thought man is distinguished from the animal. But we must not imagine that man is on one side thinking and on another side willing, as though he had will in one pocket and thought in another. Such an idea is vain. The distinction between thought and will is only that between a theoretical and a practical relation. They are not two separate faculties. The will is a special way of thinking; it is thought translating itself into reality; it is the impulse of thought to give itself reality. The distinction between thought and will may be expressed in this way. When I think an object, I make of it a thought, and take from it the sensible. Thus I make of it something which is essentially and directly mine. Only in thought am I self-contained. Conception is the penetration of the object, which is then no longer opposed to me. From it I have taken its own peculiar nature, which it had as an independent object in opposition to me. As Adam said to Eve, 'thou art flesh of my flesh and bone of my bone', so says the spirit, 'This object is spirit of my spirit, and all alienation has disappeared'. Any idea is a universalizing, and this process belongs to thinking. To make something universal is to think. The 'I' is thought and the universal. When I say 'I', I let fall all particularity of character, natural endowment, knowledge, age. The 'I' is empty, a point and simple, but in its simplicity active. The gaily colored world is before me; I stand opposed to it, and in this relation I cancel and transcend the opposition, and make the content my own. The 'I' is at home in the world, when it knows it, and still more when it has conceived it.

So much for the theoretical relation. The practical, on the other hand, begins with thinking, with the 'I' itself. It thus appears first of all as placed in opposition, because it exhibits, as it were, a separation. As I am practical, I am active; I act and determine myself; and to determine myself means to set up a distinction. But these distinctions are again mine, my own determinations come to me; and the ends are mine, to which I am impelled. Even when I let these distinctions and determinations go, setting them in the so-called external world, they remain mine. They are that which I have done and made, and bear the trace of my spirit. That is the distinction to be drawn between the theoretical and the practical relations.

And now the connection of the two must be also stated. The theoretical is essentially contained in the practical. Against the idea that the two are separate runs the fact that man has no will without intelligence. The will holds within itself the theoretical, the will determines itself, and this determination is in the first instance internal. That which I will I place before my mind, and it is an object for me. The animal acts according to instinct, is impelled by something internal, and so is also practical. But it has no will, because it cannot place before its mind what it desires. Similarly man cannot use his theoretic faculty or think without will, for in thinking we are active. The content of what is thought receives, indeed, the form of something existing, but this existence is occasioned by our activity and by it, established. These distinctions of theoretical and practical are inseparable; they are one and the same; and in every activity, whether of thought or will, both these elements are found.

It is worthwhile to recall the older way of proceeding with regard to the freedom of the will. First of all, the idea of the will was assumed, and then an effort was made to deduce from it and establish a definition of the will. Next, the method of the older empirical psychology was adopted, and different perceptions and general phenomena of the ordinary consciousness were collected, such as remorse, guilt, and the like, on the ground that these could be explained only as proceeding out of a will that is free. Then from these phenomena was deduced the so-called proof that the will is free. But it is more convenient to take a short cut and hold that freedom is given as a fact of consciousness, and must be believed in.

The nature of the will and of freedom, and the proof that the will is free, can be shown, as has already been observed, only in connection with the whole. The ground principles of the premises that spirit is in the first instance intelligence, and that the phases through which it passes in its development, namely from feeling, through imaginative thinking to thought, are the way by which it produces itself as will, which, in turn, as the practical spirit in general, is the most direct truth of intelligence—I have presented in my *Encyclopaedia of the Philosophical Sciences* (1817), and hope some day to be able to give of them a more complete exposition. There is, to my mind, so much the more need for me to give my contribution to, as I hope, the more thorough knowledge of the nature of spirit, since, as I have there said, it would be difficult to find a philosophic science in a more neglected and evil plight than is that theory of spirit, which is commonly called psychology. Some elements of the conception of will, resulting from the premises enumerated above are mentioned in this and the following paragraphs. As to these, appeal may moreover be made to every individual to see them in his own self-consciousness. Everyone will, in the first place, find in himself the ability to abstract himself from all that he is, and in this way prove himself able of himself to set every content within himself, and thus have in his own consciousness an illustration of all the subsequent phases.

The will contains (a) the element of pure indeterminateness, i.e., the pure doubling of the 'I' back in thought upon itself. In this process every limit or content, present though it be directly by way of nature, as in want, appetite or impulse, or given in any specific way, is dissolved. Thus we have the limitless infinitude of absolute abstraction, or universality, the pure thought of itself.

Those who treat thinking and willing as two special peculiar and separate faculties, and, further, look upon thought is detrimental to the will, especially the good will, show from the very start that they know nothing of the nature of willing, a remark which we shall be called upon to a number of times upon the same attitude of mind. The will on one side is the possibility of abstraction from every aspect in which the 'I' finds itself or has set itself up. It reckons any content as a limit, and flees from it. This is one of the forms of the self-direction of the will, and is by imaginative thinking insisted upon as of itself freedom. It is the negative side of the will, or freedom as apprehended by the understanding. This freedom is that of the void, which his taken actual shape, and is stirred to passion. It, while remaining purely theoretical, appears in Hindu religion as the fanaticism of pure contemplation; but becoming actual it assumes both in politics and religion the form of a fanaticism, which would destroy the established social order, remove all individuals suspected of desiring any kind of order, and demolish any organization which then sought to rise out of the ruins; only in devastation does the negative will feel that it has reality. It intends, indeed, to bring to pass some positive social condition, such as universal equality or universal religious life. But in fact it does not will the positive reality of any such condition, since that would carry in its train a system, and introduce a separation by way of institutions and between individuals. But classification and objective system attain self consciousness only by destroying negative freedom. Negative freedom is actuated by a mere solitary idea, whose realization is nothing but the fury of desolation.

This phase of will implies that I break loose from everything, give up all ends, and bury myself in abstraction. It is man alone who can let go everything, even life. He can commit suicide, an act impossible for the animal, which always remains only negative, abiding in a state foreign to itself, to which it must merely get accustomed, is pure thought of himself, and only in thinking has he the power to give himself universality and distinguish in himself all that is particular and definite.

Negative freedom, or freedom of the understanding, is one-sided, yet as this one-sidedness contains an essential feature, it is not to be discarded. But the defect of the understanding is that it exalts its one-sidedness to the sole highest place. This form of freedom frequently occurs in history. By the Hindus, e.g., the highest freedom is declared to be persistence in the consciousness of one's simple identity with himself, to abide in the empty space of one's own inner being, like the colourless light of pure intuition, and to renounce every activity of life, every purpose and every idea. In this way man becomes Brahman; there is no longer any distinction between finite man and Brahman, every difference having been swallowed up in this universality. A more concrete manifestation of this freedom is fanaticism of political and religious life. Of this nature was the terrible epoch of the French Revolution, by which all distinctions in talent and authority were to have been superseded. In this time of upheaval and commotion any specific thing was intolerable. Fanaticism wills an abstraction and not an articulate association. It finds all distinctions antagonistic to its indefiniteness, and supersedes them. Hence in the French Revolution the people abolished the institutions which they themselves had set up, since every institution is inimical to the abstract self-consciousness of equality.

(b) The 'I' is also the transition from blank indefiniteness to the distinct and definite establishment of a definite content and object, whether this content be given by nature or produced out of the conception of spirit. Through this establishment of itself as a definite thing the 'I' becomes a reality. This is the absolute element of the finitude or specialization of the 'I'.

This second element in the characterization of the 'I' is just as negative as the first, since it annuls and replaces the first abstract negativity. As the particular is contained in the universal, so this second phase is contained already in the first, and is only an establishing of what the first is implicitly. The first phase, if taken independently, is not the true infinite, i.e., the concrete universal, or the conception, but limited and one-sided. In that it is the abstraction from all definite character, it has a definite character. Its abstract and one-sided nature constitutes its definite character, its defect and finitude.

The distinct characterization of these two phases of the 'I' is found in the philosophy of Fichte as also in that of Kant. Only, in the exposition of Fichte the 'I', when taken as unlimited, as it is in the first proposition of his *Wissenschaftslehre*, is merely positive. It is the universality and identity made by the understanding. Hence this abstract 'I' is in its independence to be taken as the truth, to which by way of mere addition comes in the second proposition, the limitation, or the negative in general, whether it be in the form of a given external limit or of an activity of the 'I'. To apprehend the negative as immanent in the universal or self-identical, and also as in the 'I', was the next step, which speculative philosophy had to make. Of this want they have no presentiment, who like Fichte never apprehend that the infinite and finite are, if separated, abstract, and must be seen as immanent one in the other.

This second element makes its appearance as the opposite of the first; it is to be understood in its general form: it belongs to freedom but does not constitute the whole of it. Here the 'I' passes over from blank indeterminateness to the distinct establishment of a specific character as a content or object. I do not will merely, but I will something. Such a will, as is analysed in the preceding paragraph, wills only the abstract universal, and therefore wills nothing. Hence it is not a will. The particular thing which the will wills is a limitation, since the will, in order to be a will, must in general limit itself. Limit or negation consists in the will willing something. Particularizing is thus as a rule named finitude. Ordinary reflection holds the first element, that of the indefinite, for the absolute and higher, and the limited for a mere negation of this indefiniteness. But this indefiniteness is itself only a negation, in contrast with the definite and finite. The 'I' is solitude and absolute negation. The indefinite will is thus quite as much one-sided as the will, which continues merely in the definite.

(c) The will is the unity of these two elements. It is particularity turned back within itself and thus led back to universality; it is individuality; it is the self-direction of the 'I'. Thus at one and the same time it establishes itself as its own negation, that is to say, as definite and limited, and it also abides by itself, in its self-identity and universality, and in this position remains purely self-enclosed. The 'I' determines itself in so far as it is the reference of negativity to itself; and yet in this self-reference it is indifferent to its own definite character. This it knows as its own, that is, as an ideal or a mere possibility, by which it is not bound, but rather exists in it merely because it establishes itself there. This is the freedom of the will, constituting its conception or substantive reality. It is its gravity, as it were, just as gravity is the substantive reality of a body.

Every self-consciousness knows itself as at once universal, or the possibility of abstracting itself from everything definite, and as particular, with a fixed object, content or aim. These two elements, however, are only abstractions. The concrete and true, and all that is true is concrete, is the universality, to which the particular is at first opposed, but, when it has been turned back into itself, is in the end made equal. This unity is individuality, but it is not a simple unit as is the individuality of imaginative thought, but a unit in terms of the conception. In other words, this individuality is properly nothing else than the conception. The first two elements of the will, that it can abstract itself from everything, and that it is definite through either its own activity or something else, are easily admitted and comprehended, because in their separation they are untrue, and characteristic of the mere understanding. But into the third, the true and speculative—and all truth, as far as it is conceived, must be thought speculatively—the understanding declines to venture, always calling the conception the inconceivable. The proof and more detailed explanation of this inmost reserve of speculation, of infinitude as the negativity which refers itself to itself, and of this ultimate source of all activity, life and consciousness, belong to logic, as the purely speculative philosophy. Here it can be noticed only in passing that, in the sentences, 'The will is universal .... The will directs itself', the will is already regarded as presupposed subject or substratum; but it is not something finished and universal before it determines itself, nor yet before this determination is superseded and idealized. It is will only when its activity is self-occasioned, and it has returned into itself.

What we properly call will contains the two above-mentioned elements. The 'I' is, first of all, as such, pure activity, the universal which is by itself. Next this universal determines itself, and so far is no longer by itself, but establishes itself as another, and ceases to be the universal. The third step is that the will, while in this limitation, i.e., in this other, is by itself. While it limits itself, it yet remains with itself, and does not lose its hold of the universal. This is, then, the concrete conception of freedom, while the other two elements have been thoroughly abstract and one-sided. But this concrete freedom we already have in the form of perception, as in friendship and love: here a man is not one-sided, but limits himself willingly in reference to another, and yet in this limitation knows himself as himself. In this determination he does not feel himself determined, but in the contemplation of the other as another has the feeling of himself. Freedom also lies neither in indeterminateness nor in determinateness, but in both. The willful man has a will which limits itself wholly to a particular object, and if he has not this will, he supposes himself not to be free. But the will is not bound to a particular object, but must go further, for the nature of the will is not to be one-sided and confined. Free will consists in willing a definite object, but in so doing to be by itself and to return again into the universal.

If we define this particularizing further, we reach a distinction in the forms of the will. *(a)* In so far as the definite character of the will consists in the formal opposition of the subjective to the objective or external direct existence, we have the formal will as a self consciousness which finds an outer world before it. The process, by which individuality turns back in its definiteness into itself, is the translation of the subjective end, through the intervention of an activity and a means, into objectivity. In the absolute spirit, in which all definite character is thoroughly its own and true, consciousness is only one side, namely, the manifestation or appearance of the will, a phase which does not require detailed consideration here.

The consideration of the definite nature of the will belongs to the understanding, and is not in the first instance speculative. The will as a whole, not only in the sense of its content, but also in the sense of its form, is determined. Determinate character on the side of form is the end, and the execution of the end. The end is at first merely something internal to me and subjective, but it is to be also objective and to cast away the defect of mere subjectivity. It may be asked why it has this defect. When that which is deficient does not at the same time transcend its defect, the defect is for it not a defect at all. The animal is to us defective, but not for itself. The end, in so far as it is at first merely ours, is for us a defect, since freedom and will are for us the unity of subjective and objective. The end must also be established as objective; but does not in that way attain a new one-sided character, but rather its realization.

(b) In so far as the definite phases of will are its own peculiar property or its particularization turned back into itself, they are content. This content, as content of the will, is for it, by virtue of the form given in *(a)*, an end, which exists on its inner or subjective side as the imaginative will, but by the operation of the activity, which converts the subjective into the objective, it is realized, completed end.

The content or determinate phase of will is in the first instance direct or immediate. Then the will is free only in itself or for us, i.e., it is the will in its conception. Only when it has itself as an object is it also for itself, and its implicit freedom becomes realized.

At this standpoint the finite implies that whatever is in itself, or according to its conception, has an existence or manifestation different from what it is for itself. For example the abstract separateness of nature is in itself space, but for itself time. Here, two things are to be observed,

(*i*) that because the truth is the idea, when any object or phase is apprehended only as it is in itself or in conception, it is not as yet apprehended in its truth, and yet

(*ii*) that, whatever exists as conception or in itself, at the same time exists, and this existence is a peculiar form of the object, as, e.g., space.

The separation of existence in-itself or implicit existence from existence-for-itself or explicit existence is a characteristic of the finite, and constitutes its appearance or merely external reality. An example of this is to hand in the separation of the natural will from formal right. The understanding adheres to mere implicit existence, and in accordance with this position calls freedom a capacity, since it is at this point only a possibility. But the understanding, regards this phase as absolute and perennial, and considers the relation of the will to what it wills or reality as an application to a given material, which does not belong to the essence of freedom. In this way the understanding occupies itself with mere abstractions, and not with the idea and truth.

The will, which is will only according to the conception, is free implicitly, but is at the same time not free. To be truly free it must have a truly fixed content; then it is explicitly free, has freedom for its object, and is freedom. What is at first merely in conception, i.e., implicit, is only direct and natural. We are familiar with this in pictorial thought also. The child is implicitly a man, at first has reason implicitly, and is at first the possibility of reason and freedom. He is thus free merely according to the conception. That which is only implicit does not yet exist in actuality. A man, who is implicitly rational, must create himself by working through and out of himself and by reconstructing himself within himself, before he can become also explicitly rational.

The will, which is at first only implicitly free, is the direct or natural will. The distinctive phases, which the self-determining conception sets up in the will, appear in the direct will, as a directly present content. They are impulses, appetites, inclinations, by which the will finds itself determined by nature. Now this content, with all its attendant phases, proceeds from the rationality of the will, and is therefore implicitly rational; but let loose in its immediate directness it has not as yet the form of rationality. The content is indeed for me and my own, but the form and the content are yet different. The will is thus in itself finite.

Empirical psychology enumerates and describes these impulses and inclinations, and the wants which are based upon them. It takes, or imagines that it takes this material from experience, and then seeks to classify it in the usual way. It will be stated below what the objective side of impulse is, and what impulse is in its truth, apart from the form of irrationality which it has as an impulse, and also what shape it assumes when it reaches existence.

Impulse, appetite, inclination are possessed by the animal also, but it has not will; it must obey impulse, if there is no external obstacle. Man, however, is the completely undetermined, and stands above impulse, and may fix and set it up as his. Impulse is in nature, but it depends on my will whether I establish it in the 'I'. Nor can the will be unconditionally called to this action by the fact that the impulse lies in nature.

The system of this content, as it occurs directly in the will, exists only as a multitude or multiplicity of impulses, every one of which is mine in a general way along with others, but is at the same time universal and undetermined, having many objects and ways of satisfaction. The will, by giving itself in this two-fold indefiniteness the form of individuality, resolves, and only as resolving is it actual.

Instead of to 'resolve', i.e., to supersede the indefinite condition in which a content is merely possible, our language has the expression 'decide' ('unfold itself'). The indeterminate condition of the will, as neutral but infinitely fruitful germ of all existence, contains within itself its definite character and ends, and brings them forth solely out of itself.

By resolution, will fixes itself as the will of a definite individual, and as thereby distinguishing itself from another. However, apart from this finite character which it has as consciousness, the immediate will is in virtue of the distinction between its form and its content formal. Hence its resolution as such is abstract, and its content is not yet the content and work of its freedom.

To the intelligence, as thinking, the object or content remains universal; the intelligence retains the form merely of a universal activity. Now the universal signifies in will that which is mine, i.e., it is individuality. And yet, also, the direct and formal will is abstract; its individuality is not yet filled with its free universality. Hence at the beginning the peculiar finitude of the intelligence is in will, and only by exalting itself again to thought and giving itself intrinsic universality does the will transcend the distinction of form and content and make itself objective infinite will. It is therefore a misunderstanding of the nature of thought and will to suppose that in the will man is infinite, while in thought and even in reason he is limited. In so far as thought and will are still distinct, the reverse is rather the case, and thinking reason, when it becomes will, assigns itself to finitude.

A will which resolves nothing is not an actual will; that which is devoid of definite character never reaches a volition. The reason for hesitation may lie in a sensitiveness, which is aware that in determining itself it is engaged with what is finite, is assigning itself a limit, and abandoning its infinity; it may thus hold to its decision not to renounce the totality which it intends. Such a feeling is dead, even when it aims to be something beautiful. 'Who will be great', says Goethe, 'must be able to limit himself'. By volition alone man enters actuality, however distasteful it may be to him; for indolence will not desert its own self-brooding, in which it clings to a universal possibility. But possibility is not yet actuality. Hence the will, which is secure simply of itself, does not as yet lose itself in any definite reality.

The finite will, which has merely from the standpoint of form doubled itself back upon itself, and has become the infinite and self-secluded 'I', stands above its content of different impulses and also above the several ways by which they are realized and satisfied. At the same time, as it is only formally infinite, it is confined to this very content as the decisive feature of its nature and external actuality, although it is undetermined and not confined to one content rather than another. As to the return of the 'I' into itself such a will is only a possible will, which may or may not be mine, and the 'I' is only the possibility of deputing itself to this or that object. Hence amongst these definite phases, which in this light are for the 'I' external, the will chooses.

Freedom of the will is, in this view of it, caprice, in which are contained both a reflection, which is free and abstracted from everything and a dependence upon a content or matter either internally or externally provided. Since the content is in itself or implicitly necessary as all end, and in opposition to this reflection is a definite possibility, caprice, when it is will, is in its nature contingent.

The usual idea of freedom is that of caprice. It is a midway stage of reflection between the will as merely natural impulse and the will as free absolutely. When it is said that freedom as a general thing consists in doing what one likes, such an idea must be taken to imply an utter lack of developed thought, containing as yet not even the suspicion of what is meant by the absolutely free will, right, the ethical system, etc. Reflection, being the formal universality and unity of self-consciousness, is the will's abstract certitude of its freedom, but it is not yet the truth of it, because it has not as yet itself for content and end; the subjective side is still different from the objective. Thus the content in such a case remains purely and completely finite. Caprice, instead of being will in its truth, is rather will in its contradiction.

In the controversy carried on, especially at the time of the metaphysics of Wolf, as to whether the will is really free or our consciousness of its freedom is a delusion, it was this caprice which was in the minds of both parties. Against the certitude of abstract self-direction, determinism rightly opposed a content, which was externally presented, and not being contained in this certitude came from without. It did not matter whether this 'without' were impulse, imagination, or in general a consciousness so filled that the content was not the peculiar possession of the self-activity as such. Since only the formal element of free self-direction is immanent in caprice, while the other element is something given to it from without, to take caprice as freedom may fairly be named a delusion. Freedom in every philosophy of reflection, whether it be the Kantian or the Friesian, which is the Kantian superficialized, is nothing more than this formal self-activity.

Since I have the possibility of determining myself in this or that way, I have the power of choice, possess caprice, or what is commonly called freedom. This choice is due to the universality of the will, enabling me to make my own this thing or another. This possession is a particular content, which is therefore not adequate to me, but separated from me, and is mine only in possibility; just as I am the possibility of bringing myself into coincidence with it. Hence choice is due to the indeterminateness of the 'I', and to the determinateness of a content. But as to this content the will is not free, although it has in itself formally the side of infinitude. No such content corresponds to will; in no content can it truly find itself. In caprice it is involved that the content is not formed by the nature of my will, but by contingency. I am dependent upon this content. This is the contradiction contained in caprice. Ordinary man believes that he is free when he is allowed to act capriciously, but precisely in caprice is it inherent that he is not free. When I will the rational, I do not act as a particular individual but according to the conception of ethical life in general. In an ethical act I establish not myself but the thing. A man, who acts perversely, exhibits particularity. The rational is the highway on which every one travels, and no one is specially marked. When a great artist finishes a work we say: 'It must be so'. The particularity of the artist has wholly disappeared and the work shows no mannerism. Phidias has no mannerism; the statue itself lives and moves. But the poorer is the artist, the more easily we discern himself, his particularity all caprice. If we adhere to the consideration that in caprice a man can will what he pleases, we have certainly freedom of a kind; but again, if we hold to the view that the content is given, then man must be determined by it, and in this light is no longer free.

What is resolved upon and chosen the will may again give up. Yet, even with the possibility of transcending any other content which it may substitute, and of proceeding in this way *ad infinitum*, the will does not advance beyond finitude, because every content in turn is different from the form and is finite. The opposite aspect, namely indeterminateness, irresolution or abstraction, is also one-sided.

Since the contradiction involved in caprice is the dialectic of the impulses and inclinations, it is manifested in their mutual antagonism. The satisfaction of one demands the subjection and sacrifice of the satisfaction of another. Since an impulse is merely the simple tendency of its own essential nature, and has no measure in itself, to subject or sacrifice the satisfaction of any impulse is a contingent decision of caprice. In such a case caprice may act upon the calculation as to which impulse will bring the greater satisfaction, or may have some other similar purpose.

Impulses and inclinations are in the first instance the content of will, and only reflection transcends them. But these impulses are self-directing, crowding upon and jostling one another, and all seeking to be satisfied. To set all but one in the background, and put myself into this one, is to limit and distort myself, since I, in so doing, renounce my universality, which is a system of the impulses. Just as little help is found in a mere subordination of them, a course usually followed by the understanding. There is available no criterion by which to make such an arrangement, and hence the demand for a subordination is usually sustained by tedious and irrelevant allusions to general savings.

With regard to the moral estimate of impulses, dialectic appears in this form. The phases of the direct or natural will are immanent and positive, and thus good. Hence man is by nature good. But natural characteristics, since they are opposed to freedom and the conception of the spirit, and are, hence, negative, must be eradicated. Thus man is by nature evil. To decide for either view is a matter of subjective caprice.

The Christian doctrine that man is by nature evil is loftier than the opposite that he is naturally good, and is to be interpreted philosophically in this way. Man as spirit is a free being, who need not give way to impulse. Hence in his direct and unformed condition, man is in a situation in which he ought not to be, and he must free himself. This is the meaning of the doctrine of original sin, without which Christianity would not be the religion of freedom.

In the demand that impulses must be purified is found the general idea that they must be freed from the form of direct subjection to nature, and from a content that is subjective and contingent, and must be restored to their substantive essence. The truth contained in this indefinite demand is that impulses should be phases of will in a rational system. To apprehend them in this way as proceeding from the conception is the content of the science of right.

The content of this science may, in all its several elements, right, property, morality, family, state, be represented in this way, that man has by nature the impulse to right, the impulse to property, to morality, to sexual love, and to social life. If instead of this form, which belongs to empirical psychology, a philosophic form be preferred, it may be obtained cheap from what, in modern times was reputed and still is reputed to be philosophy. He will then say that man finds in himself as a fact of consciousness that he wills right, property, the state, etc. Later will be given still another form of the content which appears here in the shape of impulses, namely, of duties.

The reflection which is brought to bear upon impulses, placing them before itself, estimating them, comparing them with one another, and contrasting them with their means and consequences, and also with a whole of satisfaction, namely happiness, brings the formal universal to this material, and in an external way purifies it of its crudity and barbarism. This propulsion by the universality of thought is the absolute worth of civilization.

In happiness thought has already the upper hand with the force of natural impulse, since it is not satisfied with what is momentary, but requires happiness as a whole. This happiness is dependent upon civilization to the extent to which civilization confirms the universal. But in the ideal of happiness there are two elements. There is a universal that is higher than all particulars; yet, as the content of this universal is in turn only universal pleasure, there arises once more the individual, particular and finite, and retreat must be made to impulse. Since the content of happiness lies in the subjective perception of each individual, this universal end is again particular; nor is there present in it any true unity of content and form.

But the truth of this formal universality, which taken by itself is undetermined and finds definite character in externally given material, is the self-directing universality which is will or freedom. Since the will has as its object, content and end, universality itself, and thus assumes the form of the infinite, it is free not only in itself or implicitly, but for itself or explicitly. It is the true idea.

The self-consciousness of the will in the form of appetite or impulse is sensible, the sensible in general indicating the externality of self-consciousness, or that condition in which self-consciousness is outside of itself. Now this sensible side is one of the two elements of the reflecting will, and the other is the abstract universality of thought. But the absolute will has as its object the will itself as such in its pure universality. In this universality the directness of the natural will is superseded, and so also is the private individuality which is produced by reflection and infects the natural condition. But to supersede these and lift them into the universal constitutes the activity of thought. Thus the self-consciousness, which purifies its object, content or end, and exalts it to universality, is thought carrying itself through into will. It is at this point that it becomes clear that the will is true and free only as thinking intelligence. The slave knows not his essence, his infinitude, his freedom; he does not know himself in his essence, and not to know himself is not to think himself. The self-consciousness, which by thought apprehends that itself is essence, and thus puts away from itself the accidental and untrue, constitutes the principle of right, morality, and all forms of ethical life. They who, in speaking philosophically of right, morality, and ethical life, would exclude thought and turn to feeling, the heart, the breast, and inspiration, express the deepest contempt for thought and science. And science itself, overwhelmed with despair and utter insipidity, makes barbarism and absence of thought a principle, and so far as in it lay robbed men of all truth, dignity, and worth.

In philosophy truth is had when the conception corresponds to reality. A body is the reality, and soul is the conception. Soul and body should be adequate to each other. A dead man is still an existence, but no longer a true existence; it is a reality void of conception. For that reason the dead body decays. So with the true will; that which it wills, namely, its content, is identical with it, and so freedom wills freedom.

The will which exists absolutely is truly infinite, because its object being the will itself, is for it not another or a limitation. In the object the will has simply reverted into itself. Moreover, it is not mere possibility, capacity, potentiality (potential, but infinitely actual), because the reality of the conception or its visible externality is internal to itself.

Hence when the free will is spoken of without the qualification of absolute freedom, only the capacity of freedom is meant, or the natural and finite will, and, notwithstanding all words and opinions to the contrary, not the free will. Since the understanding comprehends the infinite only in its negative aspect, and hence as a beyond, it thinks to do the infinite all the more honour the farther it removes it into the vague distance, and the more it takes it as a foreign thing. In free will the true infinite is present and real; it is itself the actually present self-contained idea.

The infinite has rightly been represented as a circle. The straight line goes out farther and farther, and symbolizes the merely negative and bad infinite, which, unlike the true, does not return into itself. The free will is truly infinite, for it is not a mere possibility or disposition. Its external reality is its own inner nature, itself.

Only in this freedom is the will wholly by itself, because it refers to nothing but itself, and all dependence upon any other thing falls away. The will is true, or rather truth itself, because its character consists in its being in its manifested reality, or correlative opposite, what it is in its conception. In other words, the pure conception has the perception or intuition of itself as its end and reality.

The will is universal, because in it all limitation and particular individuality are superseded. These one-sided phases are found only in the difference between the conception and its object or content, or, from another standpoint, in the difference between the conscious independent existence of the subject, and the will's implicit, or self-involved existence, or between its excluding and concluding individuality, and its universality.

The different phases of universality are tabulated in the *Logic*. Imaginative thinking always takes universality in an abstract and external way. But absolute universality is not to be thought of either as the universality of reflection, which is a kind of consensus or generality, or, as the abstract universality and self-identity, which is fashioned by the understanding, and keeps aloof from the individual. It is rather the concrete, self-contained, and self-referring universality, which is the substance, intrinsic genus, or immanent idea of self-consciousness. It is a conception of free will as the universal, transcending its object, passing through and beyond its own specific character, and then becoming identical with itself. This absolute universal is what is in general called the rational, and is to be apprehended only in this speculative way.

The subjective side of the will is the side of its self-consciousness and individuality, as distinguished from its implicit conception. This subjectivity is: *(a)* pure form or absolute unity of self-consciousness with itself. This unity is the equation 'I = I', consciousness being characterized by a thoroughly inward and abstract self-dependence. It is pure certitude of itself in contrast with the truth. It is *(b)* particularity of will, as caprice with its accidental content of pleasurable ends. And, *(c)* in general a one-sided form, in so far as that which is willed is at first an unfulfilled end, or a content which simply belongs to self-consciousness.

(a) In so far as free will is determined by itself, and is in accord with its conception and true, it is wholly objective will. *(b)* But objective self-consciousness, which has not the form of the infinite, is a will sunk in its object or condition, whatever the content of that may be. It is the will of the child, or the will present in slavery or superstition. *(c)* Objectivity is finally a one-sided form in opposition to the subjective phase of will; it is direct reality, or external existence. In this sense the will becomes objective only by the execution of its ends.

These logical phases of subjectivity and objectivity, since they are often made use of in the sequel, are here exposed, with the express purpose of noting that it happens with them as with other distinctions and opposed aspects of reflection; they by virtue of their finite and dialectic character pass over into their opposites. For imagination and understanding the meanings of antithetic phases are not convertible because their identity is still internal. But in will, on the contrary, these phases, which ought to be at once abstract and yet also sides of that which can be known only as concrete, lead of themselves to identity, and to an exchange of meaning. To the understanding this is unintelligible. Thus, e.g., the will, as a freedom which exists in itself, is subjectivity itself; thus subjectivity is the conception of the will, and therefore its objectivity. But subjectivity is finite in opposition to objectivity, yet in this opposition the will is not isolated, but in intricate union with the object; and thus its finitude consists quite as much in its not being subjective, etc.

It is ordinarily supposed that subjective and objective are blank opposites; but this is not the case. Rather do they pass into one another, for they are not abstract aspects like positive and negative, but have already a concrete significance. To consider in the first instance the expression 'subjective'; this may mean an end which is merely the end of a certain subject. In this sense a poor work of art that is not adequate to the thing is merely subjective. But, further, this expression may point to the content of the will, and is then of about the same meaning as capricious; the subjective content then is that which belongs merely to the subject. In this sense bad acts are merely subjective. Further, the pure, empty I may be called subjective, as it has only itself as an object, and possesses the power of abstraction from all further content. Subjectivity has, moreover, a wholly particular and correct meaning in accordance with which anything, in order to win recognition from me, has to become mine and seek validity in me. This is the infinite avarice of subjectivity, eager to comprehend and consume everything within the simple and pure I.

Similarly we may take the objective in different ways. By it we may understand anything to which we give existence in contrast to ourselves, whether it be an actual thing or a mere thought, which we place over against ourselves. By it also we understand the direct reality, in which the end is to be realized. Although the end itself is quite particular and subjective, we yet name it objective after it has made its appearance. Further, the objective will is also that in which truth is; thus, God's will, the ethical will also, are objective. Lastly, we may call the will objective, when it is wholly submerged in its object, as, e.g., the child's will, which is confiding and without subjective freedom, and the slave's will, which does not know itself as free, and is thus a will-less will. In this sense any will is objective, if it is guided in its action by a foreign authority, and has not yet completed the infinite return into itself.

The absolute character or, if you like, the absolute impulse of the free spirit is, as has been observed, that its freedom shall be for it an object. It is to be objective in a two-fold sense: it is the rational system of itself, and this system is to be directly real. There is thus actualized as idea what the will is implicitly. Hence, the abstract conception of the idea of the will is in general the free will which wills the free will.

The activity of the will, directed to the task of transcending the contradiction between subjectivity and objectivity, of transferring its end from subjectivity into objectivity, and yet while in objectivity of remaining with itself, is beyond the formal method of consciousness, in which objectivity is only direct actuality. This activity is the essential development of the substantive content of the idea. In this development the conception molds the idea, which is in the first instance abstract, into the totality of a system. This totality as substantive is independent of the opposition between mere subjective end and its realization, and in both of these forms is the same.

That a reality is the realization of the free will, this is what is meant by a right. Right, therefore, is, in general, freedom as idea.

In the Kantian doctrine, now generally accepted, 'the, highest factor is a limitation of my freedom or caprice, in order that it may be able to subsist alongside of every other individual's caprice in accordance with a universal law'. This doctrine contains only a negative phase, that of limitation. And besides, the positive phase, the universal law or so-called law of reason, consisting in the agreement of the caprice of one with that of another, goes beyond the well-known formal identity and the proposition of contradiction. The definition of right, just quoted, contains the view which has especially since Rousseau spread widely. According to this view neither the absolute and rational will, nor the true spirit, but the will and spirit of the particular individual in their peculiar caprice, are the substantive and primary basis. When once this principle is accepted, the rational can announce itself only as limiting this freedom. Hence it is not an inherent rationality, but only a mere external and formal universal. This view is accordingly devoid of speculative thought, and is rejected by the philosophic conception. In the minds of men and in the actual world it has assumed a shape, whose horror is without a parallel, except in the shallowness of the thoughts upon which it was founded.

Right in general is something holy, because it is the embodiment of the absolute conception and self-conscious freedom. But the formalism of right, and after a while of duty also, is due to distinctions arising out of the development of the conception of freedom. In contrast with the more formal, abstract and limited right, there is that sphere or stage of the spirit, in which spirit has brought to definite actuality the further elements contained in the idea. This stage is the richer and more concrete; it is truly universal and has therefore a higher right.

Every step in the development of the idea of freedom has its peculiar right, because it is the embodiment of a phase of freedom. When morality and ethical life are spoken of in opposition to right, only the first or formal right of the abstract personality is meant. Morality, ethical life, a state-interest, is every one a special right, because each of these is a definite realization of freedom. They can come into collision only in so far as they occupy the same plane. If the moral standpoint of spirit were not also a right and one of the forms of freedom, it could not collide with the right of personality or any other right. A right contains the conception of freedom which is the highest phase of spirit, and in opposition to it any other kind of thing is lacking in real substance. Yet collision also implies a limit and a subordination of one phase to another. Only the right of the world-spirit is the unlimited absolute.

The scientific method by which the conception is self-evolved, and its phases self-developed and self-produced, is not first of all an assurance that certain relations are given from somewhere or other, and then the application to this foreign material of the universal. The true process is found in the logic, and here is presupposed.

The efficient or motive principle, which is not merely the analysis but the production of the several elements of the universal, I call dialectic. Dialectic is not that process in which an object or proposition, presented to feeling or the direct consciousness, is analysed, entangled, taken hither and thither, until at last its contrary is derived. Such a merely negative method appears frequently in Plato. It may fix the opposite of any notion, or reveal the contradiction contained in it, as did the ancient skepticism, or it may in a feeble way consider an approximation to truth, or modern half-and-half attainment of it, as its goal. But the higher dialectic of the conception does not merely apprehend any phase as a limit and opposite, but produces out of this negative a positive content and result. Only by such a course is there development and inherent progress. Hence this dialectic is not the external agency of subjective thinking, but the private soul of the content, which unfolds its branches and fruit organically. Thought regards this development of the idea and of the peculiar activity of the reason of the idea as only subjective, but is on its side unable to make any addition. To consider anything rationally is not to bring reason to it from the outside, and work it up in this way, but to count it as itself reasonable. Here it is spirit in its freedom, the summit of self-conscious reason, which gives itself actuality, and produces itself as the existing world. The business of science is simply to bring the specific work of the reason, which is in the thing, to consciousness.

The phases of the development of the conception are themselves conceptions. And yet, because the conception is essentially the idea, they have the form of manifestations. Hence the sequence of the conceptions, which arise in this way, is at the same time a sequence of realizations, and are to be by science so considered.

In a speculative sense the way in which a conception is manifested in reality is identical with a definite phase of the conception. But it is noteworthy that, in the scientific development of the idea, the elements, which result in a further definite form, although preceding this result as phases of the conception, do not in the temporal development go before it as concrete realizations. Thus, as will be seen later, that stage of the idea which is the family presupposes phases of the conception, whose result it is. But that these internal presuppositions should be present in such visible realizations as right of property, contract, morality, etc., this is the other side of the process, which only in a highly developed civilization has attained to a specific realization of its elements.

The idea must always go on determining itself within itself, since at the beginning it is only abstract conception. However, this initial abstract conception is never given up, but only becomes inwardly richer, the last phase being the richest. The earlier and merely implicit phases reach in this way free self-dependence, but in such a manner that the conception remains the soul which holds everything together, and only through a procedure immanent within itself arrives at its own distinctions. Hence the last phase falls again into a unity with the first, and it cannot be said that the conception ever comes to something new. Although the elements of the conception appear to have fallen apart when they enter reality, this is only a mere appearance. Its superficial character is revealed in the process, since all the particulars finally turn back again into the conception of the universal. The empirical sciences usually analyse what they find in pictorial ideas, and if the individual is successfully brought back to the general, the general property is then called the conception. But this is not our procedure. We desire only to observe how the conception determines itself, and compels us to keep at a distance everything of our own spinning and thinking. But what we get in this way is one series of thoughts and another series of realized forms. As to these two series, it may happen that the order of time of the actual manifestations is partly different from the order of the conception. Thus it cannot, e.g., be said that property existed before the family, and yet, in spite of that it is discussed before the family is discussed. The question might also be raised here, Why do we not begin with the highest, i.e., with concrete truth? The answer is, because we desire to see truth in the form of a result, and it is an essential part of the process to conceive the conception first of all as abstract. The actual series of realizations of the conception is thus for us in due course as follows, even although in actuality the order should be the same. Our process is this, that the abstract forms reveal themselves not as self-subsistent but as untrue.

PHILOSOPHY OF HISTORY

'But even regarding History as the slaughter bench at which the happiness of peoples, the wisdom of States, and the virtue of individuals have been victimized—the question involuntarily arises—to what principle, to what final aim these enormous sacrifices have been offered'.

4

PHILOSOPHY OF HISTORY

INTRODUCTION

The subject of this course of Lectures is the Philosophical History of the World. And by this must be understood, not a collection of general observations respecting it, suggested by the study of its records, and proposed to be illustrated by its facts, but Universal History itself. To gain a clear idea at the outset, of the nature of our task, it seems necessary to begin with an examination of the other methods of treating History. The various methods may be ranged under three heads:
Original History
Reflective History
Philosophical History

ORIGINAL HISTORY

Of the first kind, the mention of one or two distinguished names will furnish a definite type. To this category belong Herodotus, Thucydides, and other historians of the same order, whose descriptions are for the most part limited to deeds, events, and states of society, which they had before their eyes, and whose spirit they shared. They simply transferred what was passing in the world around them, to the realm of representative intellect. An external phenomenon is thus translated into an internal conception. Historiographers bind together the fleeting elements of story, and treasure them up for immortality in the Temple of Mnemosyne. Legends, Ballad-stories, Traditions must be excluded from such original history. The domain of reality—actually seen, or capable of being so—affords a very different basis in point of firmness from that fugitive and shadowy element, in which were engendered those legends and poetic dreams whose historical prestige vanishes, as soon as nations have attained a mature individuality.

Such original historians, then, change the events, the deeds and the states of society with which they are conversant, into an object for the conceptive faculty. The narratives they leave us cannot, therefore, be very comprehensive in their range. What is present and living in their environment, is their proper material. The influences that have formed the writer are identical with those which have molded the events that constitute the matter of his story. The author's spirit, and that of the actions he narrates, is one and the same. He describes scenes in which he himself has been an actor, or at any rate, an interested spectator. It is short periods of time, individual shapes of persons and occurrences, single unreflected traits, of which he makes his picture. And his aim is nothing more than the presentation to posterity of an image of events as clear as that which he himself possessed in virtue of personal observation, or life-like descriptions. Reflections are none of his business, for he lives in the spirit of his subject; he has not attained an elevation above it. If, as in Caesar's case, he belongs to the exalted rank of generals or statesmen, it is the prosecution of *his own aims* that constitutes the history.

REFLECTIVE HISTORY

The second kind of history we may call the *reflective*. It is history whose mode of representation is not really confined by the limits of the time to which it relates, but whose spirit transcends the present. In this second order strongly marked variety of species may be distinguished.

(a) It is the aim of the investigator to gain a view of the entire history of a people or a country, or of the world, in short, what we call *Universal History*. In this case the working up of the historical material is the main point. The workman approaches his task with his *own* spirit; a spirit distinct from that of the element he is to manipulate. Here a very important consideration will be the principles to which the author refers, the bearing and motives of the actions and events which he describes, and those which determine the form of his narrative. This first kind of Reflective History is most nearly akin to the preceding, when it has no farther aim than to present the annals of a country complete. Such compilations (among which may be reckoned the works of Livy, Diodorus Siculus, Johannes von Müller's *History of Switzerland*) are, if well performed, highly meritorious. Among the best of the kind may be reckoned such annalist as approach those of the first class; who give so vivid a transcript of events that the reader may well fancy himself listening to contemporaries and eye-witnesses. But it often happens that the individuality of tone which must characterize a writer belonging to a different culture is not modified in accordance with the periods such a record must traverse. The spirit of the writer is quite other than that of the times of which he treats.

A history which aspires to traverse long periods of time, or to be universal, must indeed forego the attempt to give individual representations of the past as it actually existed. It must foreshorten its pictures by abstractions; and this includes not merely the omission of events and deeds, but whatever is involved in the fact that Thought is, after all, the most trenchant epitomist. A battle, a great victory, a siege, no longer maintains its original proportions, but is put off with a bare mention.

(b) A second species of Reflective History is what we may call the *Pragmatical*. This takes the occurrence out of the category of the Past and makes it virtually Present. Pragmatical (didactic) reflections, though in their nature decidedly abstract, are truly and indefeasibly of the Present, and quicken the annals of the dead Past with the life of today. Whether, indeed such reflections are truly interesting and enlivening, depends on the writer's own spirit. Moral reflections must here be specially noticed,—the moral teaching expected from history; which latter has not infrequently been treated with a direct view to the former. It may be allowed that examples of virtue elevate the soul, and are applicable in the moral instructions of children for impressing excellence upon their minds. But the destinies of peoples and states, their interests, relations, and the complicated issue of their affairs, present quite another field. Rulers, Statesmen, Nations, are wont to be emphatically commended to the teaching which experience offers in history. But what experience and history teach is this—that peoples and governments never have learned anything from history, or acted on principles deduced from it. Each period is involved in such peculiar circumstances, exhibits a condition of things so strictly idiosyncratic, that its conduct must be regulated by considerations connected with itself, and itself alone. Amid the pressure of great events, a general principle gives no help. It is useless to revert to similar circumstances in the Past. The pallid shades of memory struggle in vain with the life and freedom of the Present. Looked at in this light, nothing can be shallower than the oft-repeated appeal to Greek and Roman examples during the French Revolution. Nothing is more diverse than the genius of those nations and that of our times. It is only a thorough, liberal, comprehensive view of historical relations (such examples as we find in Montesquieu's 'Esprit des Loix'), that can give truth and interest to reflections of this order. One Reflective History therefore supersedes another. The materials are patent to every writer: each is likely enough to believe himself capable of arranging and manipulating them; and we may expect that each will insist upon his own spirit as that of the age in question. These certainly have their value; but for the most part they offer only material for history.

(c) The third form of Reflective History is the *Critical*. This deserves mention as preeminently the mode of treating history now current in Germany. It is not history itself that is here presented. We might more properly designate it as a History of History; a criticism of historical narratives and an investigation of their truth and credibility. Its peculiarity in point of fact and of intention consists in the acuteness with which the writer extorts something from the records which was not in the matters recorded. Here we have the other method of making the past a living reality; putting subjective fancies in the place of historical data; fancies whose merit is measured by their boldness, that is, the scantiness of the particulars on which they are based, and the peremptoriness with which they contravene the best established facts of history.

(d) The last species of Reflective History announces its fragmentary character on the very face of it. It adopts an abstract position; yet, since it takes general points of view (e.g., as the History of Art, of Law, of Religion), it forms a transition to the Philosophical History of the World. It must be remarked that, when Reflective History has advanced to the adoption of general points of view, if the position taken is a true one, these are found to constitute—not merely an external thread, a superficial series—but are the inward guiding soul of the occurrences and actions that occupy a nation's annals. For, like the soul-conductor Mercury, the Idea is in truth the leader of peoples and of the World; and Spirit, the rational and necessitated will of that conductor, is and has been the director of the events of the World's History. To become acquainted with Spirit in this its office of guidance, is the object of our present undertaking. This brings us to:

PHILOSOPHICAL HISTORY

The third kind of history—the *Philosophical*. No explanation was needed of the two previous classes; their nature was self-evident. It is otherwise with this last, which certainly seems to require an exposition or justification. The most general definition that can be given, is, that the Philosophy of History means nothing but the *thoughtful consideration of it*. Thought is indeed essential to humanity. It is this that distinguishes us from the brutes. In sensations, cognition and intellection; in our instincts and volitions, as far as they are truly human, Thought is an invariable element.

The only Thought which Philosophy brings with it to the contemplation of History, is the simple conception *of Reason;* that Reason is the Sovereign of the World; that the history of the world therefore, presents us with a rational process. It is there proved by speculative cognition, that Reason—and this term may here suffice us, without investigating the relation sustained by the Universe to the Divine Being—is *Substance,* as well as *Infinite Power;* its own *Infinite Material* underlying all the natural and spiritual life which it originates, as also the Infinite Form—that which sets this Material in motion. On the one hand, Reason is the *substance* of the Universe; viz. that by which and in which all reality has its being and subsistence. On the other hand, it is the *Infinite Energy* of the Universe; since Reason is not so powerless as to be incapable of producing anything but a mere ideal, a mere intention—having its place outside reality, nobody knows where; something separate and abstract, in the heads of certain human beings. It is *the infinite complex of things,* their entire Essence and Truth. It is its own material which it commits to its own Active Energy to work up; not needing, as finite action does, the conditions of an external material of given means from which it may obtain its support, and the objects of its activity. It supplies its own nourishment and is the object of its own operations. While it is exclusively its own basis of existence, and absolute final aim, it is also the energizing power realizing this aim; developing it not only in the phenomena of the Natural, but also of the Spiritual Universe—the History of the World. That this 'Idea' or 'Reason' is the True, *the Eternal,* the absolutely *powerful* essence; that it reveals itself in the World, and that in that World nothing else is revealed but this and its honour and glory—is the thesis which, as we have said, has been proved in Philosophy and is here regarded as demonstrated.

If the clear idea of Reason is not already developed in our minds, in beginning the study of Universal History, we should at least leave the firm, unconquerable faith that Reason *does* exist there; and that the World of intelligence and conscious volition is not abandoned to chance, but must show itself in the light of the self-cognizant Idea. Yet I am not obliged to make any such preliminary demand upon your faith. What I have said thus provisionally, and what I shall have further to say, is, even in reference to our branch of science, not to be regarded as hypothetical, but as a summary view of the whole; the *result of the investigation* we are about to pursue; a result which happens to be known to me, because I have traversed the entire field. It is only an inference from the history of the World, that its development has been a rational process; that the history in question has constituted the rational necessary course of the World Spirit—that Spirit whose nature is always one and the same, but which unfolds this, its one nature in the phenomena of the World's existence. This must, as before stated, present itself as the ultimate result of History. To him who looks upon the world rationally, the world in its turn, presents a rational aspect. The relation is mutual.

I will only mention two phases and points of view that concern the generally diffused conviction that Reason has ruled, and is still ruling in the world, and consequently in the world's history; because they give us, at the same time, an opportunity for more closely investigating the question that presents the greatest difficulty, and for indicating a branch of the subject, which will have to be enlarged on in the sequel.

REASON GOVERNS THE WORLD

(a) One of these points is that passage in history, which informs us that the Greek Anaxagoras was the first to enunciate the doctrine that Understanding generally, or Reason, governs the world. It is not intelligence as self-conscious Reason—not a Spirit as such that is meant; and we must clearly distinguish these from each other. The movement of the solar system takes place according to unchangeable laws. These laws are Reason, implicit in the phenomena in question. But neither the sun nor the planets, which revolve around it according to these laws, can be said to have any consciousness of them.

A thought of this kind,—that Nature is an embodiment of Reason; that it is unchangeably subordinate to universal laws, appears nowise striking or strange to us. And I have mentioned this extraordinary occurrence, partly to show how history teaches, that ideas of this kind, which may seem trivial to us, have not always been in the world; that on the contrary, such a thought makes an epoch in the annals of human intelligence. Aristotle says of Anaxagoras, as the originator of the thought in question, that he appeared as a sober man among the drunken. Socrates adopted the doctrine from Anaxagoras, and it forthwith became the ruling idea in Philosophy, except in the school of Epicurus, who ascribed all events to chance. 'I was delighted with the sentiment',—Plato makes Socrates say—'and hoped I had found a teacher who would show me Nature in harmony with Reason, who would demonstrate in each particular phenomenon its specific aim, and in the whole, the grand object of the Universe. I would not have surrendered this hope for a great deal. But how very much was I disappointed, when, having zealously applied myself to the writings of Anaxagoras, I found that he adduces only external causes, such as Atmosphere, Ether, Water, and the like'. It is evident that the defect which Socrates complains of respecting Anaxagoras's doctrine, does not concern the principle itself, but the shortcoming of the propounder in applying it to Nature in the concrete. Nature is not deduced from that principle: the latter remains in fact a mere abstraction, inasmuch as the former is not comprehended and exhibited as a development of it—an organization produced by and from Reason. I wish, at the very outset, to call your attention to the important difference between a conception, a principle, a truth limited to an *abstract* form and its determinate application, and concrete development. This distinction affects the whole fabric of philosophy; and among other bearings of it there is one to which we shall have to revert at the close of our view of Universal History, in investigating the aspect of political affairs in the most recent period.

We have next to notice the rise of this idea—that Reason directs the World—in connection with a further application of it, well known to us—in the form, viz. of the *religious truth,* that the world is not abandoned to chance and external contingent causes, but that a *Providence* controls it. To put it in another shape—this appeal is forbidden, because the science of which we have to treat, proposes itself to furnish the proof (not indeed of the abstract *Truth* of the doctrine, but) of its correctness as compared with facts. The truth, then, that a Providence (that of God) presides over the events of the World—consorts with the proposition in question; for *Divine* Providence is Wisdom, endowed with an infinite Power which realizes its aim, viz. the absolute rational-design of the World. Reason is Thought conditioning itself with perfect freedom. But a difference—rather a contradiction—will manifest itself, between this belief and our principle, just as was the case in reference to the demand made by Socrates in the case of Anaxagoras's dictum. For that belief is similarly indefinite; it is what is called a belief in a general Providence, and is not followed out into definite application, or displayed in its bearing on the grand total—the entire course of human history. But to *explain* History is to depict the passions of mankind, the genius, the active powers, that play their part on the great stage; and the providentially determined process which these exhibit, constitutes what is generally called the 'plan' of Providence.

Yet it is this very plan which is supposed to be concealed from our view: which it is deemed presumption, even to wish to recognize. The ignorance of Anaxagoras, as to how intelligence reveals itself in actual existence, was ingenuous. Neither in his consciousness, nor in that of Greece at large, had that thought been further expanded. It was Socrates who took the first step in comprehending the union of the Concrete with the Universal. Anaxagoras, then, did not take up a *hostile* position towards such an application. The common belief in Providence *does;* at least it opposes the use of the principle on the large scale, and denies the possibility of discerning the plan of Providence. In isolated cases this plan is supposed to be manifest. Pious persons are encouraged to recognize in particular circumstances, something more than mere chance; to acknowledge the guiding hand of God; e.g., when help has unexpectedly come to an individual in great perplexity and need. But these instances of providential design are of a limited kind, and concern the accomplishment of nothing more than the desires of the individual in question. But in the history of the World, the *Individuals* we have to do with are *Peoples;* Totalities that are States. We cannot, therefore, be satisfied with what we may call this 'peddling' view of Providence, to which the belief alluded to limits itself. Equally unsatisfactory is the merely abstract, undefined belief in a Providence, when that belief is not brought to bear upon the details of the process which it conducts. On the contrary, our earnest endeavour must be directed to the recognition of the ways of Providence, the means it uses, and the historical phenomena in which it manifests itself; and we must show their connection with the general principle above mentioned. But in noticing the recognition of the plan of Divine Providence generally, I have implicitly touched upon a prominent question of the day; viz. that of the possibility of knowing God: or rather—since public opinion has ceased to allow it to be a matter of *question*—the *doctrine* that it is impossible to know God. In direct contravention of what is commanded in holy Scripture as the highest duty—that we should not merely love, but know God—the prevalent dogma involves the denial of what is there said; viz. that it is the Spirit (*der Geist*) that leads into Truth, knows all things, penetrates even into the deep things of the Godhead. While the Divine Being is thus placed beyond our knowledge, and outside the limit of all human things, we have the convenient license of wandering as far as we list, in the direction of our own fancies. We are freed from the obligation to refer our knowledge to the Divine and True. I have been unwilling to leave out of sight the connection between our thesis—that Reason governs and has governed the World—and the question of the possibility of a Knowledge of God, chiefly that I might not lose the opportunity of mentioning the imputation against Philosophy of being shy of noticing religious truths, or of having occasion to be so in which is insinuated the suspicion that it has anything but a clear conscience in the presence of these truths. So far from this being the case, the fact is that in recent times Philosophy has been obliged to defend the domain of religion against the attacks of several theological systems. In the Christian religion God has revealed Himself,—that is, he has given us to understand what He is; so that He is no longer a concealed or secret existence. And this possibility of knowing Him, thus afforded us, renders such knowledge a duty. That development of the thinking spirit, which has resulted from the revelation of the Divine Being as its original basis, must ultimately advance to the intellectual comprehension of what was presented in the first instance, to *feeling* and *imagination*. The time must eventually come for understanding that rich product of active Reason, which the History of the World offers to us. It was for a while the fashion to profess admiration for the wisdom of God, as displayed in animals, plants, and isolated occurrences. But, if it be allowed that Providence manifests itself in such objects and forms of existence, why not also in Universal History? Our intellectual striving aims at realizing the conviction that what was *intended* by eternal wisdom, is actually *accomplished* in the domain of existent, active Spirit, as well as in that of mere Nature. Our mode of treating the subject is, in this aspect, a Theodicaea,—a justification of the ways of God—which Leibnitz attempted metaphysically in his method, i.e., in indefinite abstract categories—so that the ill that is found in the World may be comprehended, and the thinking Spirit reconciled with the fact of the existence of evil. Indeed, nowhere is such a harmonizing view more pressingly demanded than in Universal History; and it can be attained only by recognizing the *positive* existence, in which that negative element is a subordinate, and vanquished nullity. On the one hand, the ultimate design of the World must be perceived; and, on the other hand, the fact that this design has been actually, realized in it, and that evil has not been able permanently to assert a competing position. But this conviction involves much more than the mere belief in a superintending or in 'Providence'. An adequate definition of Reason is the first desideratum; and whatever boast may be made of strict adherence to it in explaining phenomena—without such a definition we get no farther than mere words. With these observations we may proceed to the second point of view that has to be considered in this Introduction.

ESSENTIAL DESTINY OF REASON

(b) The enquiry into the *essential destiny* of Reason—as far as it is considered in reference to the World—is identical with the question, *what is the ultimate design of the World?* And the expression implies that that design is destined to be realized. Two points of consideration suggest themselves: first, the *import* of this design—its abstract definition; and secondly, its *realization*.

It must be observed at the outset, that the phenomenon we investigate—Universal History—belongs to the realm of *Spirit*. The term 'World', includes both physical and psychical Nature. Physical Nature also plays its part in the World's History—and attention will have to be paid to the fundamental natural relations thus involved. But Spirit, and the course of its development, is our substantial object. Our task does not require us to contemplate Nature as a Rational System in itself—though in its own proper domain it proves itself such—but simply in its relation to *Spirit*. On the stage on which we are observing it—Universal History—Spirit displays itself in its most concrete reality. Notwithstanding this (or rather for the very purpose of comprehending the *general* principles which this, its form of *concrete reality,* embodies) we must premise some abstract characteristics of the *nature of spirit.*

We have therefore to mention here: *(i)* The abstract characteristics of the nature of Spirit. *(ii)* What means Spirit uses in order to realize its Idea. *(iii)* Lastly, we must consider the shape which the perfect embodiment of Spirit assumes—the State.

(i) The nature of Spirit may be understood by a glance at its direct opposite—*Matter.* As the essence of Matter is Gravity, so, on the other hand, we may affirm that the substance, the essence of Spirit is Freedom. All will readily assent to the doctrine that Spirit, among other properties, is also endowed with Freedom; but philosophy teaches that all the qualities of Spirit exist only through Freedom; that all are but means for attaining Freedom; that all seek and produce this and this alone. It is a result of speculative Philosophy that Freedom is the sole truth of Spirit. Matter possesses gravity in virtue of its tendency towards a central point. It is essentially composite; consisting of parts that *exclude* each other. It seeks its Unity; and therefore exhibits itself as self-destructive, as verging towards its opposite [an indivisible point]. If it could attain this, it would be Matter no longer, it would have perished. It strives after the realization of its Idea; for in Unity it exists *ideally.* Spirit, on the contrary, may be defined as that which has its centre in itself. It has not a unity outside itself, but has already found it; it exists *in* and *with itself.* Matter has its essence out of itself; Spirit *is self-contained existence* (*Bei-sich-selbst-seyn*). Now this is Freedom, exactly. For if I am dependent, my being is referred to something else which I am not; I cannot exist independently of something external. I am free on the contrary, when my existence depends upon myself. This self-contained existence of Spirit is none other than self-consciousness—consciousness of one's own being. Two things must be distinguished in consciousness; first, the fact *that I know*; secondly, *what I know.* In *self* consciousness these are merged in one; for Spirit *knows itself.* It involves an appreciation of its own nature, as also an energy enabling it to realize itself; to make itself actually that which it is *potentially.* According to this abstract definition it may be said of Universal History, that it is the exhibition of Spirit in the process of working out the knowledge of that which it is potentially. And as the germ bears in itself the whole nature of the tree, and the taste and form of its fruits, so do the first traces of Spirit virtually contain the whole of that History. The Orientals have not attained the knowledge that Spirit—Man *as such*—is free; and because they do not know this they are not free. They only know that *one is free.* But on this very account, the freedom of that one is only caprice; ferocity—brutal recklessness or passion, or a mildness and tameness of the desires, which is itself only an accident of Nature—mere caprice like the former. That *one* is therefore only a Despot; not a *free* man. The consciousness of Freedom first arose among the Greeks, and therefore they were free; but they, and the Romans likewise, knew only that some are free,—not man

as such. Even Plato and Aristotle did not know this. The Greeks, therefore, had slaves; and their whole life and the maintenance of their splendid liberty, was implicated with the institution of slavery: a fact moreover, which made that liberty on the one hand only an accidental, transient and limited growth; on the other hand, constituted it a rigorous thraldom of our common nature—of the Human. The German nations, under the influence of Christianity, were the first to attain the consciousness, that man, as man, is free: that it is the *freedom* of Spirit which constitutes its essence. This consciousness arose first in religion, the inmost region of Spirit; but to introduce the principle into the various relations of the actual world, involves a more extensive problem than its simple implantation; a problem whose solution and application require a severe and lengthened process of culture. In proof of this, we may note that slavery did not cease immediately on the reception of Christianity. Still less did liberty predominate in States; or Governments and Constitutions adopt a rational organization, or recognize freedom as their basis. That application of the principle to political relations; the thorough molding and interpenetration of the constitution of society by it, is a process identical with history itself. The History of the world is none other than the progress of the consciousness of Freedom; a progress whose development according to the necessity of its nature, it is our business to investigate.

The general statement given above, of the various grades in the consciousness of Freedom—and which we applied in the first instance to the fact that the Eastern nations knew only that *one* is free; the Greek and Roman world only that *some* are free; whilst *we* know that all men absolutely (man *as man*) are free—supplies us with the natural division of Universal History, and suggests the mode of its discussion.

In the process before us, the essential nature of freedom—which involves in it absolute necessity,—is to be displayed as coming to a consciousness of itself (for it is in its very nature, self-consciousness) and thereby realizing its existence. Itself is its own object of attainment, and the sole aim of Spirit. This result it is, at which the process of the World's History has been continually aiming; and to which the sacrifices that have ever and anon been laid on the vast altar of the earth, through the long lapse of ages, have been offered. This is the only aim that sees itself realized and fulfilled; the only pole of repose amid the ceaseless change of events and conditions, and the sole efficient principle that pervades them. This final aim is God's purpose with the world; but God is the absolutely perfect Being, and can, therefore, will nothing other than himself—his own Will. The Nature of His Will—that is, His Nature itself—is what we here call the Idea of Freedom; translating the language of Religion into that of Thought. The question, then, which we may next put, is: What means does this principle of Freedom use for its realization? This is the second point we have to consider.

(ii) The question of the *means* by which Freedom develops itself to a World, conducts us to the phenomenon of History itself. The first glance at History convinces us that the actions of men proceed from their needs, their passions, their

characters and talents; and impresses us with the belief that such needs, passions and interests are the sole springs of action—the efficient agents in this scene of activity. Their power lies in the fact that they respect none of the limitations which justice and morality would impose on them; and that these natural impulses have a more direct influence over man than the artificial and tedious discipline that tends to order and self-restraint, law and morality. When we look at this display of passions, and the consequences of their violence; the Unreason which is associated not, only with them, but even (rather we might say *especially*) with *good* designs and righteous aims; when we see the evil, the vice, the ruin that has befallen the most flourishing kingdoms which the mind of man ever created, we can scarce avoid being filled with sorrow at this universal taint of corruption: and, since this decay is not the work of mere Nature, but of the Human Will—a moral embitterment—a revolt of the Good Spirit (if it has a place within us) may well be the result of our reflections. Without rhetorical exaggeration, a simply truthful combination of the miseries that have overwhelmed the noblest of nations and polities, and the finest exemplars of private virtue,—forms a picture of most fearful aspect, and excites emotions of the profoundest and most hopeless sadness, counter-balanced by no consolatory result. But even regarding History as the slaughter bench at which the happiness of peoples, the wisdom of States, and the virtue of individuals have been victimized—the question involuntarily arises—to what principle, to what final aim these enormous sacrifices have been offered. From this point the investigation usually proceeds to that which we have made the general commencement of our enquiry. Starting from this we pointed out those phenomena which made up a picture so suggestive of gloomy emotions and thoughtful reflections—as *the very field* which we, for our part, regard as exhibiting only the means for realizing what we assert to be the essential destiny—the absolute aim, or—which comes to the same thing—the true *result* of the World's History. We return then to the point of view which we have adopted; observing that the successive steps (*Momente*) of the analysis to which it will lead us, will also evolve the conditions requisite for answering the enquiries suggested by the panorama of sin and suffering that history unfolds.

The *first* remark we have to make, and which—though already presented more than once—cannot be too often repeated when the occasion seems to call for it,—is that what we call *principle, aim, destiny,* or the nature and idea of Spirit, is something merely general and abstract. Principle—Plan of Existence—Law—is a hidden, undeveloped essence, which as such—however true in itself—is not completely real. Aims, principles, etc., have a place in our thoughts, in our subjective design only; but not yet in the sphere of reality. That which exists for itself only, is a possibility, a potentiality; but has not yet emerged into Existence. A *second* element must be introduced in order to produce actuality—viz. actuation, realization; and whose motive power is the Will—the activity of man in the widest sense. It is only by this activity that that Idea as well as abstract characteristics generally, are realized, actualized; for of themselves they are powerless. The motive power that puts them in operation, and gives them determinate existence, is the need, instinct, inclination, and passion of man. That some conception of mine should be developed into act and existence, is my earnest desire: I wish to assert my personality in connection with it: I wish to be satisfied by its execution. If I am to exert myself for any object, it must in some way or other be *my* object. In the accomplishment of such or such designs I must at the same time find *my* satisfaction; although the purpose for which I exert myself includes a complication of results, many of which have no interest for me. This is the absolute right of personal existence—to find *itself* satisfied in its activity and labour. Here a mistake must be avoided. We intend blame, and justly impute it as a fault, when we say of an individual, that he is 'interested' (in taking part in such or such transactions) that is, seeks only his private advantage. In reprehending this we find fault with him for furthering his personal aims without any regard to a more comprehensive design; of which he takes advantage to promote his own interest, or which he even sacrifices with this view. But he who is active in *promoting an object,* is not simply 'interested', but interested in that object itself. Nothing therefore happens, nothing is accomplished, unless the individuals concerned, seek their own satisfaction in the issue. They are particular units of society; i.e., they have special needs, instincts, and interests generally, peculiar to themselves. Among these needs are not only such as we usually call necessities—the stimuli of individual desire and volition—but also those connected with individual views and convictions; or leanings of opinion; supposing the impulses of reflection, understanding, and reason, to have been awakened.

We assert then that nothing has been accomplished without interest on the part of the actors; and—if interest be called passion, inasmuch as the whole individuality, to the neglect of all other actual or possible interests and claims, is devoted to an object with every fibre of volition, concentrating all its desires and powers upon it—we may affirm absolutely that *nothing great in the World* has been accomplished without *passion.* Two elements, therefore, enter into the object of our investigation; the first the Idea, the second the complex of human passions; the one the warp, the other the woof of the vast arras-web of Universal History. The concrete mean and union of the two is Liberty, under the conditions of morality in a State. We have spoken of the Idea of Freedom as the nature of Spirit, and the absolute goal of History. Passion is regarded as a thing of sinister aspect, as more or less immoral. Man is required to have no passions. Passion, it is true, is not quite the suitable word for what I wish to express. I mean here nothing more than human activity as resulting from private interests—special, or if you will, self-seeking designs—with this qualification, that the whole energy of will and character is devoted to their attainment; that other interests (which would in themselves constitute attractive aims), or rather all things else, are sacrificed to them. The object in question is so bound up with the man's will, that it entirely and alone determines the 'hue of resolution' and is inseparable from it. It has become the very essence of his volition. For a person is a specific existence; not man in general (a term to which no real existence corresponds), but a particular human being. I shall, therefore, use the term 'passion', understanding thereby the particular bent of character, as far as the peculiarities of volition are not limited to private interest, but supply the impelling and actuating force for accomplishing deeds shared in by the community at large. Passion is in the first instance the *subjective,* and therefore the formal side of energy, will, and activity—leaving the object or aim still undetermined.

From this comment on the second essential element in the historical embodiment of an aim, we infer—glancing at the institution of the State in passing—that a State is then well constituted and internally powerful, when the private interest of its citizens is one with the common interest of the State; when the one finds its gratification and realization in the other. But in a State many institutions must be adopted, much political machinery invented, accompanied by appropriate political arrangements,—necessitating long struggles of the understanding before what is really appropriate can be discovered,—involving, moreover, contentions with private interest and passions, and a tedious discipline of these latter, in order to bring about the desired harmony. The epoch when a State attains this harmonious condition, marks the period of its bloom, its virtue, its vigour, and its prosperity. But the history of mankind does not begin with *a conscious* aim of any kind, as it is the case with the particular circles into which men form themselves of set purpose. The mere social instinct implies a conscious purpose of security for life and property; and when society has been constituted, this purpose becomes more comprehensive. The History of the World begins with its general aim—the realization of the Idea of Spirit—only in an *implicit* form (*an sich*) that is, as Nature; a hidden, most profoundly hidden, unconscious instinct; and the whole process of History (as already observed), is directed to rendering this unconscious impulse a conscious one. Thus appearing in the form of merely natural existence, natural will—that which has been called the subjective side,—physical craving, instinct, passion, private interest, as also opinion and subjective conception,—spontaneously present themselves at the very commencement. This vast congeries of volitions, interests and activities, constitute the instruments and means of the World-Spirit for attaining its object; bringing it to consciousness, and realizing it. And this aim is none other than finding itself—coming to itself—and contemplating itself in concrete actuality. The Union of Universal Abstract Existence generally with the Individual,—the Subjective—that this alone is Truth, belongs to the department of speculation, and is treated in this general form in Logic. But in the process of the World's History itself,—as still incomplete,—the abstract final aim of history is not yet made the distinct object of desire and interest. While these limited sentiments are still unconscious of the purpose they are fulfilling, the universal principle is implicit in them, and is realizing itself through them. The question also assumes the form of the union of *Freedom* and *Necessity*; the latent abstract process of Spirit being regarded as *Necessity,* while that which exhibits itself in the conscious will of men, as their interest, belongs to the domain of *Freedom.*

Philosophy shows that the Idea advances to an infinite antithesis; that, viz. between the Idea in its free, universal form—in which it exists for itself—and the contrasted form of abstract introversion, reflection on itself, which is formal existence-for-self, personality, formal freedom, such as belongs to Spirit only. The universal Idea exists thus as the substantial totality of things on the one side, and as the abstract essence of free volition on the other side. This reflection of the mind on itself is individual self-consciousness—the polar opposite of the Idea in its general form, and therefore existing in absolute Limitation. This polar opposite is consequently limitation, particularization, for the universal absolute being; it is the side of its *definite existence;* the sphere of its formal reality, the sphere of the reverence paid to God. To comprehend the absolute connection of this antithesis, is the profound task of metaphysics. The formal volition wills itself; desires to make its own personality valid in all that it purposes and does. This pole of the antithesis, existing for itself, is—in contrast with the Absolute Universal Being—a special separate existence, taking cognizance of speciality only, and willing that alone. This is the sphere of particular purposes, in effecting which individuals exert themselves on behalf of their individuality—give it full play and objective realization. The History of the World is not the theatre of happiness. Periods of happiness are blank pages in it, for they are periods of harmony,—periods when the antithesis is in abeyance. Reflection on self,—the Freedom above described—is abstractly defined as the formal element of the activity of the absolute Idea. The realizing activity of which we have spoken is the middle term of the Syllogism, one of whose extremes is the Universal essence, the Idea, which reposes in the penetralia of Spirit; and the other, the complex of external things, objective matter. That activity is the medium by which the universal latent principle is translated into the domain of objectivity.

I will endeavour to make what has been said more vivid and clear by examples.

The building of a house is, in the first instance, a subjective aim and design. On the other hand we have, as means, the several substances required for the work,—iron, wood, stones. The elements are made use of in working up this material: fire to melt the iron, wind to blow the fire, water to set wheels in motion, in order to cut the wood, etc. The result is that the wind, which has helped to build the house, is shut out by the house; so also are the violence of rains and floods, and the destructive powers of fire, so far as the house is made fire-proof. The stones and beams obey the law of gravity,—press downwards,—and so high walls are carried up. Thus the elements are made use of in accordance with their nature, and yet to co-operate for a product, by which their operation is limited. Thus the passions of men are gratified; they develop themselves and their aims in accordance with their natural tendencies, and build up the edifice of human society; thus fortifying a position for Right and Order *against themselves.*

The connection of events above indicated, involves also the fact, that in history an additional result is commonly produced by human actions beyond that which they aim at and obtain—that which they immediately recognize and desire. An analogous example is offered in the case of a man who, from a feeling of revenge,—perhaps not an unjust one, but produced by injury on the other's part,—burns that other man's house. A connection is immediately established between the deed itself and a train of circumstances not directly included in it, taken abstractedly. In itself it consisted in merely presenting a small flame to a small portion of a beam. Events not involved in that simple act follow of themselves. The part of the beam which was set fire to is connected with its remote portions; the beam itself is united with the woodwork of the house generally, and this with other houses; so that a wide conflagration ensues, which destroys the goods and chattels of many other persons besides his against whom the act of revenge was first directed; perhaps even costs not a few men their lives. This lay neither in the deed abstractedly, nor in the design of the man who committed it. But the action has a further general bearing. In the design of the doer it was only revenge executed against an individual in the destruction of his property, but it is moreover a crime, and that involves punishment also. This may not have been present to the mind of the perpetrator, still less in his intention; but his deed itself, the general principles it calls into play, its substantial content entails it. By this example I wish only to impress on you the consideration, that in a simple act, something farther may be implicated than lies in the intention and consciousness of the agent. The example before us involves, however, this additional consideration, that the substance of the act, consequently we may say the act itself, recoils upon the perpetrator,—reacts upon him with destructive tendency. This union of the two extremes—the embodiment of a general idea in the form of direct reality, and the elevation of a speciality into connection with universal truth—is brought to pass, at first sight, under the conditions of an utter diversity of nature between the two, and an indifference of the one extreme towards the other. The aims which the agent set before them are limited and special; but it must be remarked that the agents themselves are intelligent thinking beings. The purport of their desires is interwoven with *general, essential* considerations of justice, good, duty, etc.; for mere desire—volition in its rough and savage forms—falls not within the scene and sphere of Universal History. Those general considerations, which form at the same time a norm for directing aims and actions, have determinate purport; for such an abstraction as 'good for its own sake', has no place in living reality. If men are to act, they must not only intend the Good, but must have decided for themselves whether this or that particular thing is a Good. What special course of action, however, is good or not, is determined, as regards the ordinary contingencies of private life, by the laws and customs of a State; and here no great difficulty is presented. Each individual has his position; he knows on the whole what a just, honourable course of conduct is.

It is quite otherwise with the comprehensive relations that History has to do with. In this sphere are presented those momentous collisions between existing, acknowledged duties, laws, and rights, and those contingencies which are adverse to this fixed system;—which assail and even destroy its foundations and existence;

whose tenor may nevertheless seem good,—on the large scale advantageous,—yes, even indispensable and necessary. These contingencies realize themselves in History: they involve a general principle of a different order from that on which depends the *permanence* of a people or a State. This principle is an essential phase in the development of the *creating* Idea, of Truth striving and urging towards [consciousness of] itself. Historical *men—World-Historical Individuals—*are those in whose aims such a general principle lies.

Caesar, in danger of losing a position, not perhaps at that time of superiority, yet at least of equality with the others who were at the head of the State, and of succumbing to those who were just on the point of becoming his enemies,—belongs essentially to this category. These enemies—who were at the same time pursuing *their* personal aims—had the form of the constitution, and the power conferred by an appearance of justice, on their side. Caesar was contending for the maintenance of his position, honour, and safety; and, since the power of his opponents included the sovereignty over the provinces of the Roman Empire, his victory secured for him the conquest of that entire Empire: and he thus became—though leaving the form of the constitution—the Autocrat of the State. That which secured for him the execution of a design, which in the first instance was of negative import—the Autocracy of Rome,—was, however, at the same time an independently necessary feature in the history of Rome and of the world. It was not, then, his private gain merely, but an unconscious impulse that occasioned the accomplishment of that for which the time was ripe. Such are all great historical men—whose own particular aims involve those large issues which are the will of the World-Spirit. They may be called Heroes, inasmuch as they have derived their purposes and their vocation, not from the calm, regular course of things, sanctioned by the existing order; but from a concealed fount—one which has not attained to phenomenal, present existence,—from that inner Spirit, still hidden beneath the surface, which, impinging on the outer world as on a shell, bursts it in pieces, because it is another kernel than that which belonged to the shell in question. They are men, therefore, who appear to draw the impulse of their life from themselves; and whose deeds have produced a condition of things and a complex of historical relations which appear to be only *their* interest, and *their* work.

Such individuals had no consciousness of the general Idea they were unfolding, while prosecuting those aims of theirs; on the contrary, they were practical, political men. But at the same time they were thinking men, who had an insight into the requirements of the time—what *was ripe for development.* This was the very Truth for their age, for their world; the species next in order, so to speak, and which was already formed in the womb of time. It was theirs to know this nascent principle; the necessary, directly sequent step in progress, which their world was to take; to make this their aim, and to expend their energy in promoting it. World-historical men—the Heroes of an epoch—must, therefore, be recognized as its clear-sighted ones; *their* deeds, *their* words are the best of that time. Their fellows, therefore, follow these soul-leaders; for they feel the irresistible power of their own inner Spirit thus embodied. If we go on to cast a look at the fate of these World-Historical persons, whose vocation it was to be the agents of the World-Spirit,—we shall find it to have been no happy one. They attained no calm enjoyment; their whole life was labour and trouble; their whole nature was nought else but their master—passion. When their object is attained they fall off like empty hulls from the kernel. They die early, like Alexander; they are murdered, like Caesar; transported to St. Helena, like Napoleon.

They are *great* men, because they willed and accomplished something great; not a mere fancy, a mere intention, but that which met the case and fell in with the needs of the age. This mode of considering them also excludes the so-called 'psychological' view, which—serving the purpose of envy most effectually—contrives so to refer all actions to the heart,—to bring them under such a subjective aspect—as that their authors appear to have done everything under the impulse of some passion, mean or grand,—some morbid craving,—and on account of these passions and cravings to have been not moral men.

A World-historical individual is not so unwise as to indulge a variety of wishes to divide his regards. He is devoted to the One Aim, regardless of all else. It is even possible that such men may treat other great, even sacred interests, inconsiderately; conduct which is indeed obnoxious to moral reprehension. But so mighty a form must trample down many an innocent flower—crush to pieces many an object in its path.

The special interest of passion is thus inseparable from the active development of a general principle: for it is from the special and determinate and from its negation, that the Universal results. Particularity contends with its like, and some loss is involved in the issue. It is not the general idea that is implicated in opposition and combat, and that is exposed to danger. It remains in the background, untouched and uninjured. This may be called the *cunning of reason*,—that it sets the passions to work for itself, while that which develops its existence through such impulsion pays the penalty and suffers loss. For it is *phenomenal* being that is so treated, and of this, part is of no value, part is positive and real. The particular is for the most part of too trifling value as compared with the general: individuals are sacrificed and abandoned. The Idea pays the penalty of determinate existence and of corruptibility, not from itself, but from the passions of individuals.

But though we might tolerate the idea that individuals, their desires and the gratification of them, are thus sacrificed, and their happiness given up to the empire of chance, to which it belongs; and that as a general rule, individuals come under the category of means to an ulterior end,—there is one aspect of human individuality which we should hesitate to regard in that subordinate light, even in relation to the highest; since it is absolutely no subordinate element, but exists in those individuals as inherently eternal and divine. I mean *morality, ethics, religion*. Human beings least of all, sustain the bare external relation of mere means to the great ideal aim. Not only do they in the very act of realizing it, make it the occasion of satisfying personal desires, whose purport is diverse from that aim—

but they share in that ideal aim itself; and are for that very reason objects of their own existence; not *formally* merely, as the world of living beings generally is—whose individual life is essentially subordinate to that of man, and is properly used *up* as an instrument. Men, on the contrary, are objects of existence to themselves, as regards the intrinsic import of the aim in question. That is to say, man is an object of existence in himself only in virtue of the Divine that is in him,—that which was designated at the outset as *Reason;* which, in view of its activity and power of self-determination, was called *Freedom*. And we affirm—without entering at present on the proof of the assertion—that Religion, Morality, etc. have their foundation and source in that principle, and so are essentially elevated above all alien necessity and chance. And here we must remark that individuals, to the extent of their freedom, are responsible for the depravation and enfeeblement of morals and religion. This is the seal of the absolute and sublime destiny of man—that he knows what is good and what is evil; that his destiny *is* his very ability to will either good or evil,—in one word, that he is the subject of moral imputation, imputation not only of evil, but of good; and not only concerning this or that particular matters and all that happens *ab extrâ*, but *also* the good and evil attaching to his individual freedom. The brute alone is simply innocent.

With more justice than happiness—or a fortunate environment for individuals,—it is demanded of the grand aim of the world's existence, that it should foster, nay involve the execution and ratification of good, moral, righteous purposes. What makes men morally discontented, is that they do not find the present adapted to the realization of aims which they hold to be right and just (more especially in modern times, ideals of political constitutions); they contrast unfavourably things as they are, with their idea of things as they *ought* to be. In this case it is not private interest nor passion that desires gratification, but Reason, Justice, Liberty; and equipped with this title, the demand in question assumes a lofty bearing, and readily adopts a position not merely of discontent, but of open revolt against the actual condition of the world. To estimate such a feeling and such views aright, the demands insisted upon, and the very dogmatic opinions asserted, must be examined. At no time so much as in our own, have such general principles and notions been advanced, or with greater assurance. The pretensions thus contended for as legitimate in the name of that which has been stated as the ultimate aim of Reason, pass accordingly, for absolute aims,—to the same extent as Religion, Morals, Ethics. Nothing, as before remarked, is now more common than the complaint that the *ideals* which imagination sets up are not realized—that these glorious dreams are destroyed by cold actuality. These Ideals—which in the voyage of life founder on the rocks of hard reality—may be in the first instance only subjective, and belong to the idiosyncrasy of the individual, imagining himself the highest and wisest. But by the term 'Ideal', we also understand the ideal of Reason, of the Good, of the True. Poets, as, e.g., Schiller, have painted such ideals touchingly and with strong emotion, and with the deeply melancholy conviction that they could not be realized. In affirming, on the contrary that the

Universal Reason *does* realize itself, we leave indeed nothing to do with the individual empirically regarded. The insight then to which—in contradistinction from those ideals—philosophy is to lead us, is, that the real world is as it ought to be—that the truly good - the universal divine reason—is not a mere abstraction, but a vital principle capable of realizing itself. This *Good,* this *Reason,* in its most concrete form, is God. God governs the world; the actual working of his government—the carrying out of his plan—is the History of the World. This plan philosophy strives to comprehend; for only that which has been developed as the result of it, possesses bona fide reality. That which does not accord with it, is negative, worthless existence. Before the pure light of this divine Idea—which is no mere Idea—the phantom of a world whose events are an incoherent concourse of fortuitous circumstances, utterly vanishes. Philosophy wishes to discover the substantial purport, the real side of the divine idea and to justify the so much despised Reality of things; for Reason is the comprehension of the Divine work. But as to what concerns the perversion, corruption, and ruin of religious, ethical and moral purposes, and states of society generally, it must be affirmed, that in their *essence* these are infinite and eternal; but that the forms they assume may be of a limited orders and consequently belong to the domain of mere nature, and be subject to the sway of chance. They are therefore perishable, and exposed to decay and corruption. Religion and morality—in the same way as inherently universal essences—have the peculiarity of being present in the individual soul, in the full extent of their Idea, and therefore truly and really; although they may not manifest themselves in it *in extenso,* and are not applied to fully developed relations. The religion, the morality of a limited sphere of life—that of a shepherd or a peasant, e.g.—in its intensive concentration and limitation to a few perfectly simple relations of life,—has infinite worth; the same worth as the religion and morality of extensive knowledge, and of an existence rich in the compass of its relations and actions. This inner focus—this simple region of the claims of subjective freedom,—the home of volition, resolution, and action,—the abstract sphere of conscience,—that which comprises the responsibility and moral value of the individual, remains untouched; and is quite shut out from the noisy din of the World's History—including not merely external and temporal changes, but also those entailed by the absolute necessity inseparable from the realization of the Idea of Freedom itself. But as a general truth this must be regarded as settled, that whatever in the world possesses claims as noble and glorious, has nevertheless a higher existence above it. The claim of the World-Spirit rises above all special claims.

These observations may suffice in reference to the means which the World-Spirit uses far realizing its Idea. Stated simply and abstractly, this mediation involves the activity of personal existences in whom Reason is present as their absolute substantial being; but a basis, in the first instance, still obscure and unknown to them. But the subject becomes more complicated and difficult when we regard individuals not merely in their aspect of activity, but more concretely, in conjunction with a particular manifestation of that activity in their religion and morality,—forms of existence which are intimately connected with Reason, and share in its absolute claims. Here the relation of mere means of an end disappears, and the chief hearings of this seeming difficulty in reference to the absolute aim of Spirit, have been briefly considered.

(iii) The third point to be analysed is, therefore—what is the object to be realized by these means; i.e., what is the form it assumes in the realm of reality. We have spoken of means; but in the carrying out of a subjective, limited aim, we have also to take into consideration the element of a *material*, either already present or which has to be procured. Thus the question would arise: What is the material in which the Ideal of Reason is wrought out? The primary answer would be,—Personality itself—human desires—Subjectivity generally. In human knowledge and volition, as its material element, Reason attains positive existence. We have considered subjective volition where it has an object which is the truth and essence of a reality, viz. where it constitutes a great world-historical passion. As a subjective will, occupied with limited passions, it is dependent, and can gratify its desires only within the limits of this dependence. But the subjective will has also a substantial life—a reality,—in which it moves in the region of *essential* being and has the essential itself as the object of its existence. This essential being is the union of the *subjective* with the *rational* Will: it is the moral Whole, the State, which is that form of reality in which the individual has and enjoys his freedom; but on the condition of his recognition, believing in and willing that which is common to the Whole. And this must not be understood as if the subjective will of the social unit attained its gratification and enjoyment through that common Will; as if this were a means provided for its benefit; as if the individual, in his relations to other individuals, thus limited his freedom, in order that this universal limitation—the mutual constraint of all—might secure a small space of liberty for each. Rather, we affirm, are Law, Morality, Government, and they alone, the positive reality and completion of Freedom. Freedom of a low and limited order is mere caprice; which finds its exercise in the sphere of particular and limited desires.

Subjective volition—Passion—is that which sets men in activity, that which effects 'practical' realization. The Idea is the inner spring of action; the State is the actually, existing, realized moral life. For it is the Unity of the universal, essential Will, with that of the individual; and this is 'Morality'. The Individual living in this unity has a moral life; possesses a value that consists in this substantiality alone. Sophocles in his Antigone, says, 'The divine commands are not of yesterday, nor of today; no, they have an infinite existence, and no one could say whence they came'. The laws of morality are not accidental, but are the essentially Rational. It is the very object of the State that what is essential in the practical activity of men, and in their dispositions, should be duly recognized; that it should have a manifest existence, and maintain its position. It is the absolute interest of Reason that this moral Whole should exist; and herein lies the justification and merit of heroes who have founded states,—however rude these may have been. In the history of the World, only those peoples can come under our notice which form a state. For it must be understood that this latter is the realization of Freedom, i.e., of the absolute final aim, and that it exists for its own sake. It must further be understood that all the worth which the human being possesses—all spiritual reality, he possesses only through the State. For his spiritual reality consists in this, that his own essence—Reason—is objectively present to him, that it possesses objective immediate existence for him. Thus only is he fully conscious; thus only is he a partaker of morality—of a just and moral social and political life. For Truth is the Unity of the universal and subjective Will; and the Universal is to be found in the State, in its laws, its universal and rational arrangements. The State is the Divine Idea as it exists on Earth. We have in it, therefore, the object of History in a more definite shape than before; that in which Freedom obtains objectivity, and lives in the enjoyment of this objectivity. For Law is the objectivity of Spirit; volition in its true form. Only that will which obeys law, is free; for it obeys itself—it is independent and so free. When the State or our country constitutes a community of existence; when the subjective will of man submits to laws,—the contradiction between Liberty and Necessity vanishes. The Rational has necessary existence as being the reality and substance of things, and we are free in recognizing it as law, and following it as the substance of our own being. The objective and the subjective will are then reconciled, and present one identical homogeneous whole. For the morality (*Sittlichkeit*) of the State is not of that ethical (*moralische*) reflective kind, in which one's own conviction bears sway; this latter is rather the peculiarity of the modern time, while the true antique morality is based on the principle of abiding by one's duty [to the state at large]. An Athenian citizen did what was required of him, as it were from instinct; but if I reflect on the object of any activity, I must have the consciousness that my will has been called into exercise. But morality is Duty—substantial Right—a '*second* nature' as it has been justly called; for the *first* nature of man is his primary merely animal existence.

The development *in extenso* of the Idea of the State belongs to the Philosophy of Jurisprudence; but it must be observed that in the theories of our time various errors are current respecting it, which pass for established truths, and have become fixed prejudices. The error which first meets us is the direct contradictory of our principle that the state presents the realization of Freedom; the opinion, viz., that man is free by *nature*, but that in *society,* in the State—to which nevertheless he is irresistibly impelled—he must limit this natural freedom. That man is free by Nature is quite correct in one sense; viz., that he is so according to the Idea of Humanity; but we imply thereby that he is such only in virtue of his destiny—that he has an undeveloped power to become such; for the 'Nature' of an object is exactly synonymous with its 'Idea'. But the view in question imports more than this. When man is spoken of as 'free by Nature', the mode of his existence as well as his destiny is implied. His merely natural and primary condition is intended. In this sense a 'state of Nature' is assumed in which mankind at large are in the possession of their natural rights with the unconstrained exercise and enjoyment of their freedom. This assumption is not indeed raised to the dignity of the historical fact; it would indeed be difficult, were the attempt seriously made, to point out any such condition as actually existing, or as having ever occurred.

What we find such a state of Nature to be in actual experience, answers exactly to the Idea of a *merely* natural condition. Freedom as the *ideal* of that which is original and natural, does not exist *as original and natural*. Rather must it be first sought out and won; and that by an incalculable medial discipline of the intellectual and moral powers. The state of Nature is, therefore, predominantly that of injustice and violence, of untamed natural impulses, of inhuman deeds and feelings. Limitation is certainty produced by Society and the State, but it is a limitation of the mere brute emotions and rude instincts; as also, in a more advanced stage of culture, of the premeditated self-will of caprice and passion. This kind of constraint is part of the instrumentality by which only, the consciousness of Freedom and the desire for its attainment, in its true—that is Rational and Ideal form—can be obtained. To the Ideal of Freedom, Law and Morality are indispensably requisite: and they are in and for themselves, universal existences, objects and aims; which are discovered only by the activity of thought, separating itself from the merely sensuous, and developing itself, in opposition thereto; and which must on the other hand, be introduced into and incorporated with the originally sensuous will, and that contrarily to its natural inclination. The perpetually recurring misapprehension of Freedom consists in regarding that term only in its *formal*, subjective sense, abstracted from its essential objects and aims; thus a constraint put upon impulse, desire, passion—pertaining to the particular individual as such—a limitation of caprice and self-will is regarded as a fettering of Freedom. We should on the contrary look upon such limitation as the indispensable proviso of emancipation. Society and the State are the very conditions in which Freedom is realized.

We must notice a second view, contravening the principle of the development of moral relations into a legal form. The basis of the patriarchal condition is the family relation; which develops the primary form of conscious morality, succeeded by that of the State as its *second* phase. The patriarchal condition is one of transition, in which the family has already advanced to the position of a race or people; where the union, therefore, has already ceased to be simply a bond of love and confidence, and has become one of plighted service. We must first examine the ethical principle of the Family. The Family may be reckoned as virtually a single person; since its members have either mutually surrendered their individual personality, (and consequently their legal position towards each other, with the rest of their particular interests and desires) as in the case of the Parents; or have not yet attained such an independent personality,—(the Children,—who are primarily in that merely natural condition already mentioned). They live, therefore, in a unity of feeling, love, confidence, and faith in each other. And in a relation of mutual love, the one individual has the consciousness of himself in the consciousness of the other; he lives out of self; and in this mutual self-renunciation each regains the life that had been virtually transferred to the other; gains, in fact, that other's existence and his own, as involved with that other. The farther interests connected with the necessities and external concerns of life, as well as the development that has to take place within their circle, i.e., of the children constitute a common object for the members of the Family. The Spirit of the Family—the Penates—form one substantial being, as much as the Spirit of a People in the State; and morality in both cases consists in a feeling, a consciousness, and a will, not limited to individual personality and interest, but embracing the common interests of the members generally. But this unity is in the case of the Family essentially one of *feeling;* not advancing beyond the limits of the merely *natural.* The piety of the Family relation should be respected in the highest degree by the State; by its means the State obtains as its members individuals who are already moral (for as mere *persons* they are not) and who in uniting to form a state bring with them that sound basis of a political edifice—the capacity of feeling one with a Whole. But the expansion of the Family to a patriarchal unity carries us beyond the ties of blood-relationship—the simply natural elements of that basis; and outside of these limits the members of the community must enter upon the position of independent personality. A review of the patriarchal condition, *in extenso,* would lead us to give special attention to the Theocratical Constitution. The head of the patriarchal clan is also its priest. If the Family in its general relations, is not yet separated from civic society and the state, the separation of religion from it has also not yet taken place; and so much the less since the piety of the hearth is itself a profoundly subjective state of feeling.

We have considered two aspects of Freedom,—the objective and the subjective; if, therefore, Freedom is asserted to consist in the individuals of a State all agreeing in its arrangements it is evident that only the subjective aspect is regarded. The natural inference from this principle is, that no law can be valid without the approval of all. This difficulty is attempted to be obviated by the decision that the minority must yield to the majority; the majority therefore bear the sway. But long ago J. J. Rousseau remarked, that in that case there would be no longer freedom, for the will of the *minority* would cease to be respected. At the Polish Diet each single member had to give his consent before any political step could be taken; and this kind of freedom it was that ruined the State. Besides, it is a dangerous and false prejudice, that the People *alone* have reason and insight, and know what justice is; for each popular faction may represent itself as the People, and the question as to what constitutes the State is one of advanced science, and not of popular decision.

If the principle of regard for the individual will is recognized as the only basis of political liberty, viz., that nothing should be done by or for the State to which all the members of the body politic have not given their sanction, we have, properly speaking, no *Constitution.* The only arrangement that would be necessary, would be, first, a centre having no *will* of its own but which should take into consideration what appeared to be the necessities of the State; and, secondly, a contrivance for calling the members of the State together, for taking the votes, and for performing the arithmetical operations of reckoning and comparing the number of votes for the different propositions, and thereby deciding upon them. The State is an *abstraction*, having even its generic existence in its citizens; but it is an actuality, and its simply generic existence must embody itself in individual will and activity. The want of government and political administration in general is felt; this necessitates the selection and separation from the rest of those who have to take the helm in political affairs, to decide, concerning them, and to give orders to other citizens, with a view to the execution of their plans. If, e.g., even the people in a Democracy resolve on a war, a general must head the army. It is only by a Constitution that the *abstraction*—the State—attains life and reality; but this involves the distinction between those who command and those who obey. Yet obedience seems inconsistent with liberty, and those who command appear to do the very opposite of that which the fundamental idea of the State, viz. that of Freedom, requires. It is, however, urged that,—though the distinction between commanding and obeying is absolutely necessary, because affairs could not go on without it—and indeed this seems only a compulsory limitation, external to and even contravening freedom in the abstract—the constitution should be at least so framed, that the citizens may obey as little as possible, and the smallest modicum of free volition be left to the commands of the superiors;—that the substance of that for which subordination is necessary, even in its most important bearings, should be decided and resolved on by the People—by the will of many or of all the citizens; though it is supposed to be thereby provided that the State should be possessed of vigour and strength as a reality—an individual unity. The primary consideration is, then, the distinction between the governing and the governed, and political constitutions in the abstract have been rightly divided into Monarchy, Aristocracy, and Democracy; which gives occasion, however, to the remark that Monarchy itself must be further divided into Despotism and Monarchy proper; that in all the divisions to which the leading Idea gives rise, only the generic character is to be made prominent,—it being not intended thereby that the particular category under review should be exhausted as a Form, Order, or Kind in its *concrete* development. But especially it must be observed, that the above-mentioned divisions admit of a multitude of particular modifications,—not only such as lie within the limits of those classes themselves,—but also such as are mixtures of several of these essentially distinct classes, and which are consequently misshapen, unstable, and inconsistent forms. In such a collision, the concerning question is, what is the *best constitution;* that is, by what arrangement, organization or mechanism of the power of the State its object can be most surely attained. The inquiry into the best constitution is frequently treated as if not only the theory were an affair of subjective independent conviction, but as if the introduction of a constitution recognized as the best,—or as superior to others,—could be the result of a resolve adopted in this theoretical manner; as if the form of a constitution were a matter of free choice, determined by nothing else but reflection.

In the present day, the Constitution of a country and people is not represented as so entirely dependent on free and deliberate choice. The fundamental but abstractly (and therefore imperfectly) entertained conception of Freedom, has resulted in the Republic being very generally regarded—in theory—as the only just and true political constitution. The necessity of a particular constitution is made to depend on the condition of the people in such a way as if the latter were nonessential and accidental. This representation is founded on the distinction which the reflective understanding makes between an idea and the corresponding reality; holding to an abstract and consequently untrue idea; not grasping it in its completeness, or—which is virtually, though not in point of form, the same—not taking a concrete view of a people and a state. We shall have to show further on that the constitution adopted by a people makes one substance—one spirit—with its religion, its art and philosophy, or, at least, with its conceptions and thoughts—its culture generally; not to expatiate upon the additional influences, *ab extrâ*, of climate, of neighbours, of its place in the world. A State is an individual totality, of which you cannot select any particular side—although a supremely important one, such as its political constitution—and deliberate and decide respecting it in that isolated form. Not only is that constitution most intimately connected with and dependent on those other spiritual forces; but the form of the entire moral and intellectual individuality—comprising all the forces it embodies—is only a step in the development of the grand Whole,—with its place pre-appointed in the process: a fact which gives the highest sanction to the constitution in question, and establishes its absolute necessity. The origin of a State involves imperious lordship on the one hand, instinctive submission on the other. But even obedience—lordly power, and the fear inspired by a ruler—in itself implies some degree of voluntary connection. Even in barbarous states this is the case; it is not the isolated will of individuals that prevails; individual pretensions are relinquished, and the general will is the essential bond of political union. This unity of the general and the particular is the Idea itself, manifesting itself as a *State,* and which subsequently undergoes further development within itself. The abstract yet necessitated process in the development of truly independent states is as follows: They begin with regal power, whether of patriarchal or military origin. In the next phase, particularity and individuality assert themselves in the form of Aristocracy and Democracy. Lastly, we have the subjection of these separate interests to a single power; but which can be absolutely none other than one outside of which those spheres have an independent position, viz., the Monarchical.

In a Constitution the main feature of interest is the self-development of the *rational*, that is, the *political* condition of a people; the setting free of the successive elements of the Idea: so that the several powers in the State manifest themselves as separate,—attain their appropriate and special perfection,—and yet in this independent condition, work together for one object, and are held together by it—i.e., form an organic whole. The State is thus the embodiment of rational freedom, realizing and recognizing itself in an objective form. For its objectivity consists in this,—that its successive stages are not merely ideal, but are present in an appropriate reality; and that in their separate and several working, they are absolutely merged in that agency by which the totality—the soul—the individual unity—is produced, and of which it is the result.

The State is the Idea of Spirit in the external manifestation of human Will and its Freedom. It is to the State, therefore, that change in the aspect of History indissolubly attaches itself; and the successive phases of the Idea manifest themselves in it as distinct political *principles*. The Constitutions under which World-Historical peoples have reached their culmination, are peculiar to them; and therefore do not present a generally applicable political basis. Were it otherwise, the differences of similar constitutions would consist only in a peculiar method of expanding and developing that generic basis; whereas they really originate in diversity of principle. From the comparison therefore of the political institutions of the ancient World-Historical peoples, it so happens, that for the most recent principle of a Constitution—for the principle of our own times—nothing (so to speak) can be learned. Nothing is so absurd as to look to Greeks, Romans, or Orientals, for models for the political arrangements of our time. From the East may be derived beautiful pictures of a patriarchal condition, of paternal government, and of devotion to it on the part of peoples; from Greeks and Romans, descriptions of popular liberty. Among the latter we find the idea of a Free Constitution admitting all the citizens to a share in deliberations and resolves respecting the affairs and laws of the Commonwealth. In our times, too, this is its general acceptation; only with this modification, that—since our States are so large, and there are so many of 'the Many', the latter,—direct action being impossible,—should by the indirect method of elective substitution express their concurrence with resolves affecting the common weal; that is, that for legislative purposes generally, the people should be represented by deputies. The so-called Representative Constitution is that form of government with which we connect the idea of a free constitution, and this notion has become a rooted prejudice. On this theory People and Government are separated. But there is a perversity in this antithesis; an ill-intentioned *ruse* designed to insinuate that the People are the totality of the State. Besides, the basis of this view is the principle of isolated individuality—the absolute validity of the subjective will—a dogma which we have already investigated. The great point is, that Freedom in its Ideal conception has not subjective will and caprice for its principle, but the recognition of the universal will; and that the process by which Freedom is realized is the free development of its successive stages. The subjective will is a merely formal determination—a *carte blanche*—not including what it is that is willed. Only the *rational* will is that universal principle which independently determines and unfolds its own being, and develops its successive elemental phases as organic members. Of this Gothic-cathedral architecture the ancients knew nothing.

At an earlier stage of the discussion, we established the two elemental considerations: first, the *idea* of freedom as the absolute and final aim; second, the *means* for realizing it, i.e., the subjective side of knowledge and will, with its life, movement, and activity. We then recognized the State as the moral Whole and the Reality of Freedom, and consequently as the objective unity of these two elements. For although we make this distinction into two aspects for our consideration, it must be remarked that they are intimately connected; and that their connection is involved in the idea of each when examined separately. We have, on the one hand, recognized the Idea in the definite form of Freedom conscious of and willing itself,—having itself alone as its object: involving at the same time, the pure and simple Idea of Reason, and likewise, that which we have called subject— self-consciousness—Spirit actually existing in the World. If, on the other hand, we consider Subjectivity, we find that subjective knowledge and will is Thought. But by the very act of thoughtful cognition and volition, I will the universal object—the substance of absolute Reason. We observe, therefore, an essential union between the objective side—the Idea,—and the subjective side—the personality that conceives and wills it. The *objective* existence of this union is the State, which is therefore the basis and centre of the other concrete elements of the life of a people,—of Art, of Law, of Morals, of Religion, of Science. All the activity of Spirit has only this object—the becoming conscious of this union, i.e., of its own Freedom. Among the forms of this conscious union *Religion* occupies the highest position. In it, Spirit—rising above the limitations of temporal and secular existence—becomes conscious of the Absolute Spirit, and in this consciousness of the self-existent Being, renounces its individual interest; it lays this aside in Devotion—a state of mind in which it refuses to occupy itself any longer with the limited and particular. By Sacrifice man expresses his renunciation of his property, his will, his individual feelings. The religious concentration of the soul appears in the form of feeling; it nevertheless passes also into reflection; a form of worship (*cultus*) is a result of reflection. The second form of the union of the objective and subjective in the human spirit is *Art*. This advances farther into the realm of the actual and sensuous than Religion. In its noblest walk it is occupied with representing, not indeed, the Spirit of God, but certainly the Form of God; and in its secondary aims, that which is divine and spiritual generally. Its office is to render visible the Divine; presenting it to the imaginative and intuitive faculty. But the True is the object not only of conception and feeling, as in Religion,—and of Intuition, as in Art,—but also of the thinking faculty; and this gives us the third form of the union in question—*Philosophy*. This is consequently the highest, freest, and wisest phase. Of course we are not intending to investigate these three phases here; they have only suggested themselves in virtue of their occupying the same general ground as the object here considered—the *State*.

The general principle which manifests itself and becomes an object of consciousness in the State,—the form under which all that the State includes is brought, is the whole of that cycle of phenomena which constitutes the *culture* of a nation. But the definite *substance* that receives the form of universality, and exists in that concrete reality which is the State,—is the Spirit of the People itself. The actual State is animated by this spirit, in all its particular affairs—its Wars, Institutions, etc. But man must also attain a conscious realization of this his Spirit and essential nature, and of his original identity with it. For we said that morality is the identity of the *subjective* or *personal* with the *universal* will. Now the mind must give itself an express consciousness of this; and the focus of this knowledge is *Religion*. Art and Science are only various aspects and forms of the same substantial being. In considering Religion, the chief point of enquiry is whether it recognizes the True—the Idea—only in its separate, abstract form, or in its true unity; in *separation*—God being represented in an abstract form as the Highest Being, Lord of Heaven and Earth, living in a remote region far from human actualities,—or in its unity,—God, as Unity of the Universal and Individual; the Individual itself assuming the aspect of positive and real existence in the idea of the Incarnation. Religion is the sphere in which a nation gives itself the definition of that which it regards as the True. A definition contains everything that belongs to the essence of an object; reducing its nature to its simple characteristic predicate, as a mirror for every predicate,—the generic soul Pervading all its details. The conception of God, therefore, constitutes the general basis of a people's character.

In this aspect, religion stands in the closest connection with the political principle. Freedom can exist only where Individuality is recognized as leaving its positive and real existence in the Divine Being. The connection may be further explained thus: Secular existence, as merely temporal—occupied with particular interests—is consequently only relative and unauthorized; and receives its validity only in as far as the universal soul that pervades it—its principle—receives absolute validity; which it cannot have unless it is recognized as the definite manifestation, the phenomenal existence of the Divine Essence. On this account it is that the State rests on Religion. We hear this often repeated in our times, though for the most part nothing further is meant than that individual subjects as God-fearing men would be more disposed and ready to perform their duty; since obedience to King and Law so naturally follows in the train of reverence for God. This reverence, indeed, since it exalts the general over the special, may even turn upon the latter,—become fanatical,—and work with incendiary and destructive violence against the State, its institutions, and arrangements. Religious feeling, therefore, it is thought, should be sober—kept in a certain degree of coolness,—that it may not storm against and bear down that which should be defended and preserved by it. The possibility of such a catastrophe is at least latent in it.

While, however, the correct sentiment is adopted, that the State is based on Religion, the position thus assigned to Religion supposes the State already to exist; and that subsequently, in order to maintain it, Religion must be brought into it—buckets and bushels as it were—and impressed upon people's hearts. It is quite true that men must be trained to religion, but not as to something whose existence has yet to begin. For in affirming that the State is based on Religion—that it has its roots in it—we virtually assert that the former has proceeded from the latter; and that this derivation is going on now and will always continue; i.e., the principles of the State must be regarded as valid in and for themselves, which can only be in so far as they are recognized as determinate manifestations of the Divine Nature. The form of Religion, therefore, decides that of the State and its constitution. The latter actually originated in the particular religion adopted by the nation; so that, in fact, the Athenian or the Roman State was possible only in connection with the specific form of Heathenism existing among the respective peoples; just as a Catholic State has a spirit and constitution different from that of a Protestant one.

If that outcry—that urging and striving for the implantation of Religion in the community—were an utterance of anguish and a call for help, as it often seems to be, expressing the danger of religion having vanished, or being about to vanish entirely from the State,—that would be fearful indeed—worse in fact than this outcry supposes; for it implies the belief in a resource against the evil, viz., the implantation and inculcation of religion; whereas religion is by no means a thing to be so produced; its *self-production* (and there can be no other) lies much deeper.

Another and opposite folly which we meet with in our time is that of pretending to invent and carry out political constitutions independently of religion. The Catholic confession, although sharing the Christian name with the Protestant, does not concede to the State an inherent Justice and Morality,—a concession which in the Protestant principle is fundamental. This tearing away of the political morality of the Constitution from its natural connection, is necessary to the genius of that religion, inasmuch as it does not recognize Justice and Morality as independent and substantial. But thus excluded from intrinsic worth,—torn away from their last refuge—the sanctuary of conscience—the calm retreat where religion has its abode,—the principles and institutions of political legislation are destitute of a real centre, to the same decree as they are compelled to remain abstract and indefinite.

Summing up what has been said of the State, we find that we have been led to call its vital principle, as actuating the individuals who compose it,—Morality. The State, its laws, its arrangements, constitute the rights of its members; its natural features, its mountains, air, and waters, are *their* country, their fatherland, their outward material property; the history of this State, *their* deeds; what their ancestors have produced, belongs to them and lives in their memory. All is their possession, just as they are possessed by it; for it constitutes their existence, their being.

Their imagination is occupied with the ideas thus presented, while the adoption of these laws, and of a fatherland so conditioned is the expression of their will. It is this matured totality which thus constitutes one Being, the spirit of *one* People. To it the individual members belong; each unit is the Son of his Nation, and at the same time—in as far as the State to which he belongs is undergoing development—the Son of his Age. None remains behind it, still less advances beyond it. This spiritual Being (the Spirit of his Time) is his; he is a representative of it; it is that in which he originated, and in which he lives. Among the Athenians the word Athens had a double import; suggesting primarily, a complex of Political institutions, but no less, in the second place, that Goddess who represented the Spirit of the People and its unity. This Spirit of a People is a *determinate* and particular Spirit, and is, as just stated, further modified by the degree of its historical development. This Spirit, then, constitutes the basis and substance of those other forms of a nation's consciousness, which have been noticed. For Spirit in its self-consciousness must become a object of contemplation to itself, and objectivity involves, in the first instance, the rise of differences which make up a total of distinct spheres of objective spirit; in the same way as the Soul exists only as the complex of its faculties, which in their form of concentration in a simple unity produce that Soul. It is thus *One Individuality* which, presented in its essence as God, is honoured and enjoyed in *Religion;* which is exhibited as an object of sensuous contemplation in *Art;* and is apprehended as an intellectual conception in *Philosophy*. In virtue of the original identity of their essence, purport, and object, these various forms are inseparably united with the Spirit of the State. Only in connection with this particular religion can this particular political constitution exist; just as in such or such a State, such or such a Philosophy or order of Art.

The remark next in order is that each particular National genius is to be treated as only One Individual in the process of Universal History. For that history is the exhibition of the divine, absolute development of Spirit in its highest forms,—that gradation by which it attains its truth and consciousness of itself. The forms which these grades of progress assume are the characteristic 'National Spirits' of History; the peculiar tenor of their moral life, of their Government, their Art, Religion, and Science. To realize these grades is the boundless impulse of the World-Spirit—the goal of its irresistible urging; for this division into organic members, and the full development of each, is its Idea. Universal History is exclusively occupied with showing how Spirit comes to a recognition and adoption of the Truth: the dawn of knowledge appears; it begins to discover salient principles, and at last it arrives at full consciousness.

Having, therefore, learned the abstract characteristics of the nature of Spirit, the means which it uses to realize its Idea, and the shape assumed by it in its complete realization in phenomenal existence—namely, the State—nothing further remains for this introductory section to contemplate but:

THE COURSE OF THE WORLD'S HISTORY

(c) The mutations which history presents have been long characterized in the general, as an advance to something better, more perfect. The changes that take place in Nature—how infinitely manifold so ever they may be—exhibit only a perpetually self-repeating cycle; in Nature there happens 'nothing new under the sun', and the multiform play of its phenomena so far induces a feeling of ennui; only in those changes which take place in the region of Spirit does anything new arise.

This peculiarity in the world of mind has indicated in the case of man an altogether different destiny from that of merely natural objects—in which we find always one and the same stable character, to which all change reverts;—namely, a real capacity for change, and that for the, better,—an impulse of *perfectibility.*

The principle of *Development* involves also the existence of a latent germ of being—a capacity or potentiality striving to realize itself. This formal conception finds actual existence in Spirit; which has the History of the World for its theatre, its possession, and the sphere of its realization. Development, however, is also a property of organized natural objects. Their existence presents itself, not as an exclusively dependent one, subjected to external changes, but as one which expands itself in virtue of an external unchangeable principle; a simple essence,—whose existence, i.e., as a germ, is primarily simple,—but which subsequently develops a variety of parts, that become involved with other objects, and consequently live through a continuous process of changes;—a process nevertheless, that results in the very contrary of change, and is even transformed into a *vis conservatrix* of the organic principle, and the form embodying it. Thus the organized *individuum* produces itself; it expands itself *actually* to what it was always *potentially:* So Spirit is only that which it attains by its own efforts; it makes itself *actually* what it always was *potentially.* That development (of *natural organisms)* takes place in a direct, unopposed, unhindered manner. Between the Idea and its realization—the essential constitution of the original germ and the conformity to it of the existence derived from it—no disturbing influence can intrude. But in relation to Spirit it is quite otherwise. The realization of its Idea is mediated by consciousness and will; these very faculties are, in the first instance, sunk in their primary merely natural life; the first object and goal of their striving is the realization of their merely natural destiny,—but which, since it is Spirit that animates it, is possessed of vast attractions and displays great power and [moral] richness. Thus Spirit is at war with itself; it has to overcome itself as its most formidable obstacle. What Spirit really strives for is the realization of its Ideal being; but in doing so, it hides that goal from its own vision, and is proud and well satisfied in this alienation from it.

Its expansion, therefore, does not present the harmless tranquility of mere growth, as does that of organic life, but a stern reluctant working against itself. It exhibits, moreover, not the mere formal conception of development, but the attainment of a definite result. The goal of attainment we determined at the outset: it is Spirit in its *completeness,* in its essential nature, i.e., Freedom.

Universal History exhibits the *gradation* in the development of that principle whose substantial *purport* is the consciousness of Freedom. The analysis of the successive grades, in their abstract form, belongs to Logic; in their concrete aspect to the Philosophy of Spirit. Here it is sufficient to state that the first step in the process presents that immersion of Spirit in Nature which has been already referred to; the second shows it as advancing to the consciousness of its freedom. But this initial separation from Nature is imperfect and partial, since it is derived immediately from the merely natural state, is consequently related to it, and is still encumbered with it as an essentially connected element. The third step is the elevation of the soul from this still limited and special form of freedom to its pure universal form; that state in which the spiritual essence attains the consciousness and feeling of itself. These grades are the ground-principles of the general process; but how each of them on the other hand involves within *itself* a process of formation,—constituting the links in a dialectic of transition,—to particularize this may be reserved for the sequel.

Here we have only to indicate that Spirit begins with a germ of infinite possibility, but *only* possibility,—containing its substantial existence in an undeveloped form, as the object and goal which it reaches only in its resultant—full reality. In actual existence Progress appears as an advancing from the imperfect to the more perfect; but the former must not be understood abstractly as *only* the imperfect, but as something which involves the very opposite of itself—the so-called perfect—as a *germ* or impulse. So—reflectively, at least—*possibility* points to something destined to become actual; the Aristotelian is also *potentia,* power and might. Thus the Imperfect, as involving its opposite, is a contradiction, which certainly exists, but which is continually annulled and solved; the instinctive movement—the inherent impulse in the life of the soul—to break through the rind of mere nature, sensuousness, and that which is alien to it, and to attain to the light of consciousness, i.e., to itself.

The only consistent and worthy method which philosophical investigation can adopt, is to take up History—where Rationality begins to manifest itself in the actual conduct of the World's affairs (not where it is merely an undeveloped potentiality),—where a condition of things is present in which it realizes itself in consciousness, will and action. The inorganic existence of Spirit—that of abstract Freedom—unconscious *torpidity* in respect to good and evil (and consequently to laws), or, if we please to term it so, 'blessed ignorance',—is itself not a subject of History. Freedom is nothing but the recognition and adoption of such universal substantial objects as Right and Law, and the production of a reality that is accordant with them—the State. Nations may have passed a long life before arriving at this their destination, and during this period, they may have attained considerable culture in some directions. This ante-historical period—consistently with what has been said—lies out of our plan; whether a real history followed it, or the peoples in question never attained a political constitution. It is a great discovery in history—as of a new world—which has been made within rather more than the last twenty years, respecting the Sanskrit and the connection of the European languages with it. In particular, the connection of the German and Indian peoples has been demonstrated, with as much certainty as such subjects allow of. In the connection just referred to, between the languages of nations so widely separated, we have a result before us, which proves the diffusion of those nations from Asia as a centre, and the so dissimilar development of what had been originally related, as an incontestable fact; not *as* an inference deduced by that favourite method of combining, and reasoning from, circumstances grave and trivial, which has already enriched and will continue to enrich history with so many fictions given out as facts. But that apparently so extensive range of events lies beyond the pale of history; in fact preceded it. In our language, the term *History* unites the objective with the subjective side, and denotes quite as much the *historia rerum gestarum,* as the *res gestae* themselves; on the other hand it comprehends not less what has *happened,* than the *narration* of what has happened. This union of the two meanings we must regard as of a higher order than mere outward accident; we must suppose historical narrations to have appeared contemporaneously with historical deeds and events. It is an internal vital principle common to both that produces them synchronously. It is the State which first presents subject-matter that is not only *adapted* to the prose of History, but involves the production of such history in the very progress of its own being. Instead of merely subjective mandates on the part of government,—sufficing for the needs of the moment,—a community that is acquiring a stable existence, and exalting itself into a State, requires formal commands and laws—comprehensive and universally binding prescriptions; and thus produces a record as well as an interest concerned with intelligent, definite—and, in their results—lasting transactions and occurrences is impelled to confer perpetuity.

The periods—whether we suppose them to be centuries or millennia—that were passed by nations before history was written among them,—and which may have been filled with revolutions, nomadic wanderings, and the strangest mutations,—are on that very account destitute of *objective* history, because they present no *subjective* history, no annals. We need not suppose that the records of such periods have accidentally perished; rather, because they were not possible, do we find them wanting. Only in a State cognizant of Laws, can distinct transactions take place, accompanied by such a clear consciousness of them as supplies the ability and suggests the necessity of an enduring record. It strikes every one, in beginning to form an acquaintance with the treasures of Indian literature, that a land so rich in intellectual products, and those of the profoundest order of thought, has no History; and in this respect contrasts most strongly with China—an empire possessing one so remarkable, one going back to the most ancient times. India has not only ancient books relating to religion, and splendid poetical productions, but also ancient codes; the existence of which latter kind of literature has been mentioned as a condition necessary to the origination of History—and yet History itself is not found. But in that country the impulse of organization, in beginning to develop social distinctions, was immediately petrified in the merely natural classification according to *castes;* so that although the laws concern themselves with civil rights, they make even these dependent on natural distinctions; and are especially occupied with determining the relations (Wrongs rather than Rights) of those classes towards each other, i.e., the privileges of the higher over the lower. Consequently, the element of morality is banished from the pomp of Indian life and from its political institutions. Where that iron bondage of distinctions derived from nature prevails, the connection of society is nothing but wild arbitrariness,—transient activity,—or rather the play of violent emotion without any goal of advancement or development. Therefore no intelligent reminiscence, no object for Mnemosyne presents itself; and imagination—confused though profound—expatiates in a region, which, to be capable of History, must have had an aim within the domain of Reality, and, at the same time, of substantial Freedom.

After these remarks, relating to the form of the *commencement* of the World's History, and to that ante-historical period which must be excluded from it, we have to state the direction of its course.

Universal history—as already demonstrated—shows the development of the consciousness of Freedom on the part of Spirit, and of the consequent realization of that Freedom. This development implies a gradation—a series of increasingly adequate expressions or manifestations of Freedom, which result from its Idea. The logical, and—as still more prominent—the *dialectical* nature of the Idea in general, viz. that it is self-determined—that it assumes successive forms which it successively transcends; and by this very process of transcending its earlier stages, gains an affirmative, and, in fact, a richer and more concrete shape;—this necessity of its nature, and the necessary series of pure abstract forms which the Idea successively assumes—is exhibited in the department of *Logic*. Here we need adopt only one of its results, viz. that every step in the process, as differing from any other, has its determinate peculiar principle. In history this principle is idiosyncrasy of Spirit—peculiar National Genius. It is within the limitations of this idiosyncrasy that the spirit of the nation, concretely manifested, expresses every aspect of its consciousness and will—the whole cycle of its realization. Its religion, its polity, its ethics, its legislation, and even its science, art, and mechanical skill, all bear its stamp. These special peculiarities find their key in that common peculiarity,—the particular principle that characterizes a people; as, on the other hand, in the facts which History presents in detail, that common characteristic principle may be detected. That such or such a specific quality constitutes the peculiar genius of a people, is the element of our inquiry which must be derived from experience, and historically proved. To accomplish this, presupposes not only a disciplined faculty of abstraction, but an intimate acquaintance with the Idea. The investigator must be familiar *a priori*, with the whole circle of conceptions to which the principles in question belong—just as Keppler (to name the most illustrious example in this mode of philosophizing) must have been familiar *a priori* with ellipses, with cubes and squares, and with ideas of their relations before he could discover, from the empirical data, those immortal 'Laws' of his, which are none other than forms of thought pertaining to those classes of conceptions. He who is unfamiliar with the science that embraces these abstract elementary conceptions, is as little capable—though he may have gazed on the firmament and the motions of the celestial bodies for a life-time—of *understanding* those Laws, as of *discovering* them. From this want of acquaintance with the ideas that relate to the development of Freedom, proceed a part of those objections which are brought against the philosophical consideration of a science usually regarded as one of mere experience; the so-called *a priori* method, and the attempt to insinuate ideas into the empirical data of history, being the chief points in the indictment. It must be observed that in this very process of scientific *Understanding,* it is of importance that the essential should be distinguished and brought into relief in contrast with the so-called non-essential. But in order to render this possible, we must know what *is essential;* and that is—in view of the History of the World in general—the Consciousness of Freedom, and the phases which this consciousness assumes in developing itself. The bearing of historical facts on this category, is their bearing on the truly Essential.

A similar process of reasoning is adopted, in reference to the correct assertion that genius, talent, moral virtues, and sentiments, and piety, may be found in every zone, under all political constitutions and conditions; in confirmation of which examples are forthcoming in abundance. Under such an aspect the well known Indian Epopees may be compared with the Homeric; perhaps—since it is the vastness of the imagination by which poetical genius proves itself—preferred to them; as, on account of the similarity of single strokes of imagination in the attributes of the divinities, it has been contended that Greek mythological forms may be recognized in those of India. Similarly the Chinese philosophy, as adopting the One as its basis, has been alleged to be the same as at a later period appeared as Eleatic philosophy and as the Spinozistic System; while in virtue of its expressing itself also in abstract numbers and lines, Pythagorean and Christian principles have been supposed to be detected in it. Instances of bravery and indomitable courage,—traits of magnanimity, of self-denial, and self-sacrifice, which are found among the most savage and the most pusillanimous nations,—are regarded as sufficient to support the view that in these nations as much of social virtue and morality may be found as in the most civilized Christian states, or even more. And on this ground a doubt has been suggested whether in the progress of history and of general culture mankind have become better; whether their morality has been increased,—morality being regarded in a subjective aspect and view, as founded on what the agent holds to be right and wrong, good and evil; not on a principle which is considered to be in and for itself right and good, or a crime and evil, or on a particular religion believed to be the true one.

We may fairly decline on this occasion the task of tracing the formalism and error of such a view, and establishing the true principles of morality, or rather of social virtue in opposition to false morality. For the History of the World occupies a higher ground than that on which morality has properly its position, which is personal character—the conscience of individuals,—their particular will and mode of action; *these* have a value, imputation, reward or, punishment proper to themselves. The History of the World might, on principle, entirely ignore the circle within which morality and the so much talked of distinction between the moral and the politic lies—not only in abstaining from judgments, but in leaving Individuals quite out of view and unmentioned. What it has to record is the activity of the Spirit of Peoples, so that the individual forms which that spirit has assumed in the sphere of outward reality, might be left to the delineation of special histories.

The same kind of formalism avails itself in its peculiar manner of the indefiniteness attaching to genius, poetry, and even philosophy; thinks equally that it finds these everywhere. We have here products of reflective thought; and it is familiarity with those general conceptions which single out and name real distinctions without fathoming the true depth of the matter,—that we call Culture.

We find then, it is true, among all world-historical peoples, poetry, plastic art, science, even philosophy; but not only is there a diversity in style and bearing generally, but still more remarkably in subject-matter; and this is a diversity of the most important kind, affecting the rationality of that subject-matter. Granted that the Indian Epopees might be placed on a level with the Homeric, on account of a number of those qualities of form—grandeur of invention and imaginative power, liveliness of images and emotions, and beauty of diction; yet the infinite difference of matter remains; consequently one of substantial importance and involving the interest of Reason which is immediately concerned with the consciousness of the Idea of Freedom, and its expression in individuals. In that comparison of the various systems of philosophy of which we have already spoken, the only point of importance is overlooked, namely the character of that Unity which is found alike in the Chinese, the Eleatic, and the Spinozistic philosophy—the distinction between the recognition of that Unity as abstract and as concrete—concrete to the extent of being a unity in and by itself—a unity synonymous with Spirit. But that co-ordination proves that it recognizes only such an abstract unity; so that while it gives judgment respecting philosophy it is ignorant of that very point which constitutes the interest of philosophy.

But there are also spheres which, amid all the variety that is presented in the substantial content of a particular form of culture, remain the same. The difference above mentioned in art, science, philosophy, concerns the thinking Reason and Freedom, which is the self-consciousness of the former, and which has the same one root with Thought. As it is not the brute, but only the man that thinks, he only—and only because he is a thinking being—has Freedom. *His* consciousness imports this, that the individual comprehends itself as a *person,* that is, recognizes itself in its single existence as possessing universality,—as capable of abstraction from, and of surrendering all speciality; and, therefore, as inherently infinite. Consequently, those spheres of intelligence which lie beyond the limits of this consciousness are a common ground among those substantial distinctions. Even morality, which is so intimately connected with the consciousness of freedom, can be very pure while that consciousness is still wanting; as far, that is to say, as it expresses duties and rights only as *objective* commands; or even as far as it remains satisfied with the merely formal elevation of the soul—the surrender of the sensual, and of all sensual motives—in a purely negative, self-denying fashion. The *Chinese* morality—since Europeans have become acquainted with it and with the writings of Confucius—has obtained the greatest praise and proportionate attention from those who are familiar with the Christian morality. There is a similar acknowledgment of the sublimity with which the *Indian* religion and poetry, (a statement that must, however, be limited to the higher kind), but especially the Indian philosophy, expatiate upon and demand the removal and sacrifice of sensuality. Yet both these nations are, it must be confessed, *entirely* wanting in the essential consciousness of the Idea of Freedom. To the Chinese their moral laws are just like natural laws—external, positive commands—claims established by force—compulsory duties or rules of courtesy towards each other. Freedom, through which alone the essential, determinations of Reason become moral sentiments, is wanting. Morality is a political affair, and its laws are administered by officers of government and legal tribunals. Their treatises upon it (which are not law books, but are certainly addressed to the subjective will and individual disposition) read,—as do the moral writings of the Stoics—like a string of commands stated as necessary for realizing the goal of happiness; so that it seems to be left free to men, on their part, to adopt such commands,—to observe them or not; while the conception of an abstract subject, 'a wise man' [Sapiens] forms the culminating point among the Chinese, as also among the Stoic moralists. Also in the Indian doctrine of the renunciation of the sensuality of desires and earthly interests, positive moral freedom is not the object and end, but the annihilation of consciousness—spiritual and even physical privation of life.

It is the concrete spirit of a people which we have distinctly to recognize, and since it is Spirit it can only be comprehended spiritually, that is, by thought. But for spirit, the highest attainment is self-knowledge; an advance not only to the *intuition,* but to the *thought*—the clear conception of itself. This it must and is also destined to accomplish; but the accomplishment is at the same time its dissolution, and the rise of another spirit, another world-historical people, another epoch of Universal History. This transition and connection leads us to the connection of the whole—the idea of the World's History as such—which we have now to consider more closely, and of which we have to give a representation.

History in general is therefore the development of Spirit in *Time,* as Nature is the development of the Idea in *Space.*

If then we cast a glance over the World's History generally, we see a vast picture of changes and transactions; of infinitely manifold forms of peoples, states, individuals, in unresting succession. Everything that can enter into and interest the soul of man—all our sensibility to *goodness, beauty, and greatness*—is called into play. On every hand aims are adopted and pursued, which we recognize, whose accomplishment we desire—we hope and fear for them. On every hand there is the motliest throng of events drawing us within the circle of its interest, and when one combination vanishes another immediately appears in its place.

The general thought—the category which first presents itself in this restless mutation of individuals and peoples, existing for a time and then vanishing—is that of *change* at large. The sight of the ruins of some ancient sovereignty directly leads us to contemplate this thought of change in its negative aspect. What traveller among the ruins of Carthage, of Palmyra, Persepolis, or Rome, has not been stimulated by reflections on the transiency of kingdoms and men, and to sadness at the thought of a vigorous and rich life now departed—a sadness which does not expend itself on personal losses and the uncertainty of one's own undertakings, but is a disinterested sorrow at the decay of a splendid and highly cultured national life! But the next consideration which allies itself with that of change, is, that chance while it imports dissolution, involves at the same time the rise of *a new life*—that while death is the issue of life, life is also the issue of death. This is a grand conception; one which the Oriental thinkers attained and which is perhaps the highest in their metaphysics. In the Idea of *Metempsychosis* we find it evolved in its relation to individual existence; but a myth more generally known, is that of the *Phoenix* as a type of the Life of *Nature;* eternally preparing for itself its funeral pile, and consuming itself upon it; but so that from its ashes is produced the new, renovated, fresh life. But Spirit—consuming the envelope of its existence—does not merely pass into another envelope, nor rise rejuvenescent from the ashes of its previous form; it comes forth exalted, glorified, a purer spirit. It certainly makes war upon itself—consumes its own existence; but in this very destruction it works up with existence into a new form, and each successive phase becomes in its turn a material, working on which it exalts itself to a new grade.

The very essence of Spirit is activity; it realizes its potentiality—makes itself its own deeds its own work—and thus it becomes an object to itself; contemplates itself as an objective existence. Thus is it with the Spirit of a people: it is a Spirit having strictly defined characteristics, which erects itself into an objective world, that exists and persists in a particular religious form of worship, customs, constitution and political laws,—in the whole complex of its institutions,—in the events and transactions that make up its history. That is its work—that is what this particular Nation *is*. Nations are what their deeds are. Every Englishman will say: We are the men who navigate the ocean, and have the commerce of the world; to whom the East Indies belong and their riches; who have a parliament, juries, etc. A Nation is moral—virtuous—vigorous—while it is engaged in realizing its grand objects, and defends its work against external violence during the process of giving to its purposes an objective existence. The contradiction between its potential, subjective being—its inner aim and life—and its *actual* being is removed; it has attained full reality, has itself objectively present to it. But this having been attained, the activity played by the Spirit of the people in question is no longer needed; it has its desire. The Nation can still accomplish much in war and peace at home and abroad; but the living substantial soul itself may be said to have ceased its activity. The essential, supreme interest has consequently vanished from its life, for interest is present only where there is opposition. In order that a truly universal interest may arise, the Spirit of a People must advance to the adoption of some new purpose: but whence can this new purpose originate? It would be a higher, more comprehensive conception of itself—a transcending of its principle—but this very act would involve a principle of a new order, a new National Spirit.

Such a new principle does in fact enter into the Spirit of a people that has arrived at full development and self-realization; it dies not a simply natural death—for it is not a mere single individual, but a spiritual, generic life; in its case natural death appears to imply destruction through its own agency.

It is not of the nature of the all-pervading Spirit to die this merely natural death; it does not simply sink into the senile life of mere custom but—as being a National Spirit belonging to Universal History—attains to the consciousness of what its work is; it attains to a conception of itself. In fact it is world-historical only in so far as a *universal principle* has lain in its fundamental element,—in its grand aim: only so far is the work which such a spirit produces, a moral, political organization. If it be mere desires that impel nations to activity, such deeds pass over without leaving a trace; or their traces are only ruin and destruction.

In the very element of an achievement the quality of generality, of thought, is contained; without thought it has no objectivity; that is its basis. The highest point in the development of a people is this,—to have gained a conception of its life and condition,—to have reduced its laws, its ideas of justice and morality to a science; for in this unity [of the objective and subjective] lies the most intimate unity that Spirit can attain to in and with itself. In its work it is employed in rendering itself an object of its own contemplation; but it cannot develop itself objectively in its essential nature, except in *thinking* itself.

But first we must observe how the life which proceeds from death, is itself, on the other hand, only individual life; so that, regarding the species as the real and substantial in this vicissitude, the perishing of the individual is a regress of the species into individuality. The perpetuation of the race is, therefore, none other than the monotonous repetition of the same kind of existence. Further, we must remark how perception,—the comprehension of being by thought,—is the source and birthplace of a new, and in fact higher form, in a principle which while it preserves, dignifies its material. For Thought is that *Universal*—that *Species* which is immortal, which preserves identity with itself. The particular form of Spirit not merely passes away in the world by natural causes in Time, but is annulled in the automatic self-mirroring activity of consciousness. Because this annulling is an activity of Thought, it is at the same time conservative and elevating in its operation. While then, on the one side, Spirit annuls the reality, the permanence of that which it is, it gains on the other side, the essence, the Thought, the Universal element of that which it *only was* [its transient conditions]. Its principle is no longer that immediate import and aim which it was previously, but *the essence* of that import and aim.

The result of this process is then that Spirit, in rendering itself objective and making this its being an object of thought, on the one hand destroys the determinate form of its being, on the other hand gains a comprehension of the universal element which it involves, and thereby gives a new form to its inherent principle. In virtue of this, the substantial character of the National Spirit has been altered,—that is, its principle has risen into another, and in fact a higher principle.

In this point lies the fundamental, the Ideal necessity of transition. This is the soul—the essential consideration—of the philosophical comprehension of History.

Spirit is essentially the result of its own activity; its activity is the transcending of immediate, simple, unreflected existence,—the negation of that existence, and the returning into itself. We may compare it with the seed; for with this the plant begins, yet it is also the result of the plant's entire life. But the weak side of life is exhibited in the fact that the commencement and the result are disjoined from each other. Thus also is it in the life of individuals and peoples. The life of a people ripens a certain fruit; its activity aims at the complete manifestation of the principle which it embodies. But this fruit does not fall back into the bosom of the people that produced and matured it; on the contrary, it becomes a poison-draught to it. That poison-draught it cannot let alone, for it has an insatiable thirst for it: the taste of the draught is its annihilation, though at the same time the rise of a new principle.

While we are thus concerned exclusively with the Idea of Spirit, and in the History of the World regard everything as only its manifestation, we have, in traversing the past,—however extensive its periods,—only to do with what is *present;* for philosophy, as occupying itself with the True, has to do with the *eternally present.* Nothing in the past is lost for it, for the Idea is ever present; Spirit is immortal; with it there is no past, no future, but an essential now. This necessarily implies that the present form of Spirit comprehends within it all earlier steps. These have indeed unfolded themselves in succession independently; but what Spirit is it has always been essentially; distinctions are only the development of this essential nature. The life of the ever present Spirit is a circle of progressive embodiments, which looked at in one respect still exist beside each other, and only as looked at from another point of view appear as past. The grades which Spirit seems to have left behind it, it still possesses in the depths of its present.

PHILOSOPHY OF FINE ART

'Now it is just the show and deception of this false and evanescent world which art disengages from the veritable significance of phenomena to which we have referred, implanting in the same a reality of more exalted rank born of spirit. The phenomena of art therefore are not merely not appearance and nothing more; we are justified in ascribing to them, as contrasted with the realities of our ordinary life, an actually higher reality and more veritable existence'.

5

PHILOSOPHY OF FINE ART

THE LIMITS OF AESTHETICS

The present inquiry has for its subject-matter *Aesthetics*. It is a subject co-extensive with the entire *realm of the beautiful;* more specifically described, its province is that of *Art,* or rather, we should say, of *Fine Art.*

For a subject-matter such as this the term 'Aesthetics' is no doubt not entirely appropriate, for 'Aesthetics' denotes more accurately the science of the senses of emotion. It is owing to the unsuitability or, more strictly speaking, the superficiality of this term that the attempt has been made by some to apply the name 'Callistic' to this science. Yet this also is clearly insufficient inasmuch as the science here referred to does not investigate beauty in its general signification, but the beauty of art pure and simple. For this reason we shall accommodate ourselves to the term Aesthetics, all the more so as the mere question of nomenclature is for ourselves a matter of indifference. It has as such been provisionally accepted in ordinary speech, and we cannot do better than retain it. The *term*, however, which fully expresses our science is 'Philosophy of Art', and, with still more precision, 'Philosophy of Fine Art'.

AESTHETICS CONFINED TO BEAUTY OF ART

(a) In virtue of this expression we at once exclude the beauty of nature from the scientific exposition of Fine Art. We are accustomed, no doubt, in ordinary life to speak of a beautiful colour, a beautiful heaven, a beautiful stream, to say nothing of beautiful flowers, animals, and, above all, of beautiful human beings. Without entering now into the disputed question how far the quality of beauty can justly be predicated of such objects, and consequently the beauty of Nature comes generally into competition with that of art, we are justified in maintaining categorically that the beauty of art stands *higher* than Nature. For the beauty of art is a

beauty begotten, a new birth of spirit; and to the extent that Spirit and its creations stand higher than Nature and its phenomena, to that extent the beauty of art is more exalted than the beauty of Nature.

Merely to maintain, in a general way, that spirit and the beauty of art which originates therefrom stands *higher* than the beauty of Nature is no doubt to establish next to nothing. The expression *higher* is obviously entirely indefinite; it still indicates the beauty of Nature and art as standing juxtaposed in the field of conception, and emphasizes the difference as a quantitative and accordingly external difference. But in predicating of spirit and its artistic beauty a higher place in contrast to Nature, we do not denote a distinction which is merely relative. Spirit, and spirit alone, is pervious to truth, comprehending all in itself, so that all which is beautiful can only be veritably beautiful as partaking in this higher sphere and as begotten of the same. Regarded under this point of view it is only a reflection of the beauty appurtenant to spirit, that is, we have it under an imperfect and incomplete mode, and one whose substantive being is already contained in the spirit itself.

Assuming, however, that we have, by way of prelude, limited our inquiry to the beauty of art, we are merely by this first step involved in fresh difficulties.

IS ART UNWORTHY OF SCIENTIFIC CONSIDERATION?

(b) What must first of all occur to us is the question whether Fine Art in itself is truly susceptible to a scientific treatment. It is a simple fact that beauty and art pervade all the affairs of life like some friendly genius, and embellish with their cheer all our surroundings, mental no less than material. They alleviate the strenuousness of such relations, the varied changes of actual life; they banish the tedium of our existence with their entertainment; and where nothing really worth having is actually achieved, it is at least an advantage that they occupy the place of actual vice. Yet while art prevails on all sides with its pleasing shapes, from the crude decorations of savage tribes up to the splendours of the sacred shrine adorned with every conceivable beauty of design, none the less such shapes themselves appear to fall outside the real purposes of life, and even where the imaginative work of art is not impervious to such serious objects, may, rather at times even appear to assist them, to the extent at least of removing what is evil to a distance, yet for all that art essentially belongs to the *relaxation* and *recreation* of spiritual life, whereas its substantive interests rather make a call upon its strained energy. On such grounds an attempt to treat that which on its own account is not of a serious character with all the gravity of scientific exposition may very possibly appear to be unsuitable and pedantic. In any case from such a point of view art appears a *superfluity* if contrasted with the essential needs and interests of life, even assuming that the *softening* of the soul which a preoccupation with the beauty of objects is capable of producing, does not actually prove injurious in its effeminate influence upon the serious quality of those *practical* interests. Owing to this fundamental assumption that they are a luxury it has often appeared necessary to

undertake the defence of the fine arts relatively to the necessities of practical life, and in particular relatively to morality and piety; and inasmuch as this harmlessness is incapable of demonstration, the idea has been at least to make it appear credible, that this luxury of human experience contributes a larger proportion of *advantages* than *disadvantages*. In this respect serious aims have been attributed to art, and in many quarters it has been commended as a mediator between reason and sensuous associations, between private inclinations and duty, personified in short as a reconciler of these forces in the strenuous conflict and opposition which this antagonism generates. But it is just conceivable that, even assuming the presence of such aims with all their indubitably greater seriousness, neither reason nor duty come by much profit from such mediation, for the simple reason that they are incapable by their very nature of any such interfusion or compromise, demanding throughout the same purity which they intrinsically possess. And we might add that art does not become in any respect more worthy thereby of scientific discussion, inasmuch as it remains still on two sides a menial, that is, subservient to idleness and frivolity, if also to objects of more elevated character. In such service, moreover, it can at most merely appear as a means instead of being an object for its own sake. And, in conclusion, assuming that art is a means, it still invariably labours under the formal defect, that so far as it in fact is subservient to more serious objects, and produces results of like nature, the means which actually brings this about is *deception*. For beauty is made vital in the *appearance*. Now it can hardly be denied that aims which are true and serious ought not to be achieved by deception; and though such an effect is here and there secured by this means, such ought only to be the case in a restricted degree; and even in the exceptional case we are not justified in regarding deception as the right means. For the means ought to correspond with the dignity of the aim. Neither semblance nor deception, but only what is itself real and true, possesses a title to create what is real and true. Just in the same way science has to investigate the true interests of the spirit in accordance with the actual process of the real world and the manner of conceiving it as we actually find it.

We may possibly conclude from the above grounds that the art of beauty is unworthy of philosophical examination.

But yet further in the *second* place, it is a still more plausible contention that even supposing fine art to be compatible generally with philosophical disquisition, none the less it would form no really adequate subject-matter for scientific enquiry in the strict sense. For the beauty of art is presented to sense, feeling, perception, and imagination: its field is not that of thought, and the comprehension of its activity and its creations demands another faculty than that of the scientific intelligence. Furthermore, what we enjoy in artistic beauty is just the *freedom* of its creative and plastic activity. In the production and contemplation of these we appear to escape the principle of rule and system. In the creations of art we seek for an atmosphere of repose and animation as some counterpoise to the austerity of the realm of law and the sombre self-concentration of thought; we seek for blithe and powerful reality in exchange for the shadow-world of the Idea. And, last of all, the free activity of the imagination is the source of the fair works of art, which in this world of the spirit are even more free than Nature is herself. Not only has art at its service the entire wealth of natural form in all their superabundant variety, but the creative imagination is able inexhaustibly to extend the realm of form by its *own* productions and modifications. In the presence of such an immeasurable depth of inspired creation and its free products, it may not unreasonably be supposed that thought will lose the courage to apprehend such in their apparent *range*, to pronounce its verdict thereon, and to appropriate such beneath its universal formulae.

Science, on the other hand, everyone must admit, is formally bound to occupy itself with thinking which abstracts from the mass of particulars: and for this very reason, from one point of view, the imagination and its contingency and caprice, in other words the organ of artistic activity and enjoyment, is excluded from it. On the other hand, when art gives joyous animation to just this gloomy and arid dryness of the notion, bringing its abstractions and divisions into reconciliation with concrete fact, supplementing with its detail what is wanting to the notion in this respect, even in that case a *purely* contemplative reflection simply removes once more all that has been added, does away with it, conducting the notion once again to that simplicity denuded of positive reality which belongs to it and its shadowland of abstraction. It is also a possible contention that science in respect to content is concerned with what is essentially *necessary*. If our science of Aesthetics places on one side natural beauty, not merely have we apparently made no advance, but rather separated ourselves yet further from what is necessary. The expression *Nature* implies from the first the ideas of *necessity* and *uniformity*, that is to say a constitution which gives every expectation of its proximity and adaptability to scientific inquiry. In mental operations generally, and most of all in the imagination, if contrasted in this respect with Nature, caprice and superiority to every kind of formal restriction, caprice, it is here assumed, is uniquely in its right place, and these at once put out of court the basis of a scientific inquiry.

From each and all these points of view consequently, in its origin, that is to say, in its effect and in its range, fine art, so far from proving itself fitted for scientific effort, rather appears fundamentally to resist the regulative principle of thought, and to be ill-adapted for exact scientific discussion.

Before turning away from such theories to the subject, as we ourselves conceive it, it will be a necessary and preliminary task to discuss the questions and objections raised above.

First, as to the *worthiness* of art to form the object of scientific inquiry, it is no doubt the case that art can be utilized as a mere pastime in the service of pleasure and entertainment, either in the embellishment of our surroundings, the imprinting of a delight-giving surface to the external conditions of life, or the emphasis placed by decoration on other objects. In these respects it is unquestionably no independent or free art, but an art subservient to certain objects. The kind of art, however, which *we* ourselves propose to examine is one which is *free* in its aim and its means. That art in general can serve other objects, and even be merely a pastime, is a relation which it possesses in common with thought itself. From one point of view thought likewise, as science subservient to other ends, can be used in just the same way for finite purposes and means as they chance to crop up, and as such serviceable faculty of science is not self-determined, but determined by something alien to it. But, further, as distinct from such subservience to particular objects, science is raised of its own essential resources in free independence to truth, and exclusively united with its own aims in discovering the true fulfilment in that truth.

Fine art is not art in the true sense of the term until it is also thus free, and its *highest* function is only then satisfied when it has established itself in a sphere which it shares with religion and philosophy, becoming thereby merely one mode and form through which the *Divine*, the profoundest interest of mankind, and spiritual truths of widest range, are brought home to consciousness and expressed. It is in works of art that nations have deposited the richest intuitions and ideas they possess; and not infrequently fine art supplies a key of interpretation to the wisdom and religion of peoples; in the case of many it is the only one. This is an attribute which art shares in common with religion and philosophy, the peculiar distinction in the case of art being that its presentation of the most exalted subject-matter is in sensuous form, thereby bringing them nearer to Nature and her mode of envisagement, that is closer to our sensitive and emotional life. The world, into the profundity of which thought penetrates, is a supersensuous one, a world which to start with is posited as a Beyond in contrast to the immediacy of ordinary conscious life and present sensation. It is the freedom of reflecting consciousness which disengages itself from this immersion in the *'this side'*, or immediacy, in other words sensuous reality and finitude. But the spirit is able, too, to heal the *fracture* which is thus created in its progression. From the wealth of its own resources it brings into being the works of fine art as the primary bond of mediation between that which is exclusively external, sensuous and transitory, and the medium of pure thought, between Nature and its finite reality, and the infinite freedom of a reason which comprehends. Now it was objected that the *element of art* was, if we view it as a whole, of an *unworthy* character, inasmuch as it consisted of appearance and deceptions inseparable from such. Such a contention would of course be justifiable, if we were entitled to assume that appearance had no *locus standi* at all. An appearance or show is, however, essential to actuality. There could be no such thing as truth if it did not appear, or, rather, let itself appear, were it not further true for some *one* thing or person, *for* itself as also *for* spirit. Consequently it cannot be appearance in general against which such an objection can be raised, but the particular mode of its manifestation under which art makes actual what is essentially real and true. If, then, the appearance, in the medium of which art gives determinate existence to its creations, be defined as *deception*, such an objection is in the first instance intelligible if we compare it with the *external world* of a phenomena, and its *immediate* relation to ourselves as material substance, or view it relatively to our own world of emotions, that is our inward sensuous life. Both these are worlds to which in our everyday life, the life, that is, of visible experience, we are accustomed to attach the worth and name of reality, actuality and truth as contrasted with that of art, which fails to possess such reality as we suppose. Now it is just this entire sphere of the empirical world, whether on its personal side or its objective side, which we ought rather to call in a stricter sense than when we apply the term to the world of art, merely a show or appearance, and an even more unyielding form of deception. It is only beyond the immediacy of emotional life and that world of external objects that we shall discover reality in any true sense of the term. Nothing is actually real but that which is actual in its own independent right and substance, that which is at once of the substance of Nature and of spirit, which, while it is actually *here* in present and determinate existence, yet retains under such limitation an essential and self-concentred being, and only in virtue of such is truly real. The predominance of these universal powers is precisely that which art accentuates and manifests. In the external and soul-world of ordinary experience we have also no doubt this essence of actuality, but in the chaotic congeries of particular detail, encumbered by the immediacy of sensuous envisagement, and every kind of caprice of condition, event, character, and so forth. Now it is just the show and deception of this false and evanescent world which art disengages from the veritable significance of phenomena to which we have referred, implanting in the same a reality of more exalted rank born of spirit. The phenomena of art therefore are not merely not appearance and nothing more; we are justified in ascribing to them, as contrasted with the realities of our ordinary life, an actually higher reality and more veritable existence.

If, however, it is in contrast with philosophic thought and religious and ethical principles, that the mode of appearance of the shapes of art, is described as a deception, there is certainly this in support of the view that the mode of revelation attained by a content in the realm of thought is the truest reality. In comparison, nevertheless, with the appearance of immediate sensuous existence and that of historical narration, the show of art possesses the advantage that, in its own virtue, it points beyond itself, directing us to a somewhat spiritual, which it seeks to envisage to the conceptive spirit. Immediate appearance, on the contrary, does not give itself out to be thus illusive, but rather to be the true and real, though as a matter of fact such truth is contaminated and obstructed by the immediately sensuous medium. The hard rind of Nature and the everyday world offer more difficulty to the spirit in breaking through to the Idea than do the products of art.

In all these respects art is and remains for us, on the side of its highest possibilities, a thing of the past. Herein it has further lost its genuine truth and life, and is rather transported to our world of *ideas* than is able to maintain its former necessity and its superior place in reality. What is now stimulated in us by works of art is, in addition to the fact of immediate enjoyment, our judgment. In other words we subject the content, and the means of presentation of the work of art, and the suitability and unsuitability of both, to the contemplation of our thought. A *science* of art is therefore a far more urgent necessity in our own days than in times in which art as art sufficed by itself alone to give complete satisfaction. We are invited by art to contemplate it reflectively, not, that is to say, with the object of recreating such art, but in order to ascertain scientifically its nature.

In doing our best to accept such an invitation we are confronted with the objection already adverted to, that even assuming that art is a subject adapted for philosophical investigation in a general way, yet it unquestionably is not so adapted to the systematic procedure of science. Such an objection, however, implies to start with the false notion that we can have a philosophical inquiry which is at the same time unscientific. In reply to such a point I can only here state summarily my opinion, that whatever ideas other people may have of philosophy and philosophizing, I myself conceive philosophical inquiry of any sort or kind to be inseparable from the methods of science. The function of philosophy is to examine subject-matter in the light of the principle of necessity, not, it is true, merely in accordance with its subjective necessity or external co-ordination, classification, and so forth; it has rather to unfold and demonstrate the object under review out of the necessity of its own intimate nature. Until this essential process is made explicit the scientific quality of such an inquiry is absent. In so far, however, as the objective necessity of an object subsists essentially in its logical and metaphysical nature the isolated examination of art may in such as case, at any rate, or rather inevitably, must be carried forward with a certain relaxation of scientific stringency. For art is based upon many assumptions, part of which relate to its content, part to its material or conceptive medium, in virtue of which art is never far from the borders of contingency and caprice. Consequently it is only relatively to the essential and ideal progression of its content and its means of expression that we are able to recall with advantage the formative principle of its necessity.

The objection that works of fine art defy the examination of scientific thought, because they originate in the unregulated world of imagination and temperament, and assert their effect exclusively on the emotions and the fancy with a complexity and variety which defies exact analysis, raises a difficulty which still carries genuine weight behind it. As a matter of fact the beauty of art does appear in a form which is expressly to be contrasted with abstract thought, a form which it is compelled to disturb in order to exercise its own activity in its own way. Such a result is simply a corollary of the thesis that reality anywhere and everywhere, whether the life of Nature or spirit, is defaced and slain by its comprehension; that so far from being brought more close to us by the comprehension of thinking, it is only by this means that it is in the complete sense removed apart from us, so that in his attempt to grasp through thought as a means the nature of life, man rather renders nugatory this very aim. An exhaustive discussion of the subject is here impossible; we propose merely to indicate the point of view from which the removal of this difficulty or impossibility and incompatibility might be effected.

It will at least be readily admitted that spirit is capable of self-contemplation, and of possessing a consciousness, and indeed one that implies a power of thought co-extensive with itself and everything which originates from itself. It is, in fact, precisely thought, the process of thinking, which constitutes the most intimate and essential nature of spirit. It is in this thinking-consciousness over itself and its products, despite all the freedom and caprice such may otherwise and indeed must invariably posses—assuming only spirit to be veritably pregnant therein—that spirit exhibits the activity congenial to its essential nature. Art and the creations of art, being works which originate in and are begotten of the spirit, are themselves stamped with the hall-mark of spirit, even though the mode of its presentation accept for its own the phenomenal guise of sensuous reality, permeating as it does the sensuous substance with intelligence. Viewed in this light art is placed from the first nearer to spirit and its thought than the purely external and unintelligent Nature. In the products of art spirit is exclusively dealing with that which is its own. And although works of art are not thought and notion simply as such, but an evolution of the notion out of itself, an alienation of the same in the direction of sensuous being, yet for all that the might of the thinking spirit is discovered not merely in its ability to grasp itself in its most native form as pure thinking, but also, and as completely, to recognize itself in its self-divestment in the medium of emotion and the sensuous, to retain the grasp of itself in that 'other' which it transforms but is not, transmuting the alien factor into thought-expression, and by so doing recovering it to itself. And moreover in this active and frequent relation to that 'other' than itself the reflective spirit is not in any way untrue to itself. We have here no oblivion or surrender of itself; neither is it so impotent as to be unable to comprehend what is differentiated from that other; what it actually does is to grasp in the notion both itself and its opposite. For the notion is the universal, which maintains itself in its particularizations, which covers in its grasp both itself and its 'other', and consequently contains the power and energy to cancel the very alienation into which it passes. For this reason the work of art, in which thought divests itself of itself, belongs to the realm of comprehending thought; and spirit, by subjecting it to scientific contemplation, thereby simply satisfies its most essential nature. For inasmuch as thought is its essence and notion, it can only ultimately find such a satisfaction after passing all the products of its activity through the alembic of rational thought, and in this way making them for the first time in very truth part of its own substance. But though art, as we shall eventually see with yet more distinctness, is far indeed from being the highest form of spirit, it is only in the philosophy of art that it comes into all that it may justly claim.

It is upon grounds such as these that we are also able to discover a track adapted to critical reflection through the apparently endless vistas of artistic creations and shapes.

We have now, I trust, by way of prelude, succeeded in restricting the content of our science on the lines of definition proposed. We have made it clear that neither is fine art unworthy of philosophical study, nor is such a philosophical study incapable of accepting as an object of its cognition the essence of fine art.

SCIENTIFIC METHODS WHICH APPLY TO THE BEAUTIFUL AND ART

If we now investigate the required *mode* of such scientific investigation, we are here again face to face with two contradictory modes of handling the subject, each of which appears to exclude the other and to permit us to arrive at no satisfactory result.

On the one hand we *observe* the science of art, merely so to speak, from an external point of view busying itself with actual works of art, cataloguing them in a history of art, drawing up a sort of commentary upon extant works, or propounding theories which are intended to supply the general points of view for artistic criticism no less than artistic production.

On the other hand we find science wholly giving itself up in its independence and self-assured to the contemplation of the beautiful, offering generalizations which do not concern the specific characteristics of a work of art, producing in short an abstract philosophy of the beautiful.

THE EMPIRICAL METHOD

(a) With regard to the first mentioned method of study, the starting-point of which is the *empirical* study of definite *facts,* such is the path everyone must tread who means to study art at all. And just as everyone nowadays, even though he does not actually concern himself with physical science, yet deems it indispensable to his intellectual equipment to have some kind of knowledge of the principles of that science, so too it is generally considered more or less essential to any man of real cultivation, that he should possess some general knowledge of art; and indeed the pretension to be ranked as dilettante, or even as genuine *connoisseur,* meets with comparatively few exceptions.

If however knowledge of this kind is really to claim the rank of *connoisseurship* of the first class it must be both varied in its character and of the widest range. It is an indispensable condition to such that it should possess an accurate knowledge of the wellnigh limitless field of particular works of art both of ancient and modern times, some of which have already disappeared, while others are only to be found in distant countries or portions of the globe, and which it is the misfortune of our situation to be unable to inspect. Add to this that every work of art belongs to *one* age, *one* nationality, and depends upon particular historical or other ends and ideas. On account of this it is indispensable that the finest type of art-scholarship should have at its command not merely historical knowledge of a wide range, but knowledge that is highly specialized. In other words, a work of art is associated with particular detail in a peculiar sense, and a specific treatment is imperative to the comprehension and interpretation of it. And in conclusion this connoisseurship of the finest class does not merely imply like every other a retentive memory, but also a keen imaginative sense, in order to hold clearly before the spirit the images of such artistic representations in all their characteristic lines, and above all, to have them ready for comparison with other works of art.

This then may be accepted as the first method of art study. It starts from the particular work which we have before us.

ABSTRACT REFLECTION

(b) The method or point of view to be contrasted with this, in other words an entirely theoretical reflection, which is concerned to cognize the beautiful as such from its own intrinsic wealth, and to penetrate to the idea of it, is essentially distinct from the first method. As is well known, Plato was the first to demand of philosophical inquiry in a profounder sense, that objects should not be cognized in their *particularity,* but in their *universality,* in their generic type, their essential being and its explicit manifestation. He maintained that this true essence did not consist in *particular* actions which were good, in particular true opinions, handsome men or beautiful works of art, but in *goodness, beauty,* and *truth* in their universality. Now if in fact the beautiful ought to be cognized according to its essence and notion, this can only be effected by means of the thinking notion, by means of which the logical and metaphysical nature of the *Idea as such,* as also of that of the particular *Idea of the beautiful* enters into the thinking consciousness. But the consideration of the beautiful in its self-independence and its idea may readily once more become an abstract metaphysics; and even though Plato is accepted as founder and pioneer, the Platonic abstraction no longer supplies all we require, not even for the logical Idea of the beautiful; we are bound to grasp this idea more profoundly and more in the concrete. The emptiness of content which clings to the Platonic Idea, no longer satisfies the richer philosophical requirements of the spirit today. It is no doubt the case that we also in the philosophy of art must make the Idea of the beautiful our starting point; but it is by no means inevitable that we should adhere to the Platonic ideas in their abstraction, ideas from which the philosophy of the beautiful merely dates its origins.

THE PHILOSOPHICAL IDEA OF ARTISTIC BEAUTY

(c) The philosophical idea of the beautiful to indicate at any rate its true nature provisionally, must contain both extremes which we have described mediated in itself. It must combine, that is to say, metaphysical universality with the determinate content of real particularity. It is only by this means that it is grasped in its essential no less than explicit truth. For on the one hand it is then, as contrasted with the sterility of one-sided reflection, fruit-bearing out of its own wealth. It is its function, in consonance with its own notion, to develop into a totality of definite qualities, and this essential conception itself, no less than its detailed explication, comprises the necessary coherence of its particular features as also of the progress and transition of one phase thereof into another. On the other hand,

these particulars into which the passage is made essentially carry the universality and essentiality of the fundamental notion as the particulars of which they appear. The modes of inquiry hitherto discussed lack both these aspects, and for this reason it is only the notion, as above formulated, in its completeness, which conducts us to definitive principles which are substantive, necessary, and self-contained in their completeness.

THE NOTION OF THE BEAUTY OF ART

What in the first instance is known to us under current conceptions of a work of art may be subsumed under the three following determinations:

(a) A work of art is no product of Nature. It is brought into being through the agency of man.
(b) It is created essentially *for* man; and, what is more, it is to a greater or less degree delivered from a sensuous medium, and addressed to his *senses*.
(c) It contains an *end* bound up with it.

THE ART-WORK IS A CREATION OF HUMAN ACTIVITY

(a) With regard to the first point, that a work of art is a product of human activity, an inference has been drawn from this *(i)* that such an activity, being the conscious production of an external object can also be *known* and *divulged*, and learned and reproduced by others. For that which one is able to effect, another—such is a notion—is able to effect or to imitate, when he has once simply mastered the way of doing it. In short we have merely to assume an acquaintance with the rules of art-production universally shared, and anybody may then, if he cares to do so, give effect to executive ability of the same type, and produce works of art. It is out of reasoning of this kind that the above-mentioned theories, with their provision of rules, and their prescriptions formulated for practical acceptance, have arisen. Unfortunately that which is capable of being brought into effect in accordance with suggestions of this description can only be something formally regular and mechanical. For only that which is mechanical is of so exterior a type that only an entirely empty effort of will and dexterity is required to accept it among our working conceptions, and forthwith to carry it out; an effort, in fact, which is not under the necessity to contribute out of its own resources anything concrete such as is quite outside the prescriptive power of such general rules.

This is apparent with most vividness when precepts of this kind are not limited to what is purely external and mechanical but extend their pretensions to the activity of the artist in the sense that implies wealth of significance and intelligence. In this field our rules pass off to purely indefinite generalities, such as 'the theme ought to be interesting, and each individual person must speak as is appropriate to his status, age, sex and situation'. But if rules are really to suffice for such a purpose their directions ought to be formulated with such directness of detail that, without any further cooperation of spirit, they could be executed precisely in the manner they are prescribed. Such rules being, in respect to this content, abstract, clearly and entirely fall short of their pretension of being able to complete the artistic consciousness. Artistic production is not a formal activity in accordance with a series of definitions; it is, as an activity of soul, constrained to work out of its own wealth, and to bring before the spirit's eye a wholly other and far richer content, and a more embracing and unique creation than ever can be thus prescribed. In particular cases such rules may prove of assistance, in so far, that is, as they contain something really definite and consequently useful for practice. But even here their guidance will only apply to conditions wholly external.

(ii) This above indicated tendency has consequently been wholly given up; but writers in doing so have only fallen as unreservedly into the opposite extreme. A work of art came to be looked upon, and so far rightly, as no longer the product of an activity *shared by all men*, but rather as a creation of a spirit gifted in an extraordinary degree. A spirit of this type has in view *merely* to give free vent to its peculiar endowment, regarded as a specific natural power. It has to free itself absolutely from a pursuit of rules of universal application, as also from any admixture of conscious reflection with its creative and, as thus viewed, wholly instinctive powers, or rather it should be on its guard therefrom, the assumption being that such an exercise of conscious thought can only act on its creations as an infection and a taint. Agreeably to such a view the work of art has been heralded as the product of *talent* and *genius*; and it is mainly the aspect of natural gift inseparable from of the ordinary conception of talent and genius, which has been emphasized. There is to some extent real truth in this. Talent is specific, genius universal capacity. With neither of these can a man endow himself *simply* by the exercise of his self-conscious activity. We shall consider this at greater length in a subsequent chapter.

In the present context we would merely draw attention to the false assumption in this view that in artistic production every kind of self-reflection upon the artist's own activity was regarded as not merely superfluous, but actually injurious. In such a view the process of creation by talent or genius simply is taken to be a general *state*; or we may define it more precisely as a condition of inspiration. To such a condition, it is said, genius is in some measure exalted by the subject-matter itself; it is also to some extent voluntarily able to place itself under such a condition, a process of self-inhibition in which the genial service of the champagne bottle is not forgotten.

The real and indeed sole point to maintain as essential is the thesis that although artistic talent and genius essentially implies an element of natural power, yet it is equally indispensable that it should be thoughtfully cultivated, that reflection should be brought to bear on the particular way it is exercised, and that it should be also kept alive with use and practice in actual work. The fact is that an important aspect of the creating process is merely facility in the use of a medium; that is to say, a work of art possesses a purely technical side, which extends to the borders of mere handicraft. This is most obviously the case in architecture and sculpture, less so in painting and music, least of all in poetry. A facility here is not assisted at all by inspiration; what solely indispensable is reflection, industry and practice. Such technical skill an artist simply *must* possess in order that he may be master over the external material, and not be thwarted by its obstinacy.

Add to this that the more exalted the rank of an artist the more profoundly ought he to portray depths of soul and spirit; and these are not to be known by flashlight, but are exclusively to be sounded, if at all, by the direction of the man's own intelligence on the world of souls and the objective world. In this respect, therefore, once more *study* is the means whereby the artist brings to consciousness such a content, and appropriates the material and structure of his conceptions. At the same time no doubt one art will require such a conscious reception and cognitive mastery of the content in question more than another. Music, for example, which has exclusively to deal with the entirely undefined motion of the soul within, with the musical tones of that which is, relatively, feeling denuded of positive thought, has little or no need to bring home to consciousness the substance of intellectual conception. For this very reason musical talent declares itself as a rule in very early youth, when the head is still empty and the emotions have barely had a flutter; it has, in fact, attained real distinction at a time in the artist's life when both intelligence and life are practically without experience. And for the matter of that we often enough see very great accomplishment in musical composition and execution hung together with considerable indigence of spirit and character. It is quite another matter in the case of poetry. What is of main importance here is a presentation of our humanity rich in subject-matter and reflective power, of its profounder interests, and of the forces which move it. Here at least spirit and heart must themselves be richly and profoundly disciplined by life, experience, and thought before genius itself can bring into being the fruit that is ripe, the content that has substance, and is essentially consummate. The early productions of Goethe and Schiller are characterized by an immaturity, we may even call it a rawness and barbarity, which really are appalling. This phenomenon, that in the majority of those experiments we find a preponderating mass of features which are absolutely prosaic, or at least uninspired and commonplace, is a main objection to the ordinary notion that inspiration is inseparable from youth and its sirocco season. These two men of genius were the first beyond question to give our nation true works of poetry, are, in fact, our national poets; but for all that it was only their mature manhood, which made it a present of creations profound, sterling of their kind, creations of genuine inspiration, and no less technically complete in their artistic form. We naturally recall the case of the veteran Homer, who only composed and uttered his immortal songs in his old age.

(iii) A third view, held relatively to the idea of a work of art as a product of human activity, concerns the position of such towards the phenomena of Nature. The natural tendency of ordinary thinking in this respect is to assume that the product of human art is of subordinate rank to the works of Nature. The work of art possesses no feeling of its own; it is not through and through a living thing, but, regarded as an external object, is a dead thing. It is usual to regard that which is alive of higher worth than what is dead. We may admit, of course, that the work of art is not in itself capable of movement and alive. The living, natural thing is, whether looked at within or without, an organization with the life-purpose of such worked out into the minutest detail. The work of art merely attains to the show of animation on its surface. Below this it is ordinary stone, wood, or canvas, or in the case of poetry idea, the medium of such being speech and letters. But this element of external existence is not that which makes a work a creation of fine art. A work of art is only truly such in so far as originating in the human spirit, it continues to belong to the soil from which it sprang, has received, in short, the baptism of the spirit and soul of man, and only presents that which is fashioned in consonance with such a sacrament. An interest vital to man, the spiritual values which the single event, one individual character, one action possesses in its devolution and final issue, is seized in the work of art and emphasized with greater purity and clarity than is possible on the ground of ordinary reality where human art is not. And for this reason the work of art is of higher rank than any product of Nature whatever, which has not submitted to this passage through the spirit. In virtue of the emotion and insight, for example, in the atmosphere of which a landscape is portrayed by the art of painting, this creation of the human spirit assumes a higher rank than the purely natural landscape. Everything which partakes of spirit is better than anything begotten of mere Nature. However this may be, the fact remains that no purely natural existence is able, as art is, to represent divine ideals.

And further, all that the spirit borrows from its own ideal content it is able, even in the direction of external existence, to endow with permanence. The individual living thing on the contrary is transitory; it vanishes and is unstable in its external aspect. The work of art persists. At the same time it is not mere continuation, but rather the form and pressure thereon of the mintage of soul-life which constitutes its true pre-eminence as contrasted with Nature's reality.

(iv) Assuming, then, that the work of art is a creation of man in the sense that it is the offspring of spirit or spirit we have still a further question in conclusion, which will help us to draw a more profound inference still from our previous discussion. That question is, 'What is the human *need* which stimulates art-production?' On the one hand the artistic activity may be regarded as the mere play of accident, or human conceits, which might just as well as be left alone as attempted. For, it may be urged, there are other and better means for carrying into effect the aims of art, and man bears within himself higher and more weighty interests, than art is capable of satisfying. In contrast to such a view art appears to originate in a higher impulse, and to satisfy more elevated needs, nay, at certain times the highest and most absolute of all, being, as it has been, united to the most embracing views of entire epochs and nations upon the constitution of the world and the nature of their religion.

This inquiry, however, concerning a necessity for art which shall not be merely contingent, but absolute, we are not as yet able to answer with completeness; it demands, in fact, a concreter mode of exposition than is compatible with the form of this introduction. We must accordingly deem it sufficient for the present merely to establish the following points.

The universal and absolute want from which art on its side of essential form arises originates in the fact that man is a *thinking* consciousness, in other words that he renders explicit to *himself*, and from his own substance, what he is and all in fact that exists. The objects of Nature exist exclusively in immediacy and *once for all*. Man, on the contrary, as spirit *reduplicates* himself. He is, to start with, an object of Nature as other objects; but in addition to this, and no less truly, he exists *for himself*; he observes himself, makes himself present to his imagination and thought, and only in virtue of this active power of self-realization is he actually mind or spirit. This consciousness of himself man acquires in a twofold way; in the *first* instance *theoretically*. This is so in so far as he is under a constraint to bring himself in his own inner life to consciousness—all which moves in the human heart, all that surges up and strives therein—and generally, so far as he is impelled to make himself an object of perception and conception, to fix for himself definitively that which thought discovers as essential being and in all that he summons out of himself, no less than in that which is received from without, to recognize only himself. And *secondly*, this realization is effected through a *practical* activity. In other words man possesses an impulse to assert himself in that which is presented him in immediacy, in that which is at hand as an external something to himself, and by doing so at the same time once more to recognize himself therein. This purpose he achieved by the alteration he effects in such external objects, upon which he imprints the seal of his inner life, rediscovering in them thereby the features of his own determinate nature. And man does all this, in order that he may as a free agent divest the external world of its stubborn alienation from himself—and in order that he may enjoy in the configuration of objective fact an external reality simply of himself. The very first impulse of the child implies in essentials this practical process of deliberate change in external fact. A boy throws stones into the stream, and then looks with wonder at the circles which follow in the water, regarding them as a result in which he sees something of his own doing. This human need runs through the most varied phenomena up to that particular form of self-reproduction in the external fact which is presented us in human art. And it is not merely in relation to external objects that man acts thus. He treats himself, that is, his natural form, in a similar manner: he will not permit it to remain as he finds it; he alters it deliberately. This is the rational ground of all ornament and decoration, though it may be as barbarous, tasteless, entirely disfiguring, nay, as injurious as the crushing of the feet of Chinese ladies, or the slitting of ears and lips. For it is among the really cultured alone that a change of figure, behaviour, and every mode and manner of self-expression will issue in harmony with the dictates of mental elevation.

This universal demand for artistic expression is based on the rational impulse in man's nature to exalt both the world of his soul experience and that of Nature for himself into the conscious embrace of spirit as an object in which he rediscovers himself. He satisfies the demand of this spiritual freedom by making explicit to his *inner* life all that exists, no less than from the further point of view giving a realized *external* embodiment to the self made thus explicit. And by this reduplication of what is his own he places before the vision and within the cognition of himself and others what is within him. This is the free rationality of man, in which art as also all action and knowledge originates. We shall investigate at a later stage the specific need for art as compared with that for other political and ethical action, or that for religious ideas and scientific knowledge.

THE ART-WORK IS ADDRESSED TO HUMAN SENSE

(b) We have hitherto considered the work of art under the aspect that it is fashioned by man; we will now pass over to the second part of our definition, that it is produced for his *sense-apprehension*, and consequently is to a more or less degree under obligations to a sensuous medium.

(i) This reflection has been responsible for the inference that the function of fine art is to arouse feeling, more precisely the feeling which suits us—that is, pleasant feeling. From such a point of view writers have converted the investigation of fine art into a treatise on the emotions and asked what kind of feelings art ought to excite—take fear, for example, and compassion—with the further question how such can be regarded as pleasant, how, in short, the contemplation of a misfortune can bring satisfaction. A discussion of this kind, however, did not carry the problem far. Feeling is the undefined obscure region of spiritual life. What is felt remains cloaked in the form of the separate personal experience under its most abstract persistence; and for this reason the distinctions of feeling are wholly abstract; they are not distinctions which apply to the subject-matter itself. The feeling throughout remains a purely subjective state which belongs to me, one in which the concrete fact vanishes, as though contracted to a vanishing point in the most abstract of all spheres. For this reason an inquiry over the nature of the emotions which art ought or ought not to arouse, comes simply to a standstill in the undefined; it is an investigation which deliberately abstracts from genuine content and its concrete substance and notion. Reflection upon feeling is satisfied with the observation of the personal emotional state and its singularity, instead of penetrating and sounding the matter for study, in other words the work of art, and in doing so bidding good-bye to the wholly subjective state and its conditions. In feeling, however, it is just this subjective state void of content which is not merely accepted, but becomes the main thing; and that is precisely why people are so proud of having emotions. And for no other reason that is why such an investigation is tedious owing to its indefinite nature and emptiness, and even repellant in its attention to trivial personal idiosyncrasies.

(ii) Inasmuch, however, as the work of art is not merely concerned with exciting

some kind of emotion or other—for this is an object it would share without any valid distinction with eloquence, historical composition, religious edification and much else—but is only a work of art in so far as it is beautiful, it occurred to reflective spirits to discover a *specific feeling for beauty*, and a distinct *sense-faculty* correspondent with it. In such an inquiry it soon became clear that a sense of this kind was no definite and mere instinct rigidly fixed by Nature, which was able by itself and independently to distinguish the beautiful. As a consequence the demand was made for *culture* as a condition precedent to such a sense, and the sense of beauty as thus cultivated was called *taste*, which, albeit an instructed apprehension and discovery of the beautiful, was none the less assumed to persist in the character of immediate feeling.

(iii) Following the above observations upon the modes of inquiry which were suggested by that aspect of a work of art in which, as itself an object with a material medium, it possessed an essential relation to man as himself receptive through sense, we will now examine this point of view in its more essential connection with art itself. We propose to do this partly (α) in respect to the art-product viewed as an object, partly (β) as regards the personal characteristics of the artist, his genius, talent, and so forth. We do not, however, propose to enter into matter which can in this connection exclusively proceed from the knowledge of art according to its universal concept. The truth is we are not as yet in the full sense on scientific ground; we have merely reached the province of external reflection.

(α) There is no question, then, that a work of art is presented to sensuous apprehension. It is submitted to the emotional sense, whether outer or inner, to sensuous perception and the imaged sense, precisely as the objective world is so presented around us, or as is our own inward sensitive nature. Even a speech, for example, may be addressed to the sensuous imagination and feeling. Notwithstanding this fact, however, the work of art is not exclusively directed to the *sensuous* apprehension, viewed, that is, as an object materially conditioned. Its position is of the nature, that along with its sensuous presentation it is fundamentally addressed to the *spirit*. The spirit is intended to be affected by it and to receive some kind of satisfaction in it.

This function of the work of art at once makes it clear how it is that it is in no way intended to be a natural product or, on the side where it impinges on Nature, to possess the living principle of Nature. This, at least, is a fact whether the natural product is ranked lower or higher than a *mere* work of art, as people are accustomed to express themselves in the tone of depreciation.

In other words the sensuous aspect of a work of art has a right to determinate existence only in so far as it exists for the human spirit, not, however, in so far as itself, as a material object, exists for itself independently.

If we examine more closely in what way the sensuous *materia* is presented to man we find that what is so can be placed under various relations to the spirit.

(αα) The lowest in grade and that least compatible with relation to intelligence is purely sensuous sensation. It consists primarily in mere looking, listening, just as in times of mental overstrain it may often be a relaxation to go about without thought, and merely listen and have a look round. The spirit, however, does not rest in the mere apprehension of external objects through sight and hearing; it makes them objective to its own inward nature, which thereupon is impelled itself to give effect to itself in these things as a further step under a sensuous mode, in other words, it relates itself to them as *desire*. In this appetitive relation to the external world man, as a sensuous particular thing, stands in a relation of opposition to things in general as in the same way particulars. He does not address himself to them with open mind and the universal ideas of thought; he retains an isolated position, with its personal impulses and interests, relatively to objects as fixed in their obduracy as himself, and makes himself at home in them by using them, or eating them up altogether, and, in short, gives effect to his self-satisfaction by the sacrifice he makes of them. In this negative relation desire requires for itself not merely the superficial show of external objects, but the actual things themselves in their material concrete existence. Mere pictures of the wood, which it seeks to make use of, or of the animals, which it hopes to eat up, would be of no service to desire. Just as little is it possible for desire to suffer the object to remain in its freedom; its craving is just this to force it to annihilate this self-subsistency and freedom of external facts, and to demonstrate that these things are only there to be destroyed and devoured. But at the same time the particular person is neither himself free, begirt as he is by the particular limited and transitory interests of his desires, for his definite acts do not proceed from the essential universality and rationality of his will, neither is he free relatively to the external world, for desire remains essentially determined by things and related to them.

This relation, then, of desire is not that in which man is related to the work of art. He suffers it to exist in its free independence as an object; he associates himself with it without any craving of this kind, rather as with an object reflective of himself, which exists solely for the contemplative faculty of spirit. For this reason, as we have said, the work of art, although it possesses sensuous existence, does not require sensuous concrete existence, nor yet the animated life of such objects. Or, rather, we should add, it *ought* not to remain on such a level, in so far as its true function is exclusively to satisfy spiritual interests, and to shut the door on all approach to mere desire. Hence we can understand how it is that practical desire rates the particular works of Nature in the organic or inorganic world, which are at its service, more highly than works of art, which are obviously useless in this sense, and only contribute enjoyment to other capacities of man's spirit.

(ββ) A second mode under which the externally present comes before the conscious subject is, as contrasted with the single sensuous perception and active desire, the purely theoretical relation to the *intelligence*. The theoretic contemplation of objects has no interest in consuming the same in their particularity and satisfying or maintaining itself through the sense by their means; its object is to attain a knowledge of them in their *universality*, to seek out their ideal nature and principle, to comprehend them according to their notional idea. Consequently this contemplative interest is content to leave the particular things as they are, and stands aloof from them in their objective singularity, which is not the object of such a faculty's investigation. For the rational intelligence is not a property of the particular person in the sense that desire is so; it appertains to his singularity as being itself likewise essentially universal. So long as it persists in this relation of universality to the objects in question, it is his reason in its universal potency which is attempting to discover *itself* in Nature, and thereby the inward or essential being of the natural objects, which his sensuous existence does not present under its mode of immediacy, although such existence is founded therein. This interest of contemplation, the satisfaction of which is the task of *science*, is, however, shared in this scientific form just as little by art as it shared in the common table of those impulses of the purely practical desire. Science can, it is true, take as its point of departure the sensuous thing in its singularity, and possess itself of some conception, how this individual thing is present in its specific colour or form. But for all that this isolated thing of sense as such possesses no further relation to spirit, inasmuch as the interest of intelligence makes for the universal, the law, the thought and notion of the object, and consequently not only does it forsake it in its immediate singularity, but it actually transforms it within the region of idea, converting a concrete object of sense into an abstract subject-matter of thought, that is converting it into something other than the same object of its sensuous perception actually was. The artistic interest does not follow such a process, and is distinct from that of science for this reason. The contemplation of art restricts its interest simply in the way in which the work of art, as external object, in the directness of its definition, and in the singularity wherein it appears to sense, is manifested in all its features of colour, form, and sound, or as a single isolated vision of the whole; it does not go so far beyond the immediately received objective character as to propose, as is the case with science, the ideal or conceptive thinking of this particular objectivity under the terms of the rational and universal notion which underlies it.

The interest of art, therefore, is distinguishable from the practical interest of desire in virtue of the fact that it suffers its object to remain in its free independence, whereas desire applies it, even to the point of destruction, to its own uses. The contemplation of art, on the other hand, differs from that of a scientific intelligence in an analogous way in virtue of the fact that it cherishes an interest for the object in its isolated existence, and is not concerned to transform the same into terms of universal thought and notion.

(γγ) It follows, then, that, though the sensuous *materia* is unquestionably present in a work of art, it is only as surface or *show* of the sensuous that it is under any necessity to appear. In the sensuous appearance of the work of art it is neither the concrete material stuff, the empirically perceived completeness and extension of the internal organism which is the object of desire, nor is it the universal thought of pure ideality, which in either case the spirit seeks for. Its aim is the sensuous presence, which, albeit suffered to persist in its sensuousness, is equally entitled to be delivered from the framework of its purely material substance. Consequently, as compared with the immediately envisaged and incorporated object of Nature, the sensuous presence in the work of art is transmuted to mere semblance or *show*, and the work of art occupies a midway ground, with the directly perceived objective world on one side and the ideality of pure thought on the other. It is not as yet pure thought, but, despite the element of sensuousness which adheres to it, it is no longer purely material existence, in the sense at least that stones, plants, and organic life are such. The sensuous element in a work of art is rather itself somewhat of ideal intension, which, however, as not being actually the ideal medium of thought, is still externally presented at the same time as an object. This semblance of the sensuous presents itself to the spirit externally as the form, visible appearance, and harmonious vibration of things. This is always assuming that it suffers the objects to remain in their freedom as objective facts, and does not seek to penetrate into their inward essence by abstract thought, for by doing so they would (as above explained) entirely cease to exist for it in their external singularity.

For this reason the sensuous aspect of art is only related to the two *theoretical* senses of *sight* and *hearing*; smell, on the other hand, taste, and the feeling of touch are excluded from the springs of art's enjoyment. Smell, taste, and touch come into contact with matter simply as such, and with the immediate sensuous qualities of the same; smell with the material volatization through the air; taste with the material dissolution of substance, and touch or mere bodily feeling with qualities such as heat, coldness, smoothness, and so forth. On this account these senses cannot have to do with the objects of art, which ought to subsist in their actual and very independence, admitting of no purely sensuous or rather physical relation. The pleasant for such senses is not the beauty of art. Thus art on its sensuous side brings before us deliberately merely a shadow-world of shapes, tones, and imaged conceptions, and it is quite beside the point to maintain that it is simply a proof of the impotence and limitations of man that he can only present us with the surface of the physical world, mere *schemata*, when he calls into being his creative works. In art these sensuous shapes and tones are not offered as exclusively for themselves and their form to our direct vision. They are presented with the intent to secure in such shape satisfaction for higher and more spiritual interests, inasmuch as they are mighty to summon an echo and response in the human spirit evoked from all depths of its conscious life. In this way the sensuous is *spiritualized* in art, or, in other words, the life of *spirit* comes to dwell in it under sensuous guise.

(β) For this reason, however, a product of art is only possible in so far as it has received its passage through the spirit, and has originated from the productive activity of spirit. This brings us to another question we have to answer, and it is this 'How is the sensuous or material aspect, which is imperative as a condition of art, operative in the artist as conjoined to his personal productive activity?' Now this mode or manner of artistic production contains, as an activity personal to the artist, in essentials just the same determinants which we found posited in the work of art. It must be a spiritual activity, which, however, at the same time possesses in itself the element of sensuousness and immediacy. It is neither, on the one hand, purely mechanical work, such as is purely unconscious facility in sleight of hand upon physical objects, or a stereotyped activity according to teachable rule of thumb; nor, on the other hand, is it a productive process of science, which tends to pass from sensuous things to abstract ideas and thoughts, or is active exclusively in the medium of pure thought. In contrast to these the two aspects of mental idea and sensuous material must in the artistic product be united. For example, it would be possible in the case of poetical compositions to attempt to embody what was the subject-matter in the form of prosaic thought in the first instance, and only after doing so to attach to the same imaginative ideas rhymes and so on, so that as a net result such imagery would be appendant to the abstract reflections as so much ornament and decoration. An attempt of this kind, however, could only lead us to a poor sort of poetry, for in it we should have operative a twofold kind of activity in its *separation*, which in the activity of genuine artistic work only holds good in inseparable unity. It is this true kind of creative activity which forms what is generally described as the artistic *imagination*.

A consequence of this is, that imagination of this type is based in a certain sense on a natural gift, a general talent for it, as we say, because its creative power essentially implies an aspect of sense presentation. It is no doubt not unusual to speak in the same way of scientific 'talent'. The sciences, however, merely presuppose the general capacity for thought, which does not possess, as imagination does, together with its intellectual activity, a reference to the concrete testimony of Nature, but rather precisely abstracts from the activity that form in which we find it in Nature. It would be, therefore, truer to the mark if we said there is no specific scientific talent in the sense of a purely natural endowment. Imagination, on the other hand, combines within it a mode of instinct-like creativeness. In other words the essential plasticity and material element in a work of art is subjectively present in the artist as part of his native disposition and impulse, and as his unconscious activity belongs in part to that which man receives straight from Nature. No doubt the entire talent and genius of an individual is not wholly exhausted by that we describe as natural capability. The creation of art is quite as much a spiritual and self-cognized process; but for all that we affirm that its spirituality contains an element of plastic or configurative facility which Nature confers on it. For this reason, though almost anybody can reach a certain point in art, yet, in order to pass beyond this—and it is here that the art in question really begins—a talent for art which is inborn and of a higher order altogether is indispensable.

Considered simply as a natural basis a talent of this kind asserts itself for the most part in early youth, and is manifested in the restless persistency, ever intent with vivacity and alertness, to create artistic shapes in some particular sensuous medium, and to make this mode of expression and utterance the unique one or the one of main importance and most suitable. And thus also a virtuosity up to a certain point in the technique of art which is arrived at with ease is a sign of inborn talent. A sculptor finds everything convertible into plastic shape, and from early days takes to modelling clay; and so on generally whatever men of such innate powers have in their minds, whatever excites and moves their souls, becomes forthwith a plastic figure, a drawing, a melody, or a poem.

(γ) Thirdly, and in conclusion: the *content* of art is also in some respects borrowed from the objective world perceived in sense, that is Nature; or, in any case, if the content is also of a spiritual character, it can only be grasped in such a way, that the spiritual element therein, as human relations, for example, are displayed in the form of phenomena which possess objective reality.

THE END OR INTEREST OF ART

(c) There is yet another question to solve, namely, what the interest or the *End* is, which man proposes to himself in the creation of the content embodied by a work of art. This was, in fact, the third point of view, which we propounded relatively to the art-product. Its more detailed discussion will finally introduce us to the true notional concept of art itself.

If we take a glance at our ordinary ideas on this subject, one of the most prevalent is obviously:

(i) The principle of the imitation of Nature. According to this view the essential aim or object of art consists in imitation, by which is understood a facility in copying natural forms as present to us in a manner which shall most fully correspond to such facts. The success of such an exact representation of Nature is assumed to afford us complete satisfaction.

(α) Now in this definition there is to start with absolutely nothing but the formal aim to bring about the bare repetition a second time by man, so far as his means will permit of this, of all that was already in the external world, precisely too in the way it is there. A repetition of this sort may at once be set down as:

(αα) A *superfluous* task for the reason that everything which pictures, theatrical performances represent by way of imitation—animals, natural scenery, incidents of human life—we have already elsewhere before us in our gardens or at home, or in other examples of the more restricted or extended reaches of our personal acquaintance. Looked at, moreover, more closely, such a superfluity of energy can hardly appear otherwise than a presumptuous trifling; it is so because:

(ββ) It lags so far behind Nature. In other words art is limited in its means of representation. It can only produce one-sided illusions, a semblance, to take one example, of real fact addressed exclusively to *one* sense. And, moreover, if it does wholly rely on the bare aim of *mere* imitation, instead of Nature's life all it gives us ever is the mere pretence of its substance.

In short, to sum up, we may state emphatically that in the mere business of imitation art cannot maintain its rivalry with Nature, and if it makes the attempt it must look like a worm which undertakes to crawl after an elephant.

(β) Inasmuch as, moreover, the principle of imitation is purely formal, *objective beauty* itself disappears, if that principle is accepted as the end. For the question is then no longer what is the *constitution* of that which is to be imitated, but simply whether the copy is *correct* or no. The object and the content of the beautiful comes to be regarded as a matter of indifference. When, in other words, putting the principle of mere imitation on one side, we speak, in connection with animals, human beings, places, actions, and characters, of a distinction between beauty and ugliness, it remains none the less the fact that relatively to such a principle we are referring to a distinction which does not properly belong to an art for which we have appropriated this principle of imitation to the exclusion of all others. In such a case, therefore, whenever we select objects and attempt to distinguish between their beauty and ugliness, owing to this absence of a standard we can apply to the infinite forms of Nature, we have in the final resort only left us the *personal taste*, which is fixed by no rule, and admits of no discussion. And, in truth, if we start, in the selection of objects for representation, from that which mankind *generally* discover as beautiful and ugly, and accept accordingly for artistic imitation, in other words, form their particular taste, there is no province in the domain of the objective world which is not open to us, and which is hardly likely to fail to secure its admirer. At any rate, among men we may assume that, though the case of every husband and his wife may be disputed, yet at least every bridegroom regards his bride as beautiful, very possibly being the only person who does so; and that an individual taste for a beauty of this kind admits of no fixed rules at all may be regarded as a bit of luck for both parties. If, moreover, we cast a glance wholly beyond mere individuals and their accidental taste to that of nations, this again is full of diversity and opposition. How often we hear it repeated that a European beauty would not please a Chinaman, or even a Hottentot—a Chinaman having a totally distinct notion of beauty from that of a black man, and the black man in his turn from that of a European. Indeed, if we consider the works of art of those extra-European peoples, their images of gods, for instance, which have been imaginatively conceived as worthy of veneration and sublime, they can only appear to us as frightful idols, their music will merely ring in our ears as an abominable noise, while, from the opposite point of view, such aliens will regard our sculptures, paintings, and musical compositions as having no meaning or actually ugly.

The end or object of art must therefore consist in something other than the purely formal imitation of what is given to objective sense, which invariably can merely call into being technical *legerdemain* and not *works* of art. It is no doubt an essential constituent of a work of art that it should have natural forms as a foundation, because the mode of its representation is in external form, and thereby along with it in that of natural phenomena.

(ii) And as a consequence of this we have the further question—'What is the true *content* of art, and with what aim is that content brought before us?' On this head we are confronted by the common opinion that it is the task and object of art to

bring before our sense, feeling, and power of emulation *every thing* that the spirit of man can perceive or conceive. Art has in short to realize for us the well-known saying, 'Nihil humani a me alienum puto' ['I count nothing human indifferent to me']. Its object is therefore declared to be that of arousing and giving life to slumbering emotions, inclinations, passions of *every* description, of filling the heart up to the brim; of compelling mankind, whether cultured or the reverse, to pass through all that the human soul carries in its most intimate and mysterious chambers, all that it is able to experience and reproduce, all that the heart is able to stir and evoke in its depths and its countlessly manifold possibilities; and yet further to deliver to the domain of feeling and the delight of our vision all that the spirit may possess of essential and exalted being in its thought and the Idea—that majestic hierarchy of the noble, eternal, and true; and no less to interpret for us misfortune and misery, wickedness and crime; to make the hearts of men realize through and through all that is atrocious and dreadful, no less than every kind of pleasure and blessedness; and last of all to start the imagination like a rover among the day-dream playing-fields of the fancy, there to revel in the seductive mirage of visions and emotions which captivate the senses. All this infinitely manifold content—so it is held—it is the function of art to explore, in order that by this means the experience of our external life may be repaired of its deficiencies, and yet from a further point of view that the passions we share with all men may be excited, not merely that the experiences of life may not have us unmoved, but that we ourselves may thereafter long to make ourselves open channels of a universal experience. Such a stimulus is not presented on the plane of actual experience itself, but can only come through the semblance of it, that is to say through the illusions which art, in its creations, substitutes for the actual world. And the possibility of such a deception, by means of the semblances of art, depends on the fact that all reality must for man pass through the medium of the vision and imaginative idea; and it is only after such a passage that it penetrates the emotional life and the will. In such a process it is of no consequence whether it is immediate external reality which claims his attention, or whether the result is effected by some other way, in other words by means of images, symbols, and ideas, which contain and display the content of such actuality. Men are able to imagine things, which do not actually exist, as if they did exist. Consequently it is precisely the same thing for our emotional life, whether it is the objective world or merely the show of the same, in virtue of which a situation, a relation, or any content of life, in short, is brought home to us. Either mode is equally able to stir in us an echo to the essential secret which it carries, whether it be in grief or joy, in agitation or convulsion, and can cause to flow through us the feelings and passions of anger, hate, pity, anxiety, fear, love, reverence and admiration, honour and fame.

    The awakening of every kind of emotion in us, the drawing our soul through every content of life, the realization of all these movements of soul-life by means of a presence which is only external as an illusion—this it is which, in the opinion described, is pre-eminently regarded as the peculiar and transcendent power of artistic creation.

We must not, however, overlook the fact that in this view of art as a means to imprint on the soul and the mind what is good and evil alike, to make man more strong in the pursuit of what is noblest, no less than enervate his definite course, by transporting his emotional life through the most sensuous and selfish desires, the task as yet proposed to art remains throughout of an entirely formal character; without possessing independently an assured aim all that art can offer is the empty form for every possible kind of ideal and formative content.

(iii) As a matter of fact art does not possess this formal side, namely, that it is able to bring before our senses and feeling and artistically adorn every possible kind of material, precisely as the thoughts of ordinary reflection elaborate every possible subject-matter and modes of action, supplying the same with its equipment of reasons and vindications. In the presence, however, of such a variety for content we cannot fail to observe that these diversified emotions and ideas, which it is assumed art has to stimulate or enforce, intersect each other, contradict and mutually cancel each other. Indeed, under this aspect, the more art inspires men to emotions thus opposed, to that extent precisely it merely enlarges the cleavage in their feelings and passions, and sets them staggering about in Bacchantic riot, or passes over into sophistry and skepticism precisely as your ordinary free thinkers do. This variety of the material of art itself compels us, therefore, not to remain satisfied with so formal a determination. Our rational nature forces its way into this motley array of discord, and demands to see the resurrection of a higher and more universal purpose from these elements despite their opposition, and to be conscious of its attainment. Just in a similar manner the social life of mankind and the State are no doubt credited with the aim that in them *all* human capacities and *all* individual potencies should meet with expansion and expression in *all* their features and tendencies. But in opposition to so formal a view there very quickly crops up the question in what *unity* these manifold manifestations are to be concentrated, and what *single end* they must have for their fundamental concept and ultimate end. Just as in the case of the notional concept of the human State so too there arises in that of human art the need, as to a part thereof, for an end *common* to the particular aspects, no less than in part for one which is more exalted and *substantive* in its character.

As such a substantive end the conclusion of reflection is readily brought home to us that art possesses at once the power and function to mitigate the savagery of mere desires.

(α) With regard to this first conception we have merely to ascertain what characteristic peculiar to art implies this possibility of eliminating this rawness of desire, and of fettering and instructing the impulses and passions. Coarseness in general has its ground-root in an unmitigated self-seeking of sensuous impulses, which take their plunge off and are exclusively intent on the satisfaction of their concupiscence. Sensual desire is, however, all the more brutal and domineering, in proportion as, in its isolation and confinement, it appropriates the *entire man*, so that he does not retain the power to separate himself in his universal capacity from this determinacy and to maintain the conscious presence of such universality. Even if the man in such a case exclaims, 'The passion is mightier than *I*', though it is true no doubt that the 'I', the abstract ego, is separate from the particular passion, yet it is purely so in a formal way. All that such a separation amounts to is that as against the force of the passion the ego, in its universal form or competency, is of no account at all. The savageness of passion consists therefore in the fusion of the ego as such a universal with the confined content of its desire, so that a man no longer possesses volitional power outside this single passion. Such savageness and untamed force of the possibilities of passion art mitigates in the first instance to the extent that it brings home to the mind and imagination of man what he does actually feel and carry into effect in such a condition. And even if art restricts itself to this that it places before the vision of the mind pictures of passion, nay, even assuming such to be flattering pictures, yet for all that a power of amelioration is contained therein. At least we may say, that by this means is brought before a man's intelligence what apart from such presentment he merely is. The man in this way contemplates his impulses and inclinations; and whereas apart from this they whirl him away without giving him time to reflect, he now sees them outside himself and already, for the reason that they come before him rather as objects than a part of himself, he begins to be free from them as aliens. For this reason it may often happen that an artist, under the weight of grief, mitigates and weakens the intensity of his own emotions in their effect upon him by the artistic representation of them. Comfort, too, is to be found even in tears. The man who to start with is wholly given up to and concentrated in sorrow, is able thus, at any rate, to express that which is merely felt within in a direct way. Yet more alleviating is the utterance of such inner life in words, images, musical sound, and shapes.

It was therefore a good old custom in the case of funerals and layings-out to appoint wailing women, in order to give audible expression to grief, or generally to create an external sympathy. For manifestations of sympathy bring the content of human sorrow to the sufferer in an objective form; he is by their repetition driven to reflect upon it, and the burden is thereby made lighter. And so it has from of old been considered that to weep or to speak oneself out are equally means whereby freedom is secured from the oppressing burden, or at least the heart is appreciably lifted. Consequently the mitigation of the violence of passions admits of this general explanation that man is released from his unmediated confinement in an emotion, becomes aware of it as a thing external to himself, to which he is consequently obliged to place himself in an ideal relation. Art, while still remaining within the sphere of the senses, faces man from the might of his sensitive experience by means of its representations. No doubt we frequently hear that pet phrase of many that it is man's duty to remain in immediate union with Nature. Such union is in its unmediated purity nothing more or less than savagery and wildness; and art, precisely in the way that it dissolves this unity for human beings, lifts them with gentle hands over this enclosure in Nature. The way men are occupied with the objects of art's creation remains throughout of a contemplative character; and albeit in the first instance it educates merely an attention to the actual facts portrayed, yet over and beyond this, and with a power no less decisive, it draws man's attention to their significance, it forces him to compare their content with that of others, and to receive without reserve the general conclusions of such a survey and all the ramifications such imply.

(β) To the characteristic above discussed adheres in natural sequence the second which has been predicated of art as its essential aim, namely, the *purification* of the passions, an instruction, that is, and a building to *moral* completeness. For the defining role that art has to bridle savage nature and educate the passions remained one wholly formal and general, so that the further question must arise as to a *specific* kind and an essential and *culminating* point of such an educative process.

(αα) The doctrine of the purification of the passions shares in the defect previously noted as adhering to the mitigation of desires. It does, however, emphasize more closely the fact that the representations of art needed a standard, by means of which it would be possible to estimate their comparative worth and unworth. This standard is just their effectiveness to separate what is pure from that which is the reverse in the passions. Art, therefore, requires a content which is capable of expressing this purifying power, and in so far as the power to assert such effectiveness is assumed to constitute the substantive end of art, the purifying content will consist in asserting that effective power before consciousness in its *universality* and *essentiality*.

(ββ) It is a deduction from the point of view just described that it is the end of art to *instruct*. Thus, on the one hand, the peculiar character of art consists in the movement of the emotions and in the satisfaction which is found in this movement, even in fear, compassion, in painful agitation and shock—that is to say, in the satisfying concern of the feelings and passions, and to that extent in a complacent, delighted, or enthusiastic attitude to the objects of art and their presentation and effect: while, on the other hand, this artistic object is held to discover its higher standard exclusively in its power to instruct, in the fibula docet, and thereby in the usefulness, which the work of art is able to exercise on the recipient. In this respect the Horatian adage:

> Et prodesse volunt et delectare poetae
> ['Poets aim at utility and entertainment alike']

contains, concentrated into a few words, all that in after times has been drawn out as a doctrine of art through every conceivable grade of dilution to the last extreme of insipidity.

In respect, then, to such instruction we have to ask whether the idea is that the same ought to be direct or indirect in the work of art, explicit or implicit.

Now if the question at issue is one of general importance to art about a universal rather than contingent purpose, such an ultimate end, on account of the essential spirituality of art, can only be itself of spiritual import; in other words, so far from being of accidental importance it must be true in virtue of its own nature and on its own account. An end of this kind can only apply to instruction in so far as a genuine and essentially explicit content is brought before the spirit by means of the work of art. From such a point of view we are entitled to affirm that it is the function of art to accept so much the more of a content of this nature within its compass in proportion to the nobility of its rank, and that only in the verity of such a content will it discover the standard according to which the pertinency of or the reverse of what is expressed is adjudged. Art is in truth the primary *instructress* of peoples.

But, on the other hand, if the object of instruction is so entirely treated as an *end* that the universal nature of the content presented cannot fail to be asserted and rendered bluntly and on its own account explicit as abstract thesis, prosaic reflection or general maxim, rather than merely in an indirect way contained by implication in the concrete embodiment of art, then and in that case, by means of such a separation, the sensuous, plastic configuration, which is precisely that which makes the artistic product a *work of art*, is merely an otiose accessory, a husk, a semblance, which are expressly posited as nothing more than *shell* and semblance. Thereby the very nature of a work of art is abused. For the work of art ought not to bring before the imaginative vision a content in its universality as such, but rather this universality under the mode of individual concreteness and distinctive sensuous particularity. If the work in question does not conform to such a principle, but rather sets before us the generalization of its content with the express object of instruction pure and simple, then the imaginative no less than the material aspect of it are merely an external and superfluous ornament, and the work of art is itself a shattered thing within that ornament, a ruin wherein form and content no longer appear as a mutually adherent growth. For, in the case supposed, the particular object of the senses and the ideal content apprehended by the spirit have become external to one another.

Furthermore, if the object of art is assumed to consist in utilitarian *instruction* of this kind, that other aspect of delight, entertainment, and diversion is simply abandoned on its own account as *unessential*; it has now to look for its substance to the utility of the matter of instruction, to which it is simply an accompaniment. But this amounts to saying, that art does not carry its vocation and purpose in itself, but that its fundamental conception is in something else, to which it subserves as a *means*. Art becomes, in short, merely one of the many means, which are either of use, or may be employed to secure, the aim of instruction. This brings us to the boundary line where art can only cease to be an end on its own independent account; it is deliberately deposed either to the mere plaything of entertainment, or a mere means of instruction.

(γγ) The line of this limit is most emphasized when the question is raised as to the end or object of highest rank for the sake of which the passions have to be purified or men have to be instructed. This goal has frequently in modern times been identified with *moral improvement*, and the end of art is assumed to consist in this that its function is to prepare our inclinations and impulses, and generally to conduct us to the supreme goal of moral perfection. In this view we find instruction and purification combined. The notion is that art by the insight it gives us of genuine moral goodness, in other words, through its instruction, at the same time summons us to the process of purification, and in this way alone can and ought to bring about the improvement of mankind as the right use they can make of it and its supreme object.

With reference to the relation in which art stands to the end of improvement, we may practically say the same thing as we did about the didactic end. It may readily be admitted that art as its principle ought not to make the immoral and its advance its end. But it is one thing deliberately to make immorality the aim of its presentation and another not expressly to do so in the case of morality. It is possible to deduce an excellent moral from any work of art whatever; but such depends, of course, on a particular interpretation and consequently on the individual who draws the moral. The defence is made of the most immoral representations on the ground that people ought to become acquainted with evil and sin in order to act morally. Conversely, it has been maintained that the portrayal of Mary Magdalene, the fair sinner, who afterwards repented, has seduced many into sin, because art makes repentance look so beautiful, and you must first sin before you can repent. The doctrine of moral improvement, however logically carried out, is not merely satisfied that a moral should be conceivably deducible from a work of art through interpretation; on the contrary, it would have the moral instruction clearly made to emerge as the substantive aim of the work; nay, further, it would deliberately exclude from art's products all subjects, characters, actions, and events which fail to be moral in its own sense. For art, in distinction from history and the sciences, which have their subject-matter determined for them, has a choice in the selection of its subjects.

In order that we may be in a position to estimate this view of the moral end of art on the basis of principle, we ought above all to raise the question as to the precise stand-point of the morality which is recommended for our reception by this view. If we examine more closely the standpoint of morality such as is submitted us today under an enlightened interpretation, we soon discover that its conception does not immediately coincide with that which we describe in a general way as virtue, respectability, uprightness, and so forth. To be a respectable honest man is not sufficient to make a man moral in the sense under discussion, for morality in this sense implies *reflection* and the definite consciousness of what is consonant with duty, and the acts which issue from such a consciousness. Now duty is itself the law of the will, which man, however, freely establishes out of himself, and thereon is taken to determine himself to this duty for duty's sake and its fulfilment's sake; in other words he only does good as acting under the conviction already secured that it is the good. This law—the duty which is selected and carried into effect for duty's sake to be the rule of conduct out of free conviction and the inner conscience—is, on its own account, the abstract universal of the will, which is the absolute antithesis to Nature, the impulses of sense, selfish interests, the passions and all that is commonly described collectively as emotional life and heart. In this opposition the one side is regarded as *negating* the other; and for the reason that both are present in the individual in their opposition, he is compelled, as determining himself from his own identity, to adopt the choice of one to the rejection of the other. Such a decision and the act carried out in accordance with it merely become moral from the standpoint now considered on the one hand in virtue of the free conviction of duty, and on the other by reason of the victory secured not only over the particular will, the natural motives, inclinations, passions and so on, but also in virtue of the noble feelings and higher impulses. For the modern ethic starts from the fixed opposition between the will in its spiritual universality and its sensuous natural particularity; it does not consist in the perfected mediation of these opposed aspects, but in their mutual conflict as opposed to one another, which carries with it the demand, that the impulses in their antagonism to duty ought to yield to it.

An opposition of this nature is not merely present to mind or consciousness in the restricted confines of moral action; it asserts itself as a fundamental severation and antithesis between that which is actual essentially, and on its own account, and that which is external reality and existence. Apprehended in entirely formal terms it is the contrast exposed by the universal, in so far as it is fixed in its substantive independence over against the particular, as the latter is also on its part rigidly exterior to it. In more concrete form it appears in Nature as the opposition of the abstract law to the wealth of particular phenomena, each of which possesses its specific characteristics. It appears in spirit as that between the sensuous and spiritual in man, as the conflict of spirit with the flesh; it is that of duty for duty's sake; of the cold imperative with particular impulses, the warm heart, the sensuous inclinations and impulses, in a word with man simply as individual. Or it appears as the harsh antagonism between the inward freedom and the external necessity of natural condition, and, lastly, as the contradiction of the dead, essentially emptied, concept, when confronted with the fullness of concrete life, in other words, of theory and subjective thought as contrasted with objective existence and experience.

Such are antithetical points of view, the discovery of which is not to be ascribed either to the ingenuity of reflective minds, or the pedantry of a philosophical cult. They have in all ages, if in manifold guise, occupied and disquieted the human consciousness, although it is our more modern culture which has emphasized their opposition most deliberately, and forced it in each case to the keenest edge of contradiction. Intellectual culture, or rather the rapier edge of the modern understanding, creates in man this contrast, which converts him into some amphibious animal. He is compelled to live in two worlds mutually contradictory; and in this divided house consciousness, too, wanders aimlessly; tossed over from one side to the other it is unable to discover permanent satisfaction for itself in either one side or the other. For, on the one hand, we see mankind confined within common reality and earthly temporal condition, oppressed by necessity and want, in Nature's toils, entangled in matter, in sensuous aims and their enjoyment, dominated and whirled away by impulse and passion. On the other hand he lifts himself up to eternal ideas, to a realm of thought and freedom. As Will he legislates for himself universal laws and destinations, he disrobes the world of the life and blossom of its reality; he dissolves it in abstractions, that the spirit may vindicate its right and intrinsic worth by this very dissolution of Nature's rights and such maltreatment, a process in which he brings home to her again the necessity and violence he has experienced at her hands. Such a cleavage of life and spirit is, however, accompanied for modern culture with the demand that a contradiction so deep-seated should be dissolved. The mere understanding of abstract reflection is unable to disengage itself from the obstinacy of such contradictions. The solution consequently remains here for consciousness a mere ought, and the present and reality is merely moved within the continuous unrest of a to and fro, which seeks for that reconciliation it is unable to find. The problem therefore arises whether such a many-sided and fundamental antagonism, which is unable to pass beyond the mere ought and postulate of its solution, can be the essential and wholly expressed truth, and, indeed, the final and supreme consummation. If the culture of the civilized world has fallen into such a contradiction it becomes the task of philosophy to dissolve the same, in other words to demonstrate that neither the one side or the other, in its onesided abstractness, should be held to possess truth, but that they contain within themselves the principle of their dissolution. The truth only then comes before us in the reconciliation and mediation of both; and this meditation is no mere postulate, but is, in its essential nature, and in its actual presence, at the same time accomplished and self-accomplishing. And, in fact, this view agrees directly with unwitting faith and will, which always has before its conscious life this contradiction in its resolution, and in action accepts it as its aim and carries it into effect. All that philosophy achieves is to contribute the insight of thought into the essence of such cleavage. It demonstrates, or seeks to demonstrate, how that which truth really is simply the resolution of the fracture, and, be it added, not in the sense that this antagonism and its alternative aspects in any way *are not*, but in the sense that they are *there* in reconciliation.

(*iv*) When discussing moral improvement as the ultimate end accepted for art it was found that its principle pointed to a higher standpoint. It will be necessary also to vindicate this standpoint for art.

Thereby the false position to which we have already directed attention vanishes, namely, that art has to serve as a means for moral ends and the moral end of the world generally by means of its didactive and ameliorating influence, and by doing so has its essential aim not in itself, but in something else. If we therefore continue still to speak of an end or goal of art, we must at once remove the perverse idea, which in the question, 'What is the end?' will still make it include the supplemental query, 'What is the use?' the perverseness consists in this that the work of art would then have to be regarded as related to something else, which is presented to us as what is essential and ought to be. A work of art would in that case be merely a useful instrument in the realization of an end which possessed real and independent importance outside the realm of art. As opposed to this we must maintain that it is art's function to reveal *truth* under the mode of art's sensuous or material configuration, to display the reconciled antithesis previously described, and by this means to prove that it possesses its final aim in itself, in this representation in short and self-revelation. For other ends such as instruction, purification, improvement, procuring of wealth, struggle after fame and honour have nothing whatever to do with this work of art as such, still less do they determine the fundamental idea of it.

PHILOSOPHY OF RELIGION

'As the act of rising-up to the True, religion is a departing from sensuous, finite objects'.

6

PHILOSOPHY OF RELIGION

PRELIMINARY

It has appeared to me to be necessary to make religion by itself the object of philosophical consideration, and to add on this study of it, in the form of a special part, to philosophy as a whole. By way of introduction I shall, however, first of all give some account of the severance or division of consciousness, which awakens the need our science has to satisfy, and describe the relation of this science to philosophy and religion, as also to the prevalent principles of the religious consciousness. Then, I shall give the division of the subject.

To begin with, it is necessary to recollect generally what object we have before us in the Philosophy of Religion, and what is our ordinary idea of religion. We know that in religion we withdraw ourselves from what is temporal, and that religion is for our consciousness that region in which all the enigmas of the world are solved, all the contradictions of deeper-reaching thought have their meaning unveiled, and where the voice of the heart's pain is silenced—the region of eternal truth, of eternal rest, of eternal peace. Speaking generally, it is through thought, concrete thought, or, to put it more definitely it is by reason of his being Spirit, that man is man; and from man as Spirit proceed all the many developments of the sciences and arts, the interests of political life, and all those conditions which have reference to man's freedom and will. But all these manifold forms of human relations, activities, and pleasures, and all the ways in which these are intertwined; all that has worth and dignity for man, all wherein he seeks his happiness, his glory, and his pride, finds its ultimate centre in religion, in the thought, the consciousness, and the feeling of God. Thus God is the beginning of all things, and the end of all things. As all things proceed from this point, so all return back to it again. He is the centre which gives life and quickening to all things, and which animates and preserves in existence all the various forms of being. In religion man places himself in a relation to this centre, in which all other relations concentrate themselves, and in so doing he rises up to the highest level of consciousness and to the religion which is free from relation to what is other than itself, to something which is absolutely self-sufficient, the unconditioned, what is free, and is its own object and end.

In the relation where the spirit occupies itself with this end, it unburdens itself of all finiteness, and wills for itself final satisfaction and deliverance; for here the spirit relates itself no longer to something that is other than itself, and that is limited, but to the unlimited and infinite, and this is an infinite relation, a relation of freedom and no longer of dependence. Here its consciousness is absolutely free, and is indeed true consciousness, because it is consciousness of absolute truth. In its character as feeling, this condition of freedom is the sense of satisfaction which we call blessedness, while as activity it has nothing further to do than to manifest the honour of God and to reveal His glory, and in this attitude it is no longer with himself that man is concerned with his own interests or his empty pride—but with the absolute end. All the various peoples feel that it is in the religious consciousness they possess truth, and they have always regarded religion as constituting their true dignity and the Sabbath of their life. Whatever awakens in us doubt and fear, all sorrow, all care, all the limited interests of finite life, we leave behind on the shores of time; and as from the highest peak of a mountain, far away from all definite view of what is earthly, we look down calmly upon all the limitations of the landscape and of the world, so with the spiritual eye man, lifted out of the hard realities of this actual world, contemplates it as something having only the semblance of existence, which seen from this pure region bathed in the beams of the spiritual still, merely reflects back its shades of colour, its varied tints and lights, softened away into eternal rest. In this region of spirit flow the streams of forgetfulness from which Psyche drinks, and in which she drowns all sorrow, while the dark things of this life are softened away into a dream-like vision, and become transfigured until they are a mere framework for the brightness of the Eternal.

This image of the Absolute may have a more or less present vitality and certainty for the religions and devout mind, and be a present source of pleasure; or it may be represented as something longed and hoped for, far off, and in the future. Still it always remains a certainty, and its rays stream as something divine into this present temporal life, giving the consciousness of the active presence of truth, even amidst the anxieties which torment the soul here in this region of time. Faith recognizes it in this last case he is inwardly occupied with it, and cannot free himself from it. As man, religion is essential to him, and is not a feeling foreign to his nature.

Yet the essential question is the relation of religion to his general theory of the universe, and it is with this that philosophical knowledge connects itself, and upon which it essentially works.

In this relation we have the source of the division which arises in opposition to the primary absolute tendency of the spirit toward religion, and here, too, all the manifold forms of consciousness, and their most widely differing connections with the main interest of religion, have sprung up. Before the Philosophy of Religion can sum itself up in its own peculiar conception, it must work itself through all those ramifications of the interests of the time which have at present concentrated themselves in the widely-extended sphere of religion. At first the movement of the principles of the time has its place outside of philosophical study, but this movement pushes on to the point at which it comes into contact, strife, and antagonism with philosophy.

We shall consider this opposition and its solution when we have examined the opposition as it still maintains itself outside of philosophy, and have seen it develop until it reaches that completed state where it involves philosophical knowledge in itself.

THE SEVERANCE OF RELIGION FROM THE FREE, WORLDLY CONSCIOUSNESS

In the relation in which religion, even in its immediacy, stands to the other forms of the consciousness of man, there already lie germs of division, since both sides are conceived of as in a condition of separation relatively to each other. In their simple relation they already constitute two kinds of pursuits, two different regions of consciousness, and we pass to and fro from the one to the other alternately only. Thus man has in his actual worldly life a number of working days during which he occupies himself with his own special interests, with worldly aims in general, and with the satisfaction of his needs; and then he has a Sunday, when he lays all this aside, collects his thoughts, and, released from absorption in finite occupations, lives to himself and to the higher nature which is in him, to his true essential being. But into this separateness of the two sides there directly enters a double modification.

Let us consider first of all the religion of the godly man; that is, of one who truly deserves to be so called. Faith is still presupposed as existing irrespective of, and without opposition to, anything else. To believe in God is thus in its simplicity, something different from that where a man, with reflection and with the consciousness that something else stands opposed to this faith, says, 'I *believe* in God'. Here the need of justification, of inference, of controversy, has already come in. Now that religion of the simple, godly man is not kept shut off and divided from the rest of his existence and life, but, on the contrary, it breathes its influence over all his feelings and actions, and his consciousness brings all the aims and objects of his worldly life into relation to God, as to its infinite and ultimate source. Every moment of his finite existence and activity, of his sorrow and joy, is lifted up by him out of his limited sphere, and by being thus lifted up produces in him the idea and sense of his eternal nature. The rest of his life, in like manner, is led under the conditions of confidence, of custom, of dutifulness, of habit; he is that which circumstances and nature have made him, and he takes his life, his circumstances, and rights as he receives everything, namely, as a lot or destiny which he does not understand. *It is so*. In regard to God, he either takes what is His and gives thanks, or else he offers it up to Him freely as a gift of free grace. The rest of his conscious life is thus subordinated, without reflection, to that higher region.

From the worldly side, however, the distinction involved in this relation develops until it becomes opposition. It is true that the development of this side does not seem to affect religion injuriously, and all action seems to limit itself strictly to that side in the matter. Judging from what is expressly acknowledged, religion is still looked upon as what is highest; but as a matter of fact it is not so, and starting from the worldly side, ruin and disunion creep over into religion. The development of this distinction may be generally designated as the maturing of the understanding and of human aims. While understanding awakens in human life and in science, and reflection has become independent, the will sets before itself absolute aims; for example, justice, the state, objects which are to have absolute worth, to be in and for themselves. Thus research recognizes the laws, the constitution, the order, and the peculiar characteristics of natural things, and of the activities and productions of Spirit. Now these experiences and forms of knowledge, as well as the willing and actual carrying out of these aims, is a work of man, both of his understanding and will. In them he is in presence *of what is his own*. Although he sets out from what is, from what he finds, yet he is no longer merely one who knows, who *has* these rights; but what he *makes* out of that which is given in knowledge and in will is his affair, his work, and he has the consciousness that he has produced it. Therefore these productions constitute his glory and his pride, and provide for him an immense, an infinite wealth—that world of his intelligence, of his knowledge, of his external possession, of his rights and deeds.

Thus the spirit has entered into the condition of opposition—as yet, it is true, artlessly, and without at first knowing it—but the opposition comes to be a conscious one, for the spirit now moves between two sides, of which the distinction has actually developed itself. The one side is that in which the spirit knows itself to be its own, where it lives in its own aims and interests, and determines itself on its own authority as independent and self-sustaining. The other side is that where the spirit recognizes a higher Power—absolute duties, duties without rights belonging to them, and what the spirit receives for the accomplishment of its duties is always regarded as grace alone. In the first instance it is the independence of the spirit which is the foundation, but in the second its attitude is that of humility and dependence. Its religion is accordingly distinguished from what we have in that region of independence by this, that it restricts knowledge, science, to the *worldly side,* and leaves for the sphere of religion, feeling and faith.

Knowledge so far aims at that which is, and the *necessity* of it, and apprehends this in the relation of cause and effect, reason and result, power and manifestation; in the relation of the Universal, of the species and of the individual existing things which are included in the sphere of contingency. Knowledge, science, in this manner places the manifold material in mutual relation, takes away from it the contingency which it has through its immediacy, and while contemplating the relations which belong to the wealth of finite phenomena, encloses the world of finiteness in itself so as to form a system of the universe, of such a kind that knowledge requires nothing for this system outside of the system itself. For what a thing is, what it is in its essential determinate character, is disclosed when it is perceived and made the subject of observation. From the constitution of things, we proceed to their connections in which they stand in relation to all others; not, however in an accidental, but in a determinate relation, and in which they point back to the original source from which they are a deduction. Thus we inquire after the reasons and causes of things; and the meaning of inquiry here is, that what is desired is to know the special causes. Thus it is no longer sufficient to speak of God as the cause of the lightning, or of the downfall of the Republican system of government in Rome, or of the French Revolution; here it is perceived that this cause is only an entirely general one, and does not yield the desired explanation. What we wish to know regarding a natural phenomenon, or regarding this or that law as effect or result, is, the reason as the reason of this particular phenomenon that is to say, not the reason which applies to all things, but only and exclusively to this definite thing. And thus the reason must be that of such special phenomena, and such reason or ground must be the most immediate, must be sought and laid hold of in the finite and must itself be a finite one. Therefore this knowledge does not go above or beyond the sphere of the finite, nor does it desire to do so, since it is able to apprehend all in its finite sphere, is conversant with everything, and knows its course of action. In this manner science forms a universe of knowledge, to which God is not necessary, which lies outside of religion, and has absolutely nothing to do with it. In this kingdom knowledge spreads itself out in its relations and connections, and in so doing has all determinate material and content on its side; and for the other side, the side of the infinite and the eternal, nothing whatever is left.

Thus both sides have developed themselves completely in their opposition, on the side of religion the heart is filled with what is Divine, but without freedom, or self-consciousness, and without consistency in regard to what is determinate, this latter having, on the contrary, the form of contingency. Consistent connection of what is determinate belongs to the side of knowledge, which is at home in the finite, and moves freely in the thought-determinations of the manifold connections of things, but can only create a system which is without absolute substantiality—without God. The religious side gets the absolute material and purpose, but only as something abstractly positive. Knowledge has taken possession of all finite material and drawn it into its territory, all determinate content has fallen to its share; but although it gives it a necessary connection, it is still unable to give it the absolute connection. Since finally science has taken possession of knowledge, and is the consciousness of *the necessity* of the finite, religion has become devoid of knowledge, and has shrivelled up into simple feeling, into the contentless or empty elevation of the spiritual to the Eternal. It can, however, affirm nothing regarding the Eternal for all that could be regarded knowledge would be a drawing down of the Eternal into the sphere of the finite, and of finite connections of things.

Now when two aspects of thought, which are so developed in this way, enter into relation with one another, their attitude is one of mutual distrust. Religious feeling distrusts the finiteness which lies in knowledge, and it brings against science the charge of futility, because in it the subject clings to itself, is in itself, and the 'I' as the knowing subject is independent in relation to all that is external. On the other hand, knowledge has a distrust of the totality in which feeling entrenches itself, and in which it confounds together all extension and development. It is afraid to lose its freedom should it comply with the demand of feeling and unconditionally recognize a truth which it does not definitely understand. And when religious feeling comes out of its universality, sets ends before itself, and passes over to the determinate, knowledge can see nothing but arbitrariness in this, and if it were to pass in a similar way to anything definite, would feel itself given over to mere contingency. When, accordingly, reflection is fully developed, and has to pass over into the domain of religion, it is unable to hold out in that region, and becomes impatient with regard to all that peculiarly belongs to it.

Now that the opposition has arrived at this stage of development, where the one side, whenever it is approached by the other, invariably thrusts it away from it as an enemy, the necessity for an adjustment comes in, of such a kind that the infinite shall appear in the finite, and the finite in the infinite, and each no longer form a separate realm. This would be the reconciliation of religious, genuine simple feeling, with knowledge and intelligence. This reconciliation must correspond with the highest demands of *knowledge,* and of the Notion, for these can surrender nothing of their dignity. But just as little can anything of the absolute content be given up, and that content be brought down into the region of finiteness; and when face to face with it knowledge must give up its finite form. In the Christian religion, more than in other religions, the need of this reconciliation has of necessity come into prominence, for the following reasons:

The Christian religion has its very beginning in absolute dualism, or division, and starts from that sense of suffering in which it rends the natural unity of the spirit asunder, and destroys natural peace. In it man appears as evil from his birth, and is thus in his innermost life in contradiction with himself, and the spirit, as it is driven back into itself, finds itself separated from the infinite, absolute Essence.

The Reconciliation, the need of which is here intensified to the uttermost degree, appears in the first place for Faith, but not in such a way as to allow of faith being of a merely ingenuous kind. For the spirit has left its natural simplicity behind, and entered upon an internal conflict; it is, as sinful, an Other in opposition to the truth; it is withdrawn, estranged from it. 'I', in this condition of schism, am not the truth, and this is therefore given as an independent content of ordinary thought, and the truth is in the first instance put forward upon authority.

When, however, by this means I am transplanted into an intellectual world in which the nature of God, the characteristics and modes of action which below, to God, are presented to knowledge, and when the truth of these rests on the witness and assurance of others, yet I am at the same time referred into myself, for thought, knowledge, reason are *in me,* and in the feeling of sinfulness, and in reflection upon this, my freedom is plainly revealed to me. Rational knowledge, therefore, is an essential element in the Christian religion itself.

In the Christian religion I am to retain my freedom or rather, in it I am to become free. In it the subject, the salvation of the soul, the redemption of the individual as an individual, and not only the species, is an essential end. This subjectivity, this *selfness* (not selfishness) is just the principle of rational knowledge itself.

Rational knowledge being thus a fundamental characteristic in the Christian religion, the latter gives development to its content, for the ideas regarding its general subject-matter are implicitly or in themselves thoughts, and must as such develop themselves. On the other hand, however, since the content is something, which exists essentially for the mind as forming ideas, it is distinct from unreflecting opinion and sense-knowledge, and as it were passes right beyond the distinction. In short, it has in relation to subjectivity the value of an absolute content existing in and for itself. The Christian religion therefore touches the antithesis between feeling and immediate perception on the one hand, and reflection and knowledge on the other. It contains rational knowledge as an essential element, and has supplied to this rational knowledge the occasion for developing itself to its full logical issue as Form and as a world of form, and has thus at the same time enabled it to place itself in opposition to this content as it appears in the shape of given truth. It is from this that the discord which characterizes the thought of the present day arises. Hitherto we have considered the progressive growth of the antitheses only in the form in which they have not yet developed into actual philosophy, or in which they still stand outside of it. Therefore the questions which primarily come before us are these: how does philosophy in general stand related to religion? How does the Philosophy of Religion stand related to philosophy? And, what is the relation of the philosophical study of religion to positive religion?

THE POSITION OF THE PHILOSOPHY OF RELIGION RELATIVELY TO PHILOSOPHY AND TO RELIGION

In saying above that philosophy makes religion the subject of consideration, and when further this consideration of it appears to be in the position of something which is different from its object, it would seem as if we are still occupying that attitude in which both sides remain mutually independent and separate. In taking up such an attitude in thus considering the subject, we should accordingly come out of that region of devotion and enjoyment which religion is, and the object and the consideration of it as the movement of thought would be as different as, for example, the geometrical figures in mathematics are from the mind which considers them. Such is only the relation, however, as it at first appears, when knowledge is still severed from the religious side, and is finite knowledge. On the contrary, when we look more closely, it becomes apparent that as a matter of fact the content, the need, and the interest of philosophy represent something which it has in common with religion.

The object of religion as well as of philosophy is eternal truth in its objectivity, God and nothing but God, and the explication of God. Philosophy is not a wisdom of the world, but is knowledge of what is not of the world—it is not knowledge which concerns external mass, or empirical existence and life, but is knowledge of that which is eternal, of what God is, and what flows out of His nature. For this His nature must reveal and develop itself. Philosophy, therefore, only unfolds itself when it unfolds religion, and in unfolding itself it unfolds religion. As thus occupied with eternal truth which exists on its own account, or is in and for itself, and, as in fact, a dealing on the part of the thinking spirit, and not of individual caprice and particular interest, with this object, it is the same kind of activity as religion is. The mind in so far as it thinks philosophically immerses itself with like living interest in this object, and renounces its particularity in that it permeates its object, in the same way, as religious consciousness does, for the latter also does not seek to have anything of its own, but desires only to immerse itself in this content.

Thus religion and philosophy come to be one. Philosophy is itself, in fact, worship; it is religion, for in the same way it renounces subjective notions and opinions in order to occupy itself with God. Philosophy is thus identical with religion, but the distinction is that it is so in a peculiar manner, distinct from the manner of looking at things which is commonly called religion as such. What they have in common is, that they are religion; what distinguishes them from each other is merely the kind and manner of religion we find in each. It is in the peculiar way in which they both occupy themselves with God that the distinction comes out. It is just here, however, that the difficulties lie which appear so great, that it is even regarded as an impossibility that philosophy should be one with religion. Hence comes the suspicion with which philosophy is looked upon by theology, and the antagonistic attitude of religion and philosophy. In accordance with this antagonistic attitude (as theology considers it to be) philosophy seems to act injuriously, destructively, upon religion, robbing it of its sacred character, and the way in which it occupies itself with God seems to be absolutely different from religion. Here, then, is the same old opposition and contradiction which had already made its appearance among the Greeks. Among that free democratic people, the Athenians, philosophical writings were burnt, and Socrates was condemned to death; now, however, this opposition is held to be an acknowledged fact, more so than that unity of religion and philosophy just asserted.

Old though this opposition is, however, the combination of philosophy and religion is just as old. Already to the neo-Pythagoreans and neo-Platonists, who were as yet within the heathen world, the gods of the people were not gods of imagination, but had become gods of thought. That combination had a place, too, among the most eminent of the Fathers of the Church, who in their religious life took up an essentially intellectual attitude inasmuch as they set out from the presupposition that theology is religion together with conscious thought and comprehension. It is to their philosophical culture that the Christian Church is indebted for the first beginnings of a content of Christian doctrine.

This union of religion and philosophy was carried out to a still-greater extent in the Middle Ages. So little was it believed that the knowledge which seeks to comprehend is hurtful to faith, that it was even held to be essential to the further development of faith itself. It was by setting out from philosophy that those great men, Anselm and Abelard, further developed the essential characteristics of faith.

Knowledge in constructing its world for itself, without reference to religion, had only taken possession of the finite contents; but since it has developed into the true philosophy, it has the same content as religion. If we now look provisionally for the distinction between religion and philosophy as it presents itself in this unity or content, we find it takes the following form:

A speculative philosophy is the consciousness of the Idea, so that everything is apprehended as Idea; the Idea, however, is the True in thought, and not in mere sensuous contemplation or in ordinary conception. The True in thought, to put it more precisely, means that it is something concrete, posited as divided in itself, and in such away, indeed, that the two sides of what is divided are *opposed characteristics of* thought, and the Idea must be conceived of as the unity of these. To think speculatively means to resolve anything real into its parts, and to oppose these to each other in such a way that the distinctions are set in opposition in accordance with the characteristics of thought, and the object is apprehended as unity of the two.

In sense-perception or picture-thought we have the object before us as a whole, our reflection distinguishes, apprehends different sides, recognizes the diversity in them, and severs them. In this act of distinguishing reflection does not keep firm hold of their unity. Sometimes it forgets the wholeness, sometimes the distinctions and if it has both before it, it yet separates the properties from the object, and so places both that that in which the two are one becomes a third, which is different from the object and its properties. In the case of mechanical objects which appear in the region of externality, this relation may have a place, for the object is only the lifeless substratum for the distinctions, and the quality of oneness is the gathering together of external aggregates

In the true object, however, which is not merely an aggregate, an externally united multiplicity, the object is one, although it has characteristics which are distinguished from it, and it is speculative thought which first gets a grasp of the unity in this very antithesis as such. It is in fact the business of speculative thought to apprehend all objects of pure thought, of nature and of Spirit, in the form of thought, and thus as the unity of the difference.

Religion, then, is itself the standpoint of the consciousness of the True, which is in and for itself, and is consequently the stage of Spirit at which the speculative content generally is object for consciousness. Religion is not consciousness of this or that truth in individual objects, but of the absolute truth, of truth as the Universal, the All-comprehending outside of which there lies nothing at all. The content of its consciousness is further the Universally True, which exists on its own account or in and for itself, which determines itself, and is not determined from without. While the finite required an Other for its determinateness, the True has its determinateness, the limit, its end in itself; it is not limited through an Other, but the Other is found in itself. It is this speculative element which comes to consciousness in religion. Truth is, indeed, contained in every other sphere, but not the highest absolute truth, for this exists only in perfect universality of characterization or determination, and in the fact of being determined in and for itself, which is not simple determinateness having reference to an Other, but contains the Other, the difference in its very self.

Religion is accordingly this speculative element in the form, as it were, of a state of consciousness, of which the aspects are not simple qualities of thought, but are concretely filled up. These moments can be no other than the moment of Thought, active universality, thought in operation, and reality as immediate, particular self-consciousness.

Now, while in philosophy the rigidity of these two sides loses itself through reconciliation in thought, because both sides are thoughts, and the one is not pure universal thought, and the other of an empirical and individual character, religion only arrives at the enjoyment of unity by lifting these two rigid extremes out of this state of severance, by rearranging them, and bringing them together again. But by thus stripping off the form of dualism from its extremes, rendering the opposition in the element of Universality fluid, and bringing it to reconciliation, religion remains always akin to thought, even in its form and movement; and philosophy, as simply active thought, and thought which unites opposed elements, has approached closely to religion. The contemplation of religion in thought has thus raised the determinate moments of religion to the rank of thoughts, and the question is how this contemplation of religion in thought is related generally to philosophy as forming an organic part in its system.

In philosophy, the Highest is called the Absolute, the Idea .... Accordingly, what is signified here is that we have got to specify the Concept, and thus it follows that the Concept is the signification; it is the Absolute, the nature of God as grasped by thought, the logical knowledge of this, to which we desire to attain. This, then, is the one signification of signification, and so far, that which we call the Absolute has a meaning identical with the expression God.

But we put the question again, in a second sense, according to which it is the opposite of this which is sought after. When we begin to occupy ourselves with pure thought-determinations, and not with outward ideas, it may be that the mind does not feel satisfied, is not at home, in these, and asks what this pure thought-determination signifies. For example, every one can understand for himself what is meant by the terms unity, objective, subjective, etc., and yet it may very well happen that the specific form of thought we call the unity of subjective and objective, the unity of real and ideal, is not understood. What is asked for in such a case is the meaning in the very opposite sense from that which was required before. Here it is an idea or a pictorial conception of the thought determination which is demanded, an example of the content, which has as yet only been given in thought. If we find a thought content difficult to understand, the difficulty lies in this, that we possess no pictorial idea of it; it is by means of an example that it becomes clear to us, and that the mind first feels at home with itself in this content. When, accordingly, we start with the ordinary conception of God, the Philosophy of Religion has to consider its signification—this, namely, that God is the Idea, the Absolute, the Essential Reality which is grasped in thought and in the Concept, and this it has in common with logical philosophy; the logical Idea is God as He is in Himself. But it is just the nature of God that He should not be implicit or in Himself only. He is as essentially for Himself, the Absolute Spirit, not only the Being who keeps Himself within thought, but who also manifests Himself, and gives Himself objectivity.

Thus, in contemplating the Idea of God, in the Philosophy of Religion, we have at the same time to do with the manner of His manifestation or presentation to us; He simply makes Himself apparent, represents Himself to Himself. This is the aspect of the determinate being or existence of the Absolute. In the Philosophy of Religion we have thus the Absolute as object; not, however, merely in the form of thought, but also in the form of its manifestation. The universal Idea is thus to be conceived of with the purely concrete meaning of essentiality in general, and is to be regarded from the point of view of its activity in displaying itself, in appearing, in revealing itself. Popularly speaking, we say God is the Lord of the natural world and of the realm of Spirit. He is the absolute harmony of the two, and it is He who produces and carries on this harmony. Here neither thought and Concept nor their manifestation—determinate being or existence—are wanting. This aspect, thus represented by determinate being, is itself, however, to be grasped again in thought, since we are here in the region of philosophy. Philosophy to begin with contemplates the Absolute as logical. Idea, the Idea as it is in thought, under the aspect in which its content is constituted by the specific forms of thought. Further, philosophy exhibits the Absolute in its activity, in its creations. This is the manner in which the Absolute becomes actual or 'for itself', becomes Spirit, and God is thus the result of philosophy. It becomes apparent, however, that this is not merely a result, but is something which eternally creates itself, and is that which precedes all else. The onesidedness of the result is abrogated and absorbed in the very result itself. Nature, finite Spirit, the world of consciousness, of intelligence, and of will, are embodiments of the divine Idea, but they are definite shapes, special modes of the appearance of the Idea, forms, in which the Idea has not yet penetrated to itself, so as to be absolute Spirit.

In the Philosophy of Religion, however, we do not contemplate the implicitly existing logical Idea merely, in its determinate character as pure thought, nor in those finite determinations where its mode of appearance is a finite one, but as it is in itself or implicitly in thought, and at the same time as it appears, manifests itself, and thus in infinite manifestation as Spirit,—which reflects itself in itself; for Spirit which does not appear, is not. In this characteristic of appearance *finite* appearance is also included—that is, the world of nature, and the world of finite spirit,—but Spirit is regarded as the power or force of these worlds, as producing them out of itself, and out of them producing itself.

This, then, is the position of the Philosophy of Religion in relation to the other parts of philosophy. Of the other parts, God is the result; here, this End is made the Beginning, and becomes our special Object, is the simply concrete Idea, with its infinite manifestations; and this characteristic concerns the content of the Philosophy of Religion. We look at this content, however, from the point of view of rational thought, and this concerns the form, and brings us to consider the position of the Philosophy of Religion with regard to religion as this latter appears in the shape of positive religion.

Now to the relation of the Philosophy of Religion to positive religion. It is well known that the faith of the Church, more especially of the Protestant Church, has taken a fixed form as a system of doctrine. This content has been universally accepted as truth; and as the description of what God is, and of what man is in relation to God, it has been called the *Creed,* that is, in the subjective sense that which is believed, and objectively, what is to be known as content, in the Christian Church, and what God has revealed Himself to be. Now as universal established doctrine this content is partly laid down in the Apostolic *Symbolum* or Apostles' Creed, partly in later symbolical books. And moreover, in the Protestant Church the Bible has always been characterized as the essential foundation of doctrine.

Accordingly, in the apprehension and determination of the content of doctrine, the influence of reason, as 'argumentation' has made itself felt. At first indeed, this was so much the case that the doctrinal content, and the Bible as its positive foundation, were to remain unquestioned, and thought was only to take up the thoughts of the Bible as Exegesis. But as a matter of fact understanding had previously established its opinions and its thoughts for itself, and then attention was directed towards observing how the words of Scripture could be explained in accordance with these. The words of the Bible are a statement of truth which is not systematic; they are Christianity as it appeared in the beginning; it is Spirit which grasps the content, which unfolds its meaning.

God is not emptiness, but Spirit; and this characteristic of Spirit does not remain for it a word only, or a superficial characteristic; on the contrary, the nature of Spirit unfolds itself for rational thought, inasmuch as it apprehends God as essentially the Triune God. Thus God is conceived of as making Himself an object to Himself, and further, the object remains in this distinction in identity with

God; in it God loves Himself. Without this characteristic of Trinity, God would not be Spirit, and Spirit would be an empty word. But if God be conceived as Spirit, then this conception includes the *subjective* side in itself or even develops itself so as to reach to that side, and the Philosophy of Religion, as the contemplation of religion by thought, binds together again the determinate content of religion in its entirety.

The Philosophy of Religion cannot, therefore, in the fashion of that metaphysics of the Understanding and exegesis of inferences, put itself in opposition to positive religion, and to such doctrine of the Church as has still preserved its content. On the contrary, it will become apparent that it stands infinitely nearer to positive doctrine than it seems at first sight to do. Indeed, the re-establishment of the doctrines of the Church, reduced to a minimum by the Understanding, is so truly the work of philosophy, that it is decried by that so-called Theology of Reason, which is merely a Theology of the Understanding, as a darkening of the mind, and this just because of the true content possessed by it. The fears of the Understanding, and its hatred of philosophy, arise from a feeling of apprehension, based on the fact that it perceives how philosophy carries back its reflecting process to its foundation, that is, to the affirmative in which it perishes, and yet that philosophy arrives at a content, and at a knowledge of the nature of God, after all content seemed to be already done away with. Every content appears to this negative tendency to be a darkening of the mind, its only desire being to continue in that nocturnal darkness which it calls enlightenment, and hence the rays of the light of knowledge must be necessarily regarded by it as hostile. It is sufficient here merely to observe regarding the supposed opposition of the Philosophy of Religion and positive religion, that there cannot be two kinds of reason and two kinds of Spirit; there cannot be a Divine reason and a human, there cannot be a Divine Spirit and a human, which are *absolutely different.* Human reason—the consciousness of one's being is indeed reason; it is the divine in man, and Spirit, in so far as it is the Spirit of God, is not a spirit beyond the stars, beyond the world. On the contrary, God is present, omnipresent, and exists as Spirit in all spirits. God is a living God, who is acting and working. Religion is a product of the Divine Spirit; it is not a discovery of man, but a work of divine operation and creation in him. The expression that God as reason rules the world, would be irrational if we did not assume that it has reference also to religion, and that the Divine Spirit works in the special character and form assumed by religion. But the development of reason as perfected in thought does not stand in opposition to this Spirit, and consequently it cannot be absolutely different from the work which the Divine Spirit has produced in religion. The more a man in thinking rationally lets the true thing or fact itself hold sway with him, renounces his particularity, acts as universal consciousness, while his reason does not seek its own in the sense of something special, the less will he as the embodiment of this reason, get into that condition of opposition; for it, namely, reason, is itself the essential fact or thing, the spirit, the Divine Spirit. The Church or the theologians may disdain this aid, or may take it amiss when their doctrine is made reasonable; they may even repel the exertions of philosophy with proud irony, though these are not directed in a hostile spirit against religion, but, on the contrary, seek to fathom its truth; and they may ridicule the manufactured truth—but this scorn is no longer of any avail, and is, in fact, idle when once the need of true rational knowledge, and the sense of discord between it and religion, have been awakened. The intelligence has here its rights, which can in no way be longer denied to it, and the triumph of knowledge is the reconciliation of the opposition.

Although then, philosophy, as the Philosophy of Religion is so very different from those tendencies of the understanding, which are at bottom hostile to religion, and is in no way such a spectral thing as it has usually been represented to be, yet even at the present day we still see the belief in the absolute opposition between philosophy and religion made one of the shibboleths of the time. All those principles of the religious consciousness which have been developed at the present time, however widely distinguished their forms may be from one another, yet agree in this, that they are at enmity with philosophy, and endeavour at all hazards to prevent it from occupying itself with religion; and the work that now lies before us is to consider philosophy in its relation to these *principles of the time.* From this consideration of the subject we may confidently promise ourselves success, all the more that it will become apparent how, in presence of all that enmity which is shown to philosophy, from however many sides it way come—indeed, it comes from almost every side of consciousness in its present form—the time has nevertheless arrived when philosophy can, partly in an unprejudiced and partly in a favourable and successful manner, occupy itself with religion. For, the opposition takes one or other of those forms of the divided consciousness which we considered above. They occupy partly the standpoint of the metaphysics of the Understanding, for which God is emptiness, and content has vanished, partly the standpoint of feeling, which after the loss of absolute content has withdrawn itself into its empty subjectivity, but is in accord with that metaphysics in coming to the result that every characterization is inadequate to the eternal content—for this indeed is only an abstraction. Or we may even see that the assertions of the opponents of philosophy contain nothing else than what philosophy itself contains as its principle, and as the foundation of its principle. This contradiction, namely, that the opponents of philosophy are the opponents of religion who have been overcome by it, and that they yet implicitly possess the principle of philosophical knowledge in their reflections, has its foundation in this, that they represent the historical element out of which philosophical thought in its complete shape has been formed.

DIVISION OF THE SUBJECT

There can be but one method in all science, since the method is the self-unfolding Concept (*Begriff*) and nothing else, and this latter is only one.

In accordance, therefore, with the moments of the Concept, the exposition and development of religion will be presented in three parts. In the first place, the notion or conception of religion will be considered in its universal aspect; then, secondly, in its particular form as the self-dividing and self-differentiating notion, that is, under the aspect of judgment [*Ur-theil = separation of subject from predicate*] of limitation, of difference, and of finiteness; and thirdly, we shall consider the notion, which encloses itself within itself, the syllogism, or the return of the notion to itself out of the particularity in which it is unequal to itself, so that it arrives at equality with its form, and does away with its limitation. This is the rhythm, the pure eternal life of Spirit itself; and had it not this movement, it would be something dead. It is of the essential nature of Spirit to have itself as object, and thence arises its manifestation. But here Spirit is to begin with in the relation of objectivity, and in this relation it is something finite. The third stage is reached when it is object to itself in such a way that it reconciles itself with itself in the object, is 'with itself', and in being so has attained its freedom. For freedom means to be self-contained, or at home with oneself.

Such, then, is the division of the subject, representing the movement, nature, and action of Spirit itself, of which we, so to speak, are only spectators. It is necessitated by the Notion; the necessity of the progression has, however, to present, explicate, prove itself in the development itself. The division, the different parts and content of which we shall now indicate in a more definite way, is therefore simply historical.

First, the general Concept (*Begriff*) of Religion. What comes first is the notion in its universal aspect, what follows in the second place is the determinateness of the notion, the notion in its definite forms.

For the philosophical way of looking at things, too, the notion occupies the first place, but here the notion is the content itself, the absolute subject-matter, the substance, as in the case of the germ, out of which the whole tree develops itself. All specifications or determinations are contained in this, the whole nature of the tree, the kind of sap it has, the way in which the branches grow; but in a spiritual manner, and not pre-formed so that a microscope could reveal its boughs, its leaves, in miniature. It is thus that the notion contains the whole nature of the object, and knowledge itself is nothing else than the development of the notion, of that which is implicitly contained in the notion, and has not yet come into existence, has not been unfolded, displayed. Thus we begin with the notion or conception of religion.

In the notion or conception of religion the purely universal, again, does indeed take the first place; that is, the moment of thought in, its complete universality.

It is not this or that that is thought, but *Thought thinks itself*. The object is the Universal, which, as active, is Thought. As the act of rising-up to the True, religion is a departing from sensuous, finite objects.

If we now say that religion has the moment of thought in its complete Universality in itself, and that the Unlimited Universal is supreme absolute Thought, we do not as yet make the distinction here between subjective and objective Thought. The Universal is object, and is thought pure and simple, but not as yet thought developed and made determinate in itself. All distinctions are as yet absent, and exist potentially only. In this ether of thought all that is finite has passed away, everything has disappeared, while at the same time everything is included in it. But this element of the Universal has not as yet taken those more explicit forms. Out of this liquid element, and in this transparency, nothing has as yet fashioned itself into distinct shape.

Now the further advance consists in this, that this Universal determines itself for itself, and this self-determination constitutes the development of the Idea of God. In the sphere of Universality the Idea itself is, to begin with, the material of determination, and the progress is revealed in divine figures, but as yet the second element—form—is retained in the divine Idea, which is still in its substantiality, and under the character of eternity it remains in the bosom of the Universal.

The particularization, therefore, which is as yet retained in the sphere of the Universal, when it actually manifests itself outwardly as such, constitutes the Other as against the extreme of Universality, and this other extreme is consciousness in its individuality as such. It is the subject in its immediacy, and with its needs, conditions, sins—in fact, in its wholly empirical, temporal character.

In religion, I am myself the *relation* of the two sides as thus determined. I who think, who am that which lifts myself up, the active Universal, and Ego, the immediate subject, are one and the same 'I' And further, the *relation* of these two sides which are so sharply opposed—the absolutely finite consciousness and being on the one hand, and the infinite on the other—exists in religion for *me*. In thinking I lift myself up to the Absolute above all that is finite, and am infinite consciousness, while I am at the same time finite consciousness, and indeed am such in accordance with my whole empirical character. Both sides, as well as their relation, exist for me. Both sides seek each other, and both flee from each other. At one time, for example, I accentuate my empirical, finite consciousness, and place myself in opposition to infiniteness; at another I exclude myself from myself, condemn myself, and give the preponderance to the infinite consciousness. The middle term contains nothing else than the characteristics of both the extremes.

I am thus the relation of these two sides, which are not abstract determinations, as 'finite and infinite'. On the contrary, each is itself totality. Each of the two extremes is itself 'I', what relates them; and the holding together, the relating is itself this which is at once in conflict with itself, and brings itself to unity in the conflict. Or, to put it differently, I am the conflict, for the conflict is just this antagonism, which is not any indifference of the two as different, but is their being bound together. I am not *one* of those taking part in the strife, but I am both the combatants, and am the strife itself. I am the fire and the water which touch each other, and am the contact and union of what flies apart, and this very contact itself is this double, essentially conflicting relation, as the relation of what is now separated, severed, and now reconciled and in unity with itself.

The movement in the preceding sphere is just that of the notion of God, of the Idea, in becoming objective to itself. We have this movement before us in the language of ordinary thought, in the expression 'God is a Spirit'. Spirit is not something having a single existence, but is Spirit only in being objective to itself, and in beholding itself in the 'Other', as itself. The highest characteristic of Spirit is self-consciousness, which includes this objectivity in itself. God, as Idea, is subjective for what is objective, and is objective for what is subjective. When the moment of subjectivity defines itself further, so that the distinction is made between God as Object and the knowing spirit, the subjective side defines itself in this distinction as that which belongs to the side of finiteness, and the two stand at first so contrasted, that the separation constitutes the antithesis of finiteness and infiniteness. This infinitude, however, being still encumbered with this opposition, is not the true infinitude; to the subjective side, which exists for itself, the absolute object remains still an Other, and the relation in which it stands to it is not self-consciousness. Such an attitude, however, also involves the relation which is expressed by saying, that the finite knows itself as a nullity in its state of separation, and knows its object as the Absolute, as its Substance. And here the first attitude toward the absolute object is that of fear; for individuality knows itself as in regard to the absolute object only as accidental, or as something which is transient and vanishing. But this standpoint of separation is not the true relation. On the contrary, it is what knows itself to be a nullity, and, therefore, something which is to be done away with and absorbed and its attitude is not merely a negative one, but is in itself, or implicitly, positive. The subject recognizes the absolute substance, in which it has to annul or lose itself, as being at the same time its essence, its substance, in which, therefore, self-consciousness is inherently contained. It is this unity, reconciliation, restoration of the subject and of its self-consciousness, the positive feeling of possessing a share in, of partaking in this Absolute, and making unity with it actually one's own—this abolition of the dualism, which constitutes the sphere of worship. Worship comprises this entire inward and outward action, which has this restoration to unity as its object. The expression 'worship' is usually taken merely in the limited sense in which it is understood to mean only outward public acts, and the inward action of the heart does not get so much prominence. We, however, shall conceive of worship as that action which includes both inwardness and outward manifestation, and which in fact produces restoration of unity with the Absolute, and in so doing is also essentially an inward conversion of the spirit and soul. Thus Christian worship does not only include the sacraments and the acts and duties pertaining to the Church, but it also includes the so-called 'way of salvation' as a matter of absolutely inward history, and as a series of actions on the part of the inner life—in fact, a movement which goes forward in the soul, and has its right place there.

But we shall always find these two sides, that of self-consciousness, that is, of worship, and that of consciousness or of idea, corresponding with each other at every stage of religion. According as the content of the notion or conception of God or consciousness is determined, so too is the attitude of the subject to Him; or to put it otherwise, so too is self-consciousness in worship determined. The one moment is always a reflection or copy of the other, the one points to the other. Both modes, of which the one holds fast to objective consciousness only, and the other to pure self-consciousness, are one-sided, and each brings about its own abrogation.

It was, therefore, a one-sided view if the natural theology of former times looked upon God as' Object of consciousness only. Such a mode of contemplating the Idea of God, although the words 'Spirit' or 'Person' might be made use of, could never in reality get beyond the idea of an Essence. It was inconsistent, for if actually carried out it must have led to the other, the subjective side, that of self-consciousness.

It is just as one-sided to conceive of religion as something subjective only, thus in fact making the subjective aspect the only one. So regarded, worship is absolutely bald and empty; its action is a movement which makes no advance, its attitude toward God a relation to a nullity, an aiming at nothing. But even this merely subjective action has inconsistency inherent in it, and must of necessity annul itself. For if the subjective side also is to be in any way determined or qualified, it is involved too in the very conception of Spirit, that it is consciousness, and that its determinate character becomes object to it. The richer the feeling, the more fully determined or specialized it is, the richer must the object be for it too. And further, the absoluteness of that feeling which is supposed to be substantial, would, in accordance with its very nature, require to get itself free from its subjectivity; for the substantial character which is supposed to belong to it, is specially directed against the accidental element of opinion and of inclination, is in fact something permanent and fixed in and for itself, independent of our feeling or experience. It is the Objective, what exists in and for itself. If this substantial element remains shut up in the heart only, it is not recognized as the something higher than ourselves, and God Himself becomes something merely subjective, while the efforts of subjectivity remain at the most, as it were a drawing of lines into empty space. For the recognition of a something higher than ourselves, which is capable too of being described, this recognition of One who is undefined, and these lines which are to be drawn in accordance with such recognition, possess no support, no connecting element, derived from what is objective, and are and remain merely our act, our lines, something subjective and the finite never attains to a true real renunciation of itself; while Spirit ought, on the contrary, in worship to liberate itself from its finiteness, and to feel and know itself in God. In the absence of that which is self-existent and commands our obedience, all worship shrinks up into subjectivity.

Worship is essentially made up of dealings with and enjoyment of a something higher than ourselves, and includes assurances, evidences, and confirmation of the existence of this higher Being; but such definite dealings, such actual enjoying and assurances can have no place if the objective, obligatory moment be wanting to them, and worship would, in fact, be annihilated if the subjective side were taken to be the whole. The possibility of getting out of the subjective heart into action would thus be as much precluded as the possibility of consciousness attaining to objective knowledge. The one is connected in the closest manner with the other. What a man believes he has to do in relation to God, corresponds with the idea which he has formed of God. His consciousness of self answers to his consciousness, and conversely he cannot believe himself to have any definite duties toward God if he neither have nor suppose himself to have any definite idea of Him as an Object. Not until religion is really relation, and contains the distinction involved in consciousness, does worship attain to a definite form as the lifting up into a higher unity of the severed elements, and become a vital process. This movement of worship does not, however, confine itself to the inner life alone in which consciousness frees itself from its finiteness, is the consciousness of its essence, and the subject as knowing itself in God has penetrated into the foundation of its life. But this its infinite life now develops towards what is outside too, for the worldly life which the subject leads has that substantial consciousness as its basis, and the way and manner in which the subject defines its ends depends on the consciousness of its essential truth. It is in connection with this side that religion reflects itself into worldly or secular life, and that knowledge of the world shows itself. This going out into the actual world is essential to religion, and in this transition religion appears as morality in relation to the State and to the entire life of the State. According, as the religion of nations is constituted, so also is their morality and their government. The shape taken by these latter depends entirely on whether the conception of the freedom of Spirit which a people has reached is a limited one, or on whether the nation has the true consciousness of freedom.

If in the first part we have considered religion in its notion or conception, the simple conception of religion, the character of the content, the Universal, it is now necessary to leave this sphere of Universality and go on to treat of determinateness in religion.

The notion as such is not as yet unfolded; the determinate qualities, the moments are contained in it, but are not as yet openly displayed, and have not received the right distinction or difference which belongs to them. It is only by means of the judgment (i.e., the act of differentiation) that they receive this. It is when God, the Notion, performs the act of judgment, and the category of determinateness enters, that we first come to have existing religion, which is at the same time definitely existing religion.

The course followed in passing from the abstract to the concrete is based upon our method, upon the notion, and not on the fact that much special content is present. There is a complete distinction between this and our point of view. Spirit, to which belongs Being which is absolute and supreme, is, exists only as activity; that is to say, in so far as it posits itself, is actual or for itself, and produces itself. But in this its activity it has the power of *knowing*, and only as it thus knows is it that which it is. It is thus essential to religion not only to exist in its notion, but also to be the consciousness of that which the notion is, and the material in which the notion as the plan, so to speak, realizes itself, which it makes its own, which it molds in accordance with itself, is human consciousness. So too, Right, for example, only is when it exists in the spirit, when it takes possession of the wills of men, and they know of it as the determination of their wills. And it is in this way that the Idea first realizes itself, having before only been posited as the form of the notion.

Spirit, in short, is not immediate; natural things are immediate, and remain in this condition of immediate Being. The Being of Spirit is not thus immediate, but is, exists only as producing itself, as making itself for itself by means of negation as Subject; otherwise it would be substance only. And this coming to itself on the part of Spirit is movement, activity, and mediation of itself with itself.

A stone is immediate, it is complete. Wherever there is life, however, this activity is already to be found. Thus the first form of the existence of plants is the feeble existence of the germ, and out of this it has to develop itself and to produce itself. Finally the plant epitomizes itself when it has unfolded itself in the seed; this beginning of the plant is also its ultimate product. In like manner man is at first a child, and as belonging to Nature he describes this round in order to beget another.

In plants there are two kinds of individual forms this germ which begins, is different from the one which is the completion of its life, and in which this evolution reaches maturity. But it is the very nature of Spirit, just because it is living, to be at first only potential, to be in its notion or conception, then to come forward into existence, to unfold, produce itself, become mature, bringing forth the notion of itself, that which it implicitly is, so that what it is in itself or implicitly may be its notion actually or for itself. The child is not as yet a reasonable person; it has capacities only, it is at first reason, Spirit, potentially only. It is by means of education and development that it becomes Spirit.

This, then, is what is called self-determination entering into existence, being 'for other', bringing one's moments into distinction, and unfolding one's self. These distinctions are no other than the characteristics which the notion itself implicitly contains.

The development of these distinctions, and the course of the tendencies which result from them, are the way by which Spirit comes to itself; it is itself, however, the goal. The absolute end, which is that Spirit should know itself, comprehend itself, should become object to itself as it is in itself, arrive at perfect knowledge of itself, first appears as its true Being. Now this process, followed by self-producing Spirit, this path taken by it, includes distinct moments; but the path is not as yet the goal, and Spirit does not reach the goal without having traversed the path; it is not originally at the goal; even what is most perfect must traverse the path to the goal in order to attain it. Spirit, in these halting places of its progress, is not as yet perfect; its knowledge, its consciousness regarding itself, is not what is true, and it is not as yet revealed to itself. Spirit being essentially this activity of self-production, it follows that there are stages of its consciousness, but its consciousness of itself is always in proportion only to the stage which has been reached. Now these stages supply us with definite religion; here religion is consciousness of the universal Spirit, which is not as yet fully developed as absolute; this consciousness of Spirit at each stage is definite consciousness of itself, it is the path of the education of Spirit. We have therefore to consider the definite forms of religion. These, as being stages on the road followed by Spirit, are imperfect.

The different forms or specific kinds of religion are, in one aspect, moments of religion in general, or of perfected religion. They have, however, an independent aspect too, for in them religion has developed itself in time, and historically.

Religion, in so far as it is definite, and has not as yet completed the circle of its determinateness—so far that is as it is finite religion, and exists as finite—is historical religion, or a particular form of religion. Its principal moments, and also the manner in which they exist historically, being exhibited in the progress of religion from stage to stage, and in its development, there thus arises a series of forms of religion, or a history of religion. That which is determined by means of the Notion must of necessity have existed, and the religions, as they have followed upon one another, have not arisen accidentally. It is Spirit which rules inner life, and to see only, chance here, after the fashion of the historical school, is absurd.

The essential moments of the notion or conception of religion show themselves and make their appearance at every stage in which religion exists at all. It is only because the moments are not as yet posited in the totality of the notion that any difference between it and its true form arises. These definite religions are not indeed our religion, yet they are included in ours as essential, although as subordinate moments, which cannot miss having in them absolute truth. Therefore in them we have not to do with what is foreign to us, but with what is our own, and the knowledge that such is the case is the reconciliation of the true religion with the false. Thus the moments of the notion or conception of religion appear on lower stages of development, though as yet in the shape of anticipations or presentiments, as natural flowers and creations of fancy which have, so to speak, blossomed forth by chance. What determines the characteristics of these stages, however, through their entire history, is the determinateness of the notion itself, which can at no stage be absent. The thought of the Incarnation, for example, pervades every religion. Such general conceptions make their presence felt too in other spheres of Spirit. What is substantial in moral relations, as, for example, property, marriage, protection of the sovereign and of the State, and the ultimate decision which rests with subjectivity regarding that which is to be done for the whole, all this is to be found in an uneducated society as well as in the perfect state; only the definite form of this substantial element differs according to the degree of culture which such a society has reached. What is here of special importance, however, is that the notion should also become actually known in its totality, and in exact accordance with the degree in which this knowledge is present, is the stage at which the religious spirit is, higher or lower, richer or poorer. Spirit may have something in its possession without having a developed consciousness of it. It actually has the immediate, proper nature of Spirit, has a physical, organic nature, but it does not know that nature in its essential character and truth, and has only an approximate, general idea of it. Men live in the State, they are themselves the life, activity, actuality of the State, but the positing, the becoming conscious of what the State is, does not on that account take place, and yet the perfected State just means that everything which is *potentially* in it, that is to say, in its notion or conception should be developed, posited, and made into rights and duties, into law. In like manner the moments of the notion or conception are actually present in the definite religions, in mental pictures, feelings, or immediate imagery; but the *consciousness* of these moments is not as yet evolved, or, in other words, they have not as yet been elevated to the point at which they are the determination of the absolute object, and God is not as yet actually represented under these determinations of the totality of the conception of religion.

It is undoubtedly true that the definite religions of the various peoples often enough exhibit the most distorted, confused, and abortive ideas of the divine Being, and likewise of duties and relations as expressed in worship. But we must not treat the matter so lightly, and conceive of it in so superficial a manner, as to reject these ideas and these rites as superstition, error, and deceit, or only trace back their origin to pious feeling, and thus value them as merely representing some sort of religious feeling without caring how they may chance to be constituted. The mere collection and elaboration of the external and visible elements cannot satisfy us either. On the contrary, something higher is necessary, namely, to recognize the meaning, the truth, and the connection with truth; in short, to get to know what is rational in them They are human beings who have hit upon such religions, therefore there must be *reason* in them, and amidst all that is accidental in them a higher necessity. We must do them this justice, for what is human, rational in them, is our own too, although it exists in our higher consciousness as a moment only. To get a grasp of the history of religions in this sense means to reconcile ourselves even with what is horrible, dreadful, or absurd in them, and to justify it. We are on no account to regard it as right or true, as it presents itself in its purely immediate form—there is no question of doing this—but we are at least to recognize its beginning, the source from which in it has originated as being in human nature. Such is the reconciliation with this entire sphere, the reconciliation which completes itself in the notion. Religions, as they follow upon one another, are determined by means of the notion. Their nature and succession are not determined from without; on the contrary, they are determined by the nature of Spirit which has entered into the world to bring itself to consciousness of itself. Since we look at these definite religions in accordance with the notion, this is a purely philosophical study of what actually is or exists. Philosophy indeed treats of nothing which is not and does not concern itself with what is so powerless as not even to have the energy to force itself into existence.

Now in development as such, in so far as it has not as yet reached its goal, the moments of the notion are still in a state of separation or mutual exclusion, so that the reality has not as yet come to be equal to the notion or conception. The finite religions are the appearance in history of these moments. In order to grasp these in their truth, it is necessary to consider them under two aspects; on the one hand, we have to consider how God is known, how He is characterized; and on the other, how the subject at, the same time knows itself. For the two aspects the objective and subjective have but one foundation for their further determination, and but one specific character pervades them both. The idea which a man has of God corresponds with that which he has of himself, of his freedom. Knowing himself in God, he at the same time knows his imperishable life in God; He knows of the truth of his Being, and therefore the idea of the *immortality of the soul* here enters as an essential moment into the history of religion. The ideas of God and of immortality have a necessary relation to each other; when a man knows truly about God, he knows truly about himself too: the two sides correspond with each other. At first God is something quite undetermined; but in the course of the development of the human mind, the consciousness of that which God is gradually forms and matures itself, losing more and more of its initial indefiniteness, and with this the development of true *self*-consciousness advances also. The Proofs of the Existence of God fall to be included also within the sphere of this progressive development, it being their aim to set forth the necessary elevation of the spirit to God. For the diversity of the characteristics which in this process of elevation are attributed to God, is fixed by the diversity of the points of departure, and this diversity again has its foundation in the nature of the historical stage of actual self-consciousness which has been reached. The different forms which this elevation of the spirit takes will always indicate the metaphysical spirit of the period in question, for this corresponds with the prevalent idea of God and the sphere of worship. If we now attempt to indicate in a more precise way the divisions of this stage of definite religion, we find that what is of primary importance here is the manner of the divine manifestation. God is manifestation, not in a general sense merely, but as being Spirit He determines Himself as appearing to Himself; that is to say, He is not Object in the general sense, but is Object to Himself.

As for manifestation generally, or abstract manifestation, it is Nature in General. Manifestation is Being for Other, an externalization of things mutually distinct, and not yet reflected and one, in fact, which is immediate into itself. This logical determination is taken here in its concrete sense as the natural world. What is for an 'Other', exists for this very reason in a sensuous form. The thought, which is for another thought, which, as having Being, is to be posited as distinct, that is to say, as something which exists as an independent subject in reference to the other, is only capable of being communicated by the one to the other through the sensuous medium of sign or speech, in fact, by bodily means.

But since God exists essentially only as appearing to Himself, that abstract attitude of man to nature does not belong to religion; on the contrary, in religion nature is only a moment of the Divine, and therefore must, as it exists for the religious consciousness, have also the characteristic note of the spiritual mode of existence in it. It thus does not remain in its pure, natural element, but receives the characteristic quality of the Divine which dwells in it. It cannot be said of any religion that in it men have worshipped the sun, the sea, or nature; when they worship these objects, the latter no longer have for the worshippers the prosaic character which they have for ourselves. Even while these objects are for them divine, they still, it is true, remain natural; but when they become objects of religion, they at once assume a spiritual aspect. The contemplation of the sun, the stars, etc., as individual natural phenomena, is outside the sphere of religion. The so-called prosaic manner of looking at nature, as the latter exists for consciousness when regarding it through the understanding, betokens a separation which comes later; its presence is consequent on much deeper and more thorough-going reflection. Not till the spirit or mind has posited itself independently for itself, and as free from nature, does the latter appear to it as an Other, as something external.

The first mode of manifestation then, in the form of Nature namely, has the subjectivity, the spiritual nature of God as its centre in a general sense only, and consequently these two determinations have not as yet come into relation through reflection. When this takes place, it constitutes the second mode of manifestation.

In Himself or potentially God is Spirit; this is our notion or conception of Him. But for this very reason He must be posited too as Spirit, and this means that the manner of His manifestation must be itself a *spiritual* one, and consequently the negation of the natural. And for this it is necessary that His determinateness, the Idea on the side of reality, be equal to the conception; and the relation of reality to the divine conception is complete when Spirit exists as Spirit; that is to say, when both the conception and reality exist as this Spirit. To begin with, however, we see that the form of nature constitutes that determinateness of the conception of God, or the aspect of reality belonging to the Idea. The emergence of the spiritual element of subjectivity out of nature, accordingly appears at first merely as a conflict between the two sides, which are still entangled with one another in that conflict. Therefore this stage of definite religion too remains in the sphere of what is natural, and in fact constitutes, in common with the preceding one, the stage of the Religion of Nature.

It is actually within the definite religions as they succeed each other that Spirit in its movement attempts to make the determinateness correspond with the notion or conception, but this determinateness appears here as still abstract, or, to put it otherwise, the notion appears as still the finite notion. These attempts, in which the principle of the preceding stages, namely, Essence, or essential Being, strives to grasp itself together into infinite inwardness are: 1. the Jewish religion; 2. the Greek; 3. the Roman. The God of the Jews is Oneness or soleness, which as such continues to be abstract unity, and is not as yet concrete in itself. This God is indeed God in the Spirit, but does not exist as yet *as* Spirit. He is something not presented to sense, an abstraction of Thought, which has not as yet that fullness in itself which constitutes it Spirit. The freedom which the notion seeks to reach through self-development in the Greek religion, still lives under the sway of up sceptre of necessity of Essence; and the notion as it appears in and seeks to win its independence in the Roman religion is still limited, since it is related to an external world which stands opposite to it, in which it is only to be objective, and is, therefore, external adaptation to an end, or external utility.

These are the principal specific forms which here present themselves as the modes of the Reality of Spirit. As *determinate* they are inadequate to the notion or conception of Spirit, and are finite in character, and this infinitude, namely, that there is one God, this abstract affirmation, is finite also. This determination of the manifestation of God in consciousness as pure ideality of the One, as abolition of the manifold character of external manifestation, might perhaps be contrasted, as being that which is true, with the religion of nature, but it is really only one form of determinateness as against the totality of the notion of Spirit. It corresponds with this totality just as little as its opposite does. These definite relations are not in fact as yet the true religion, and in them God is not as yet known in His true nature, since there is wanting to them the absolute content of Spirit.

Manifestation, development, and determination or specification do not go on *ad infinitum,* and do not cease *accidentally.* True progress consists rather in this, that this reflection of the notion into itself stops short, inasmuch as it really returns into itself. Thus manifestation is itself infinite in nature; the content is in accordance with the conception of Spirit, and the manifestation is, like Spirit, in and for itself. The notion or conception of religion has in religion become objective to itself. Spirit, which is in and for itself, has now no longer individual forms, determinations of itself, before it, as it unfolds itself. It knows itself no longer as Spirit in any definite form or limitation, but has now overcome those limitations, this finiteness, and is actually, what it is potentially. This knowledge of Spirit for itself or actually, as it is in itself or potentially, is the being in-and-for-itself of Spirit as exercising knowledge, the perfect, absolute religion, in which it is revealed what Spirit, what God is; this is the Christian religion.

That Spirit, as it does in all else, must in religion also run through its natural course, is necessarily bound up with the conception of Spirit. Spirit is only Spirit when it exists for itself as the negation of all finite forms, as this absolute ideality.

I form ideas, I have perceptions, and here there is a certain definite content, as, for instance, this house, and so on. They are my perceptions, they present themselves to me I could not, however, present them to myself if I did not grasp this particular content in myself, and if I had not posited it in a simple, ideal manner in myself. Ideality means that this definite external existence, these conditions of space, of time, and matter, this separateness of parts, is done away with in something higher; in that I know this external existence, these forms of it are not ideas which are mutually exclusive, but are comprehended, grasped together in me in a simple manner.

Spirit is knowledge; but in order that knowledge should exist, it is necessary that the content of that which it knows should have attained to this ideal form, and should in this way have been negated. What Spirit is must in that way have become its own, it must have described this circle; and these forms, differences, determinations, finite qualities, must have existed in order that it should make them its own.

This represents both the way and the goal—that Spirit should have attained to its own notion or conception, to that which it implicitly is, and in this way only, the way which has been indicated in its abstract moments, does it attain it. Revealed religion is manifested religion, because in it God has become wholly manifest. Here all is proportionate to the notion; there is no longer anything secret in God. Here, then, is the consciousness of the developed conception of Spirit, of reconciliation, not in beauty, in joyousness, but *in the Spirit*. Revealed religion, which was hitherto still veiled, and did not exist in its truth, came at its own time. This was not a chance time, dependent on some one's liking, or caprice, but determined on in the essential, eternal counsel of God; that is, in the eternal reason, wisdom of God; it is the notion of the reality or fact itself, the divine notion, the notion of God Himself, which determines itself to enter on this development, and has set its goal before it.

This course thus followed by religion is the true theodicy; it exhibits all products of Spirit, every form of its self-knowledge, as necessary, because Spirit is something living, working, and its impulse is to press on through the series of its manifestations towards the consciousness of itself as embracing all truth.

HISTORY OF PHILOSOPHY

'Thus the Idea, and it alone is Truth. Now it is essentially in the nature of the Idea to develop, and only through development to arrive at comprehension of itself, or to become what it is. That the Idea should have to make itself what it is, seems like a contradiction; it may be said that it is what it is'.

7

HISTORY OF PHILOSOPHY

INTRODUCTION

There are various aspects under which the History of Philosophy may possess interest. We shall find the central point of this interest in the essential connection existing between what is apparently past and the present stage reached by Philosophy. That this connection is not one of the external considerations which may be taken into account in the history of Philosophy, but really expresses its inner character: that the events of this history, while they perpetuate themselves in their effects like all other events, yet produce their results in a special way—this it is which is here to be more clearly expounded.

 The acts of thought appear at first to be a matter of history, and, therefore, things of the past and outside our real existence. But in reality we are what we are through history: or, more accurately, as in the history of Thought, what has passed away is only one side, so in the present, what we have as a permanent possession is essentially bound up with our place in history. The possession of self-conscious reason, which belongs to us of the present world, did not arise suddenly, nor did it grow only from the soil of the present. This possession must be regarded as previously present, as an inheritance, and as the result of labour—the labour of all past generations of men. Just as the arts of outward life, the accumulated skill and invention, the customs and arrangements of social and political life, are the result of the thought, care, and needs, of the want and the misery, of the ingenuity, the plans and achievements of those who preceded us in history, so, likewise, in science, and specially in Philosophy, do we owe what we are to the tradition which, as Herder has put it like a holy chain, runs through all that was transient, and has therefore passed away. Thus has been preserved and transmitted to us what antiquity produced.

 The ideas and questions which may be present to our mind regarding the character and ends of the history of Philosophy, depend on the nature of the relationship here given. In this lies the explanation of the fact that the study of the history of Philosophy is an introduction to Philosophy itself. The guiding principles for the formation of this history are given in this fact, the further discussion of which must thus be the main object of this introduction. We must also, however, keep in mind, as being of fundamental importance, the conception of the aim of Philosophy. And since, as already mentioned, the systematic exposition of this conception cannot here find a place, such discussion as we can now undertake, can only propose to deal with the subject provisionally and not to give a thorough and conclusive account of the nature of the Becoming of Philosophy.

This Becoming is not merely a passive movement, as we suppose movements such as those of the sun and moon to be. It is no mere movement in the unresisting medium of space and time. What we must represent to ourselves is the activity of free thought; we have to present the history of the world of thought as it has arisen and produced itself.

There are, therefore, the following points with which I wish to deal in this introduction.

The first of these will be to investigate the character of the history of Philosophy, its significance, its nature, and its aim, from which will follow inferences as to its treatment. In particular, we shall get an insight into the relation of the history of Philosophy to the science of Philosophy, and this will be the most interesting point of all. That is to say, this history represents, not merely the external, accidental, events contained within it, but it shows how the content, or that which appears to belong to mere history, really belongs to the science of Philosophy. The history of Philosophy is itself scientific, and thus essentially becomes the science of Philosophy.

In the second place, the Notion of Philosophy must be more adequately determined, and from it must be deduced what should be excluded from the history of Philosophy out of the infinite material and the manifold aspects of the intellectual culture of the nations. Religion, certainly, and the thoughts contained in and regarding it, particularly when these are in the form of mythology, are, on account of their matter, and the sciences with their ideas on the state, duties and laws, on account of their form, so near Philosophy that the history of the science of Philosophy threatens to become quite indefinite in extent. It might be supposed that the history of Philosophy should take account of all these ideas. Has not everything been called Philosophy and philosophizing? On the other hand, when the province of Philosophy has been correctly defined, we reach, with the determination of what Philosophy is and what pertains to it, the starting-point of its history, which must be distinguished from the commencements of religious ideas and mere thoughtful conjectures.

From the idea of the subject which is contained in these first two points of view, it is necessary to pass on to the consideration of the third point, to the general review of this history and to the division of its progress into natural periods—such an arrangement to exhibit it as an organic, progressive whole, as a rational connection through which this history attains the dignity of a science. And I will not occupy further space with reflections on the use of the history of Philosophy, and other methods of treating it. The use is evident.

THE NOTION OF THE HISTORY OF PHILOSOPHY

It is easy to comprehend the aim of Philosophy, which is in thought and in conception to grasp the Truth, and not merely to discover that nothing can be known, or that at least temporal, finite truth, which also is an untruth, can alone be known and not the Truth indeed. Further we find that in the history of Philosophy we have to deal with Philosophy itself. The facts within that history are not adventures and contain no more romance than does the history of the world. They are not a mere collection of chance events, of expeditions of wandering knights, each going about fighting, struggling purposelessly, leaving no results to show for all his efforts. Nor is it so that one thing has been thought out here, another there, at will; in the activity of thinking mind there is real connection, and what there takes place is rational. It is with this belief in the spirit of the world that we must proceed to history, and in particular to the history of Philosophy.

The above statement, that the Truth is only one, is still abstract and formal. In the deeper sense it is our starting point. But the aim of Philosophy is to know this one Truth as the immediate source from which all else proceeds, both all the laws of nature and all the manifestations of life and consciousness of which they are mere rejections or to lead these laws and manifestations in ways apparently contrary, back to that single source, and from that source to comprehend them, which is to understand their derivation. Thus what is most essential is to know that the single truth is not merely a solitary, empty thought, but one determined within itself. To obtain this knowledge we must enter into some abstract Notions which, as such, are quite general and dry, and which are the two principles of Development and of the Concrete. We could, indeed, embrace the whole in the single principle of development; if this were clear, all else would result and follow of its own accord. The product of thinking is the thought; thought is, however, still formal; somewhat more defined it becomes Notion, and finally Idea is Thought in its totality, implicitly and explicitly determined. Thus the Idea, and it alone is Truth. Now it is essentially in the nature of the Idea to develop, and only through development to arrive at comprehension of itself, or to become what it is. That the Idea should have to make itself what it is, seems like a contradiction; it may be said that it is what it is.

The idea of development is well known, but it is the special characteristic of Philosophy to investigate such matters as were formerly held as known. The further discussion of this idea belongs to the science of Logic.

In order to comprehend what development is, what may be called two different states must be distinguished. The first is what is known as capacity, power, what I call being-in-itself (*potentia*); the second principle is that of being-for-itself, actuality (*actus*). If we say, for example, that man is by nature rational, we would mean that he has reason only inherently or in embryo: in this sense, reason, understanding, imagination, will, are possessed from birth or even from the mother's womb. But while the child only has capacities or the actual possibility of reason, it is just the same as if he had no reason; reason does not yet exist in him since he cannot yet do anything rational, and has no rational consciousness. Thus what man is at first implicitly becomes explicit, and it is the same with reason. If, then, man has actuality on whatever side, he is actually rational; and now we come to reason.

What is the real meaning of this word? That which is in itself must become an object, to mankind, must arrive at consciousness, thus becoming for man. What has become an object to him is the same as what he is in himself through the becoming objective of this implicit being, man first becomes for himself; he is made double, is retained and not changed into another. For example, man is thinking, and thus he thinks out thoughts. In this way it is in thought alone that thought is object; reason produces what is rational: reason is its own object. The fact that thought may also descend to what is destitute of reason is a consideration involving wider issues, which do not concern us here. But even though man, who in himself is rational, does not at first seem to have got further on since he became rational for himself—what is implicit having merely retained itself—the difference is quite enormous: no new content has been produced, and yet this form of being for self makes all the difference. The whole variation in the development of the world in history is founded on this difference. This alone explains how since all mankind is naturally rational, and freedom is the hypothesis on which this reason rests, slavery yet has been, and in part still is, maintained by many peoples, and men have remained contented under it. The only distinction between the Africans and the Asiatics on the one hand, and the Greeks, Romans, and moderns on the other, is that the latter know and it is explicit for them, that they are free, but the others are so without knowing that they are, and thus without existing as being free. This constitutes the enormous difference in their condition. All knowledge, and learning, science, and even commerce have no other object than to draw out what is inward or implicit and thus to become objective.

Because that which is implicit comes into existence, it certainly passes into change, yet it remains one and the same, for the whole process is dominated by it. The plant, for example, does not lose itself in mere indefinite change. From the germ much is produced when at first nothing was to be seen but the whole of what is brought forth, if not developed, is yet hidden and ideally contained within itself. The principle of this projection into existence is that the germ cannot remain merely implicit, but is impelled towards development, since it presents the contradiction of being only implicit and yet not desiring so to be. But this coming without itself has an end in view; its completion fully reached, and its previously determined end is the fruit or produce of the germ, which causes a return to the first condition. The germ will produce itself alone and manifest what is contained in it, so that it then may return to itself once more thus to renew the unity from which it started. With nature it certainly is true that the subject which commenced and the matter which forms the end are two separate units, as in the case of seed and fruit. The doubling process has apparently the effect of separating into two things that which in content is the same. Thus in animal life the parent and the young are different individuals although their nature is the same.

In Spirit it is otherwise: it is consciousness and therefore it is free, uniting in itself the beginning and the end. As with the germ in nature, Spirit indeed resolves itself back into unity after constituting itself another. But what is in itself becomes for Spirit and thus arrives at being for itself. The fruit and seed newly contained within it on the other hand, do not become for the original germ, but for us alone; in the case of Spirit both factors not only are implicitly the same in character, but there is a being for the other and at the same time a being for self. That for which the 'other' is, is the same as that 'other'; and thus alone Spirit is at home with itself in its 'other'. The development of Spirit lies in the fact that its going forth and separation constitutes its coming to itself.

This being-at-home-with-self, or coming-to-self of Spirit may be described as its complete and highest end: it is this alone that it desires and nothing else. Everything that from eternity has happened in heaven and earth, the life of God and all the deeds of time simply are the struggles for Spirit to know itself, to make itself objective to itself, to find itself, be for itself, and finally unite itself to itself; it is alienated and divided, but only so as to be able thus to find itself and return to itself. Only in this manner does Spirit attain its freedom, for that is free which is not connected with or dependent on another. True self-possession and satisfaction are only to be found in this, and in nothing else but Thought does Spirit attain this freedom. In sense-perception, for instance, and in feeling, I find myself confined and am not free; but I am free when I have a consciousness of this my feeling. Man has particular ends and interests even in will; I am free indeed when this is mine. Such ends, however, always contain 'another', or something which constitutes for me 'another', such as desire and impulse. It is in Thought alone that all foreign matter disappears from view, and that Spirit is absolutely free. All interest which is contained in the Idea and in Philosophy is expressed in it.

It is shown from what has been said regarding the formal nature of the Idea, that only a history of Philosophy thus regarded as a system of development in Idea, is entitled to the name of Science: a collection of facts constitutes no science. Only thus as a succession of phenomena established through reason, and having as content just what is reason and revealing it, does this history show that it is rational: it shows that the events recorded are in reason. How should the whole of what has taken place in reason not itself be rational? That faith must surely be the more reasonable in which chance is not made ruler over human affairs, and it is the business of Philosophy to recognize that however much its own manifestations may be history likewise, it is yet determined through the Idea alone.

Through these general preliminary conceptions the categories are now determined, the more immediate application of which to the history of Philosophy we have now to consider. This application will bring before us the most significant aspects in this history.

The first result which follows from what has been said, is that the whole of the history of Philosophy is a progression impelled by an inherent necessity, and one which is implicitly rational and *a priori* determined through its Idea; and this the history of Philosophy has to exemplify. Contingency must vanish on the appearance of Philosophy. Its history is just as absolutely determined as the development of Notions, and the impelling force is the inner dialectic of the forms. The finite is not true, nor is it what it is to be—its determinate nature is bound up with its existence. But the inward Idea abolishes these finite forms: a philosophy which has not the absolute form identical with the content must pass away because its form is not that of truth.

What follows secondly from what we have said, is that every philosophy has been and still is necessary. Thus none have passed away, but all are affirmatively contained as elements in a whole. But we must distinguish between the particular principle of these philosophies as particular, and the realization of this principle throughout the whole compass of the world. The principles are retained, the most recent philosophy being the result of all preceding, and hence no philosophy has ever been refuted. What has been refuted is not the principle of this philosophy, but merely the fact that this principle should be considered final and absolute in character. The atomic philosophy, for example, has arrived at the affirmation that the atom is the absolute existence, that it is the indivisible unit which is also the individual or subject; seeing, then, that the bare unit also is the abstract being-for-self, the Absolute would be grasped as infinitely many units. The atomic theory has been refuted, and we are atomists no longer. Spirit is certainly explicitly existent as a unit or atom, but that is to attribute to it a barren character and qualities incapable of expressing anything of its depth. The principle is indeed retained, although it is not the absolute in its entirety. This same contradiction appears in all development. The development of the tree is the negation of the germ, and the blossom that of the leaves, in so far as that they show that these do not form the highest and truest existence of the tree. Last of all, the blossom finds its negation in the fruit. Yet none of them can come into actual existence excepting as preceded by all the earlier stages. Our attitude to a philosophy must thus contain an affirmative side and a negative; when we take both of these into consideration, we do justice to a philosophy for the first time. We get to know the affirmative side later on both in life and in science; thus we find it easier to refute than to justify.

In the third place, we shall limit ourselves to the particular consideration of the principle itself. Each principle has reigned for a certain time, and when the whole system of the world has been explained from this special form, it is called a philosophical system. Its whole theory has certainly to be learned, but as long as the principle is abstract it is not sufficient to embrace the forms belonging to our conception of the world. The Cartesian principles, for instance, are very suitable for application to mechanism, but for nothing further; their representation of other manifestations in the world, such as those of vegetable and animal nature, are insufficient, and hence uninteresting. Therefore we take into consideration the principles of these philosophies only, but in dealing with concrete philosophies we must also regard the chief forms of their development and their applications. The subordinate philosophies are inconsistent; they have had bright glimpses of the truth, which are, however, independent of their principles. This is exemplified in the *Timæus* of Plato, a philosophy of nature, the working out of which is empirically very barren because its principle does not as yet extend far enough, and it is not to its principle that we owe the deep gleams of thought there contained.

In the fourth place it follows that we must not regard the history of Philosophy as dealing with the past, even though it is history. The scientific products of reason form the content of this history, and these are not past. What is obtained in this field of labour is the True, and, as such, the Eternal; it is not what exists now, and not then; it is true not only today or tomorrow, but beyond all time, and in as far as it is in time, it is true always and for every time. The bodily forms of those great minds who are the heroes of this history, the temporal existence and outward lives of the philosophers, are, indeed, no more, but their works and thoughts have not followed suit, for they neither conceived nor dreamt of the rational import of their works. Philosophy is not somnambulism, but is developed consciousness; and what these heroes have done is to bring that which is implicitly rational out of the depths of Spirit, where it is found at first as substance only, or as inwardly existent, into the light of day, and to advance it into consciousness and knowledge. This forms a continuous awakening. Such work is not only deposited in the temple of Memory as forms of times gone by, but is just as present and as living now as at the time of its production. The effects produced and work performed are not again destroyed or interrupted by what succeeds, for they are such that we must ourselves be present in them. They have as medium neither canvas, paper, marble, nor representation or memorial to preserve them. These mediums are themselves transient, or else form a basis for what is such. But they do have Thought, Notion, and the eternal Being of Spirit, which moths cannot corrupt, nor thieves break through and steal. The conquests made by Thought when constituted into Thought form the very Being of Spirit. Such knowledge is thus not learning merely, or a knowledge of what is dead, buried and corrupt: the history of Philosophy has not to do with what is gone, but with the living present.

THE RELATION OF PHILOSOPHY TO OTHER DEPARTMENTS OF KNOWLEDGE

The History of Philosophy has to represent this science in that form of time and individualities from which its outward form has resulted. Such a representation has, however, to shut out from itself the external history of the time, and to take into account only the general character of the people and time, and likewise their circumstances as a whole. But as a matter of fact, the history of Philosophy does present this character and that indeed in the highest possible degree; its connection with it is of the closest kind, and the particular appearance presented by a philosophy belonging to one special period, is only a particular aspect or element in the character. Because of this inward correspondence we have partly to consider more closely the particular relation borne by a philosophy to its historical surroundings, and partly, but pre-eminently, what is proper to itself, from which alone, after separating everything related however closely, we can fix our standpoint. This connection, which is not merely external but essential, has thus two sides, which we must consider. The first is the distinctly historical side, the second is the connection with other matters—the connection of Philosophy with Religion, for instance, by which we at once obtain a deeper conception of Philosophy itself.

But men do not at certain epochs, merely philosophize in general, for there is a definite Philosophy which arises among a people, and the definite character of the standpoint of thought is the same character which permeates all the other historical sides of the spirit of the people, which is most intimately related to them, and which constitutes their foundation. The particular form of a Philosophy is thus contemporaneous with a particular constitution of the people amongst whom it makes its appearance, with their institutions and forms of government, their morality, their social life and the capabilities, customs and enjoyments of the same; it is so with their attempts and achievements in art and science, with their religions, warfares and external relationships, likewise with the decadence of the States in which this particular principle and form had maintained its supremacy, and with the origination and progress of new States in which a higher principle finds its manifestation and development. Spirit in each case has elaborated and expanded in the whole domain of its manifold nature the principle of the particular stage of self-consciousness to which it has attained. Thus the Spirit of a people in its richness is an organization, and, like a Cathedral, is divided into numerous vaults, passages, pillars and vestibules, all of which have proceeded out of one whole and are directed to one end. Philosophy is one form of these many aspects. And which is it? It is the fullest blossom, the Notion of Spirit in its entire form, the consciousness and spiritual essence of all things, the spirit of the time as spirit present in itself. The multifarious whole is reflected in it as in the single focus, in the Notion which knows itself.

The Philosophy which is essential within Christianity could not be found in Rome, for all the various forms of the whole are only the expression of one and the same determinate character. Hence political history, forms of government, art and religion are not related to Philosophy as its causes, nor, on the other hand, is Philosophy the ground of their existence - one and all have the same common root, the spirit of the time. It is one determinate existence, one determinate character which permeates all sides and manifests itself in politics and in all else as in different elements; it is a condition which hangs together in all its parts, and the various parts of which contain nothing which is really inconsistent, however diverse and accidental they may appear to be, and however much they may seem to contradict one another. This particular stage is the product of the one preceding. But to show how the spirit of a particular time molds its whole actuality and destiny in accordance with its principle, to show this whole edifice in its conception, is far from us—for that would be the object of the whole philosophic world-history. Those forms alone concern us which express the principle of the Spirit in a spiritual element related to Philosophy.

This is the position of Philosophy amongst its varying forms, from which it follows that it is entirely identical with its time. But if Philosophy does not stand above its time in content, it does so in form, because, as the thought and knowledge of that which is the substantial spirit of its time, it makes that spirit its object. In as far as Philosophy is in the spirit of its time, the latter is its determined content in the world, although as knowledge, Philosophy is above it, since it places it in the relation of object. But this is in form alone, for Philosophy really has no other content. This knowledge itself undoubtedly is the actuality of Spirit, the self-knowledge of Spirit which previously was not present: thus the formal difference is also a real and actual difference. Through knowledge, Spirit makes manifest a distinction between knowledge and that which is; this knowledge is thus what produces a new form of development. The new forms at first are only special modes of knowledge, and it is thus that a new Philosophy is produced: yet since, it already is a wider kind of spirit, it is the inward birth-place of the spirit which will later arrive at actual form. We shall deal further with this in the concrete below, and we shall then see that what the Greek Philosophy was, entered, in the Christian world, into actuality.

The history of the other Sciences, of culture and above all the history of art and of religion are, partly in regard to the elements contained in them, and partly to their particular objects, related to the history of Philosophy. It is through this relationship that the treatment of the history of Philosophy has been so confused. If it is to concern itself with the possession of culture generally and then with scientific culture, and then again with popular myths and the dogmas contained only in them, and yet farther with the religious reflections which are already thoughts of a speculative kind, and which make their appearance in them, no bounds are left to Philosophy at all. This is so, partly on account of the amount of material itself and the labour required in working it up and preparing it, and partly because it is in immediate connection with so much else. But the separation must not be made arbitrarily or as by chance, but must be derived from fundamental determinations. If we merely look at the name of Philosophy, all this matter will pertain to its history.

I shall speak of this material from three points of view, for three related aspects are to be eliminated and separated from Philosophy. The first of these is that which is generally considered to be the domain of science, and in which are found the beginnings of understanding thought. The second region is that of mythology and religion; the relation of Philosophy to them seems often to be inimical both in the time of the Greeks and of the Christians. The third is that of philosophizing and the metaphysics of the understanding. While we distinguish what is related to Philosophy, we must also take note of the elements in this related matter which belong to the Notion of Philosophy, but which appear to us to be partially separated from it: and thus we may become acquainted with the Notion of Philosophy.

RELATION OF PHILOSOPHY TO RELIGION

As the first department of knowledge was related to Philosophy principally by means of formal and independent knowledge, Religion, though in its content quite different from this first kind or sphere of knowledge, is through it related to Philosophy. Its object is not the earthly and worldly, but the infinite. In the case of art and still more in that of Religion, Philosophy has in common a content composed entirely of universal objects; they constitute the mode in which the highest Idea is existent for the unphilosophical feeling, the perceiving and imagining consciousness. Inasmuch as in the progress of culture in time the manifestation of Religion precedes the appearance of Philosophy, this circumstance must really be taken account of, and the conditions requisite for beginning the History of Philosophy have to depend on this, because it has to be shown in how far what pertains to Religion is to be excluded from it, and that a commencement must not be made with Religion.

In Religion, races of men have undoubtedly expressed their idea of the nature of the world, the substance of nature and of intellect and the relation of man thereto. Absolute Being is here the object of their consciousness; and as such, is for them pre-eminently the 'other', a 'beyond', nearer or further off, more or less friendly or frightful and alarming. In the act and forms of worship this opposition is removed by man, and he raises himself to the consciousness of unity with his Being, to the feeling of, or dependence on, the Grace of God, in that God has reconciled mankind to Himself. In conception, with the Greeks, for instance, this existence is to man one which is already in and for itself and friendly, and thus worship is but the enjoyment of this unity. This existence is now reason which is existent in and for itself, the universal and concrete substance, the Spirit whose first cause is objective to itself in consciousness; it thus is a representation of this last in which not only reason in general, but the universal infinite reason is. We must, therefore, comprehend Religion, as Philosophy, before everything else, which means to know and apprehend it in reason; for it is the work of self-revealing reason and is the highest form of reason. Such ideas as that priests have framed a people's Religion in fraud and self-interest are consequently absurd; to regard Religion as an arbitrary matter or a deception is as foolish as it is perverted. Priests have often profaned Religion—the possibility of which is a consequence of the external relations and temporal existence of Religion. It can thus, in this external connection, be laid hold of here and there, but because it is Religion, it is really that which stands firm against finite ends and their complications and constitutes a region exalted high above them. This region of Spirit is really the Holy place of Truth itself, the Holy place in which are dissolved the remaining illusions of the sensuous world, of finite ideas and ends, and of the sphere of opinion and caprice.

Inasmuch as it really is the content of religions, this rational matter might now seem to be capable of being abstracted and expressed as a number of historical theorems. Philosophy stands on the same basis as Religion and has the same object: the universal reason existing in and for itself. Spirit desires to make this object its own, as is done with Religion in the act and form of worship. But the form, as it is present in Religion, is different from what is found to be contained in Philosophy, and on this account a history of Philosophy is different from a history of Religion. Worship is only the operation of reflection; Philosophy attempts to bring about the reconciliation by means of thinking knowledge, because Spirit desires to take up its Being into itself. Philosophy is related in the form of thinking consciousness to its object; with Religion it is different. But the distinction between the two should not be conceived of so abstractly as to make it seem that thought is only in Philosophy and not in Religion. The latter has likewise ideas and universal thoughts. Because both are so nearly related, it is an old tradition in the history of Philosophy to deduce Philosophy from Persian, Indian, or similar philosophy, a custom which is still partly retained in all histories of Philosophy. For this reason, too, it is a legend universally believed that Pythagoras, for instance, received his Philosophy from India and Egypt; the fame of the wisdom of these people, which wisdom is understood also to contain Philosophy, is an old one. The Oriental ideas and religious worship which prevailed throughout the West up to the time of the Roman Empire, likewise bear the name of Oriental Philosophy. The Christian Religion and Philosophy are thought of in the Christian world, as more definitely divided; in these Eastern days, on the other hand, Religion and Philosophy are still conceived of as one in so far as that the content has remained in the form in which it is Philosophy. Considering the prevalence of these ideas and in order to have a definite limit to the relations between a history of Philosophy and religious ideas, it is desirable to note some further considerations as to the form which separates religious ideas from philosophical theorems.

Religion has not only universal thought as inward content implicitly contained in its myths, ideas, imaginations and in its exact and positive histories, so that we require first of all to dig this content out of such myths in the form of theorems, but it often has its content explicit in the form of thought. In the Persian and Indian Religions very deep, sublime and speculative thoughts are even expressed. Indeed, in Religion we even meet philosophies directly expressed, as in the Philosophy of the Fathers. The scholastic Philosophy really was Theology; there is found in it a union or, if you will, a mixture of Theology and Philosophy which may very well puzzle us. The question which confronts us on the one side is, how Philosophy differs from Theology, as the science of Religion, or from Religion as consciousness? And then, in how far have we in the history of Philosophy to take account of what pertains to Religion?

Religion is also the point of view from which this existence is known. But as regards the different forms of knowledge existing in Religion and Philosophy, Philosophy appears to be opposed to the conception in Religion that the universal mind first shows itself as external, in the objective mode of consciousness. Worship, commencing with the external, then turns against and abrogates it as has just been said, and thus Philosophy is justified through the acts and forms of worship, and only does what they do. Philosophy has to deal with two different objects; first as in the Religion present in worship, with the substantial content, the spiritual soul, and secondly with bringing this before consciousness as object, but in the form of thought. Philosophy thinks and conceives of that which Religion represents as the object of consciousness, whether it is as the work of the imagination or as existent facts in history. The form of the knowledge of the object is, in religious consciousness, such as pertains to the ordinary idea, and is thus more or less sensuous in nature. In Philosophy we do not say that God begot a Son, which is a relation derived from natural life. Thought, or the substance of such a relation, is therefore still recognized in Philosophy. Since Philosophy thinks its object, it has the advantage of uniting the two stages of religious consciousness—which in Religion are different moments—into one unity in philosophic thought.

It is these two forms which are different from one another and which, as opposed, may therefore seem to be mutually conflicting; and it is natural and it necessarily seems to be the case, that on first definitely coming to view they are so to speak conscious of their diversity, and hence at first appear as inimical to one another. The first stage in the order of manifestation is definite existence, or a determinate Being-for-self as opposed to the other. The later form is that Thought embraces itself in the concrete, immerses itself in itself, and Spirit, as such, comes in it to consciousness. In the earlier stage, Spirit is abstract, and in this constraint it knows itself to be different, and in opposition to the other. When it embraces itself in the concrete, it is no more simply confined in determinate existence, only knowing or possessing itself in that diversity, but it is the Universal which, inasmuch as it determines itself, contains its 'other' within itself. As concrete intelligence, Spirit thus comprehends the substantial in the form which seemed to differ from it, of which it had only grasped the outward manifestation and had turned away from it; it recognizes itself in its inward content, and so it for the first time grasps its object, and deals justice to its opposite.

Generally speaking, the course of this antithesis in history is that Thought first of all comes forth within Religion, as not free and in separate manifestations. Secondly, it strengthens itself, feels itself to be resting upon itself, holds and conducts itself inimically towards the other form, and does not recognize itself therein. In the third place, it concludes by acknowledging itself as in this other. Or else Philosophy has to begin with carrying on its work entirely on its own account, isolating Thought from all popular beliefs, and taking for itself quite a different field of operation, a field for which the world of ordinary ideas lies quite apart, so that the two exist peacefully side by side, or, to put it better, so that no reflection on their opposition is arrived at. Just as little did the thought of reconciling them occur, since in the popular beliefs the same content appeared as in any external form other than the notion—the thought that is, of explaining and justifying popular belief, in order thus to be able again to express the conceptions of free thought in the form of popular religion.

Thus we see Philosophy first restrained and confined within the range of the Greek heathen world; then resting upon itself, it goes forth against popular religion and takes up an unfriendly attitude to it, until it grasps that religion in its innermost and recognizes itself therein. Thus the ancient Greek philosophers generally respected the popular religion, or at least they did not oppose it, or reflect upon it. Those coming later, including even Xenophanes, handled popular ideas most severely, and thus many so-called atheists made their appearance. But as the spheres of popular conception and abstract thought stood peacefully side by side, we also find Greek philosophers of even a later period in development, in whose case speculative thought and the act of worship, as also the pious invocation upon and sacrifice to the gods, coexist in good faith, and not in mere hypocrisy. Socrates was accused of teaching other gods than those belonging to the popular religion; his *daimonion* was indeed opposed to the principles of Greek morals and religion, but at the same time he followed quite honestly the usages of his religion, and we know besides that his last request was to ask his friends to offer a cock to Aesculapius—a desire quite inconsistent with his conclusions regarding the existence of God and above all regarding morality. Plato declaimed against the poets and their gods. It was in a much later time that the Neo-Platonists first recognized in the popular mythology rejected earlier by the philosophers, the universal content; they transposed and translated it into what is significant for thought, and thus used mythology itself as a symbolical imagery for giving expression to their formulas.

Similarly do we see in the Christian Religion, thought which is not independent first placing itself in conjunction with the form belonging to this Religion and acting within it—that is to say, taking the Religion as its groundwork, and proceeding from the absolute assumption of the Christian doctrine. We see later on the opposition between so-called faith and so-called reason; when the wings of thought have become strengthened, the young eaglet flies away for himself to the sun of Truth; but like a bird of prey he turns upon Religion and combats it. Latest of all Philosophy permits full justice to be done to the content of Religion through the speculative Notion, which is through Thought itself. For this end the Notion must have grasped itself in the concrete and penetrated to concrete spirituality. This must be the standpoint of the Philosophy of the present time; it has begun within Christianity and can have no other content than the world-spirit. When that spirit comprehends itself in Philosophy, it also comprehends itself in that form which formerly was inimical to Philosophy.

Thus Religion has a content in common with Philosophy, the forms alone being different; and the only essential point is that the form of the Notion should be so far perfected as to be able to grasp the content of Religion. The Truth is just that which has been called the mysteries of Religion. These constitute the speculative element in Religion such as were called by the Neo-Platonists being initiated, or being occupied with speculative Notions. By mysteries is meant, superficially speaking, the secret, what remains such and does not arrive at being known. But in the Eleusinian mysteries there was nothing unknown; all Athenians were initiated into them, Socrates alone shut himself out. Openly to make them known to strangers was the one thing forbidden, as indeed it was made a crime in the case of certain people. Such matters however, as being holy, were not to be spoken of. Herodotus often expressly says that he would speak of the Egyptian Divinities and mysteries in as far as it was pious so to do: he knew more, but it would be impious to speak of them. In the Christian Religion dogmas are called mysteries. They are that which man knows about the Nature of God. Neither is there anything mysterious in this; it is known by all those who are partakers in that Religion, and these are thus distinguished from the followers of other Religions. Hence mystery here signifies nothing unknown, since all Christians are in the secret. Mysteries are in their nature speculative, mysterious certainly to the understanding but not to reason; they are rational, just in the sense of being speculative. The understanding does not comprehend the speculative which simply is the concrete because it holds to the differences in their separation; their contradiction is indeed contained in the mystery, which, however, is likewise the resolution of the same.

The form of Religion is necessary to Spirit as it is in and for itself; it is the form of truth as it is for all men, and for every mode of consciousness. This universal mode is first of all for men in the form of sensuous consciousness, and then, secondly, in the intermingling of the form of the universal with sensuous manifestation or reflection—the representing consciousness, the mythical, positive and historical form, is that pertaining to the understanding. The essential truth contained in the testimony of Spirit only becomes object to consciousness when it appears in the form of the understanding, that is to say, consciousness must first be already acquainted with these forms from life and from experience. Now, because thinking consciousness is not the outward universal form for all mankind, the consciousness of the true, the spiritual and the rational, must have the form of Religion, and this is the universal justification of this form.

COMMENCEMENT OF PHILOSOPHY AND OF ITS HISTORY

Now that we have thus defined the Notion of Philosophy to be the Thought which, as the universal content, is complete Being, it will be shown in the history of Philosophy how the determinations in this content make their appearance little by little. At first we only ask where Philosophy and its History begin.

The general answer is in accordance with what has been said. Philosophy begins where the universal is comprehended as the all-embracing existence, or where the existent is laid hold of in a universal form, and where thinking about thought first commences. Where, then, has this occurred? Where did it begin? That is a question of history. Thought must be for itself, must come into existence in its freedom, liberate itself from nature and come out of its immersion in mere sense-perception; it must as free, enter within itself and thus arrive at the consciousness of freedom. Philosophy is properly to be commenced where the Absolute is no more in the form of ordinary conception, and free thought not merely thinks the Absolute but grasps its Idea. That is to say where Thought grasps as Thought, the Being (which may be Thought itself), which it recognizes as the essence of things, the absolute totality and the immanent essence of everything, and does so as an external being. The simple existence which is not sensuous and which the Jews thought of as God (for all Religion is thinking), is thus not a subject to be treated of by Philosophy, but just such a proposition as that 'The existence or principle of things is water', fire or thought.

Thought, this universal determination which sets forth itself, is an abstract determinateness; it is the beginning of Philosophy, but this beginning is at the same time in history, the concrete form taken by a people, the principle of which constitutes what we have stated above. If we say that the consciousness of freedom is connected with the appearance of Philosophy, this principle must be a fundamental one with those with whom Philosophy begins; a people having this consciousness of freedom founds its existence on that principle seeing that the laws and the whole circumstances of the people are based only on the Notion that Spirit forms of itself, and in the categories which it has. Connected with this on the practical side, is the fact that actual freedom develops political freedom, and this only begins where the individual knows himself as an independent individual to be universal and real, where his significance is infinite, or where the subject has attained the consciousness of personality and thus desires to be esteemed for himself alone. Free, philosophic thought has this direct connection with practical freedom, that as the former supplies thought about the absolute, universal and real object, the latter, because it thinks itself, gives itself the character of universality. Thinking means the bringing of something into the form of universality; hence Thought first treats of the universal, or determines what is objective and individual in the natural things which are present in sensuous consciousness, as the universal, as an objective Thought. Its second attribute is that in recognizing and knowing this objective and infinite universal, I, at the same time, remain confronting it from the standpoint of objectivity.

On account of this general connection between political freedom and the freedom of Thought, Philosophy only appears in History where and in as far as free institutions are formed. Since Spirit requires to separate itself from its natural will and engrossment in matter if it wishes to enter upon Philosophy, it cannot do so in the form with which the world-spirit commences and which takes precedence of that separation. This stage of the unity of Spirit with Nature which as immediate is not the true and perfect state, is mainly found in the Oriental conception of existence, therefore Philosophy first begins in the Grecian world.

Some explanations have to be given regarding this first form. Since Spirit in it, as consciousness and will, is but desire, self-consciousness still stands upon its first stage in which the sphere of its idea and will is finite. As intelligence is thus finite too, its ends are not yet a universal for themselves; but if a people makes for what is moral, if laws and justice are possessed, the character of universality underlies its will. This presupposes a new power in Spirit with which it commences to be free, for the universal will as the relation of thought to thought or as the universal, contains a thought which is at home with itself. If a people desire to be free, they will subordinate their desires to universal laws, while formerly that which was desired was only a particular. Now finitude of the will characterizes the orientals, because with them the will has not yet grasped itself as universal, for thought is not yet free for itself. Hence there can but be the relation of lord and slave, and in this despotic sphere fear constitutes the ruling category. Because the will is not yet free from what is finite, it can therein be comprehended and the finite can be shown forth as negative. This sensation of negation, that something cannot last, is just fear as distinguished from freedom which does not consist in being finite but in being for itself, and this cannot be laid hold of. Religion necessarily has this character, since the fear of the Lord is the essential element beyond which we cannot get. 'The fear of the Lord is the beginning of wisdom' is indeed a true saying; man must begin with this in order to know the finite ends in their negative character. But man must also have overcome fear through the relinquishment of finite ends, and the satisfaction which that Religion affords is confined to what is finite, seeing that the chief means of reconciliation are natural forms which are impersonated and held in reverence.

The oriental consciousness raises itself, indeed, above the natural content to what is infinite; but it only knows itself as accidental in reference to the power which makes the individual fear. This subordination may take two forms and must indeed from one extreme pass to the other. The finite, which is for consciousness, may have the form of finitude as finite, or it may become the infinite, which is however an abstraction. The man who lives in fear, and he who rules over men through fear, both stand upon the same platform; the difference between them is only in the greater power of will which can go forth to sacrifice all that is finite for some particular end. The despot brings about what his caprice directs, including certainly what is good, not as law, but as arbitrary will: the passive will, like that of slavery, is converted into the active energy of will, which will, however, is arbitrary still. In Religion we even find self-immersion in the deepest sensuality represented as the service of God, and then there follows in the East a flight to the emptiest abstraction as to what is infinite, as also the exaltation attained through the renunciation of everything, and this is specially so amongst the Indians, who torture themselves and enter into the most profound abstraction. The Indians look straight before them for ten years at a time, are fed by those around, and are destitute of other spiritual content than that of knowing what is abstract, which content therefore is entirely finite. This, then, is not the soil of freedom.

In the East, Spirit indeed begins to dawn, but it is still true of it that the subject is not presented as a person, but appears in the objectively substantial, which is represented as partly supersensuous and partly, and even more, material, as negative and perishing. The highest point attainable by the individual, the everlasting bliss, is made an immersion into substance, a vanishing away of consciousness, and thus of all distinction between substance and individuality—hence an annihilation. A spiritually dead relation thus comes into existence, since the highest point there to be reached is insensibility. So far, however, man has not attained that bliss, but finds himself to be a single existent individual, distinguished from the universal substance. He is thus outside the unity, has no significance, and as being what is accidental and without rights, is finite only; he finds himself limited through Nature—in caste for instance. The will is not here the substantial will; it is the arbitrary will given up to what is outwardly and inwardly contingent, for substance alone is the affirmative. With it greatness, nobility, or exaltitude of character, are certainly not excluded, but they are only present as the naturally determined or the arbitrary will, and not in the objective forms of morality and law to which all owe respect, which hold good for all, and in which for that same reason all are recognized. The oriental subject thus has the advantage of independence, since there is nothing fixed; however undetermined is the substance of the Easterns, as undetermined, free and independent may their character be. What for us is justice and morality is also in their state, but in a substantial, natural, patriarchal way, and not in subjective freedom. Conscience does not exist nor does morality. Everything is simply in a state of nature, which allows the noblest to exist as it does the worst.

The conclusion to be derived from this is that no philosophic knowledge can be found here. To Philosophy belongs the knowledge of Substance, the absolute Universal, that whether I think it and develop it or not, confronts me still as for itself objective; and whether this is to me substantial or not, still just in that I think it, it is mine, that in which I possess my distinctive character or am affirmative: thus my thoughts are not mere subjective determinations or opinions, but, as being my thoughts, are also thoughts of what is objective, or they are substantial thoughts. The Eastern form must therefore be excluded from the History of Philosophy, but still, upon the whole, I will take some notice of it. I have touched on this elsewhere, for some time ago we for the first time reached a position to judge of it. Earlier a great parade was made about the Indian wisdom without any real knowledge of what it was; now this is for the first time known, and naturally it is found to be in conformity with the rest.

Philosophy proper commences in the West. It is in the West that this freedom of self-consciousness first comes forth; the natural consciousness, and likewise Spirit disappear into themselves. In the brightness of the East the individual disappears; the light first becomes in the West the flash of thought which strikes within itself, and from thence creates its world out of itself. The blessedness of the

West is thus so determined that in it the subject as such endures and continues in the substantial; the individual mind grasps its Being as universal, but universality is just this relation to itself This being at home with self, this personality and infinitude of the 'I' constitutes the Being of Spirit; it is thus and can be none else. For a people to know themselves as free, and to be only as universal, is for them to be; it is the principle of their whole life as regards morality and all else. To take an example, we only know our real Being in so far as personal freedom is its first condition, and hence we never can be slaves. Were the mere arbitrary will of the prince a law, and should he wish slavery to be introduced, we would have the knowledge that this could not be. To sleep, to live, to have a certain office, is not our real Being, and certainly to be no slave is such, for that has come to mean the being in nature. Thus in the West we are upon the soil of a veritable Philosophy.

Because in desire I am subject to another, and my Being is in a particularity, I am, as I exist, unlike myself; for I am 'I', the universal complete, but hemmed in by passion. This last is self-will or formal freedom, which has desire as content. Amongst the Greeks we first find the freedom which is the end of true will, the equitable and right, in which I am free and universal, and others, too, are free, are also 'I' and like me; where a relationship between free and free is thus established with its actual laws, determinations of the universal will, and justly constituted states. Hence it is here that Philosophy began.

In Greece we first see real freedom flourish, but still in a restricted form, and with a limitation, since slavery was still existent, and the states were by its means conditioned. In the following abstractions we may first of all superficially describe the freedom of the East, of Greece, and of the Teutonic world. In the East only one individual is free, the despot; in Greece the few are free; in the Teutonic world the saying is true that all are free, that is, man is free as man. But since the one in Eastern countries cannot be free because that would necessitate the others also being free to him, impulse, self-will, and formal freedom, can there alone be found. Since in Greece we have to deal with the particular, the Athenians, and the Spartans, are free indeed, but not the Messenians or the Helots. The principle of the 'few' has yet to be discovered, and this implies some modifications of the Greek point of view which we must consider in connection with the History of Philosophy. To take these into consideration means simply to proceed to the dividing up of Philosophy.

DIVISION OF THE HISTORY OF PHILOSOPHY

Since we set to work systematically this division must present itself as necessary. Speaking generally, we have properly only two epochs to distinguish in the history of Philosophy, as in ancient and modern art—these are the Greek and the Teutonic. The Teutonic Philosophy is the Philosophy within Christendom in so far as it belongs to the Teutonic nations; the Christian–European people, inasmuch as they belong to the world of science possess collectively Teutonic culture; for Italy, Spain, France, England, and the rest, have through the Teutonic nations, received a new form. The influence of Greece also reaches into the Roman world, and hence we have to speak of Philosophy in the territory of the Roman world; but the Romans produced no proper Philosophy any more than any proper poets. They have only received from and imitated others, although they have often done this with intelligence; even their religion is derived from the Greek, and the special character that it has, makes no approach to Philosophy and Art, but is unphilosophical and inartistic.

A further description of these two outstanding opposites must be given. The Greek world developed thought as far as to the Idea; the Christian Teutonic world, on the contrary, has comprehended Thought as Spirit; Idea and Spirit are thus the distinguishing features. More particularly the facts are as follows. Because God, the still undetermined and immediate Universal, Being, or objective Thought, jealously allowing nothing to exist beside Him, is the substantial groundwork of all Philosophy, which never alters, but ever sinks more deeply within itself, and through the development of determinations manifests itself and brings to consciousness, we may designate the particular character of the development in the first period of Philosophy by saying that this development is a simple process of determinations, figurations, abstract qualities, issuing from the one ground that potentially already contains the whole.

The second stage in this universal principle is the gathering up of the determinations manifested thus, into ideal, concrete unity, in the mode of subjectivity. The first determinations as immediate, were still abstractions, but now the Absolute, as the endlessly self-determining Universal, must furthermore be comprehended as active Thought, and not as the Universal in this determinate character. Hence it is manifested as the totality of determinations and as concrete individuality. Thus, with the *nous* of Anaxagoras, and still more with Socrates, there commences a subjective totality in which Thought grasps itself, and thinking activity is the fundamental principle.

The third stage, then, is that this totality, which is at first abstract, in that it becomes realized through the active, determining, distinguishing thought, sets itself forth even in the separated determinations, which, as ideal, belong to it. Since these determinations are contained unseparated in the unity, and thus each in it is also the other, these opposed moments are raised into totalities. The quite general forms of opposition are the universal and the particular, or, in another form, Thought as such, external reality, feeling or perception. The Notion is the identity of universal and particular; because each of these is thus set forth as concrete in itself, the universal is in itself at once the unity of universality and particularity, and the same holds good of particularity. Unity is thus posited in both forms, and the abstract moments can be made complete through this unity alone; thus it has come to pass that the differences themselves are each raised up to a system of totality, which respectively confront one another as the Philosophy of Stoicism and of Epicureanism. The whole concrete universal is now Spirit; and the whole concrete individual, Nature. In Stoicism pure Thought develops into a totality; if we make the other side from Spirit—natural being or feeling—into a totality, Epicureanism is the result. Each determination is formed into a totality of thought, and, in accordance with the simple mode which characterizes this sphere, these principles seem to be for themselves and independent, like two antagonistic systems of Philosophy. Implicitly both are identical, but they themselves take up their position as conflicting, and the Idea is also, as it is apprehended, in a one-sided determinateness.

The higher stage is the union of these differences. This may occur in annihilation, in skepticism; but the higher point of view is the affirmative, the Idea in relation to the Notion. If the Notion is, then, the universal—that which determines itself further within itself, but yet remains there in its unity and in the ideality and transparency of its determinations which do not become independent—the further step is, on the other hand, the reality of the Notion in which the differences are themselves brought to totalities. Thus the fourth stage is the union of the Idea, in which all these differences, as totalities, are yet at the same time blended into one concrete unity of Notion. This comprehension first takes place without constraint, since the ideal is itself only apprehended in the element of universality.

The Greek world got as far as this Idea, since they formed an ideal intellectual world; and this was done by the Alexandrian Philosophy, in which the Greek Philosophy perfected itself and reached its end.

Grecian Philosophy in the Neo-Platonists finds its end in a perfect kingdom of Thought and of bliss, and in a potentially existent world of the ideal, which is yet unreal because the whole only exists in the element of universality. This world still lacks individuality as such, which is an essential moment in the Notion; actuality demands that in the identity of both sides of the Idea, the independent totality shall be also posited as negative. Through this self-existent negation, which is absolute subjectivity, the Idea is first raised into Spirit. Spirit is the subjectivity of self-knowledge; but it is only Spirit inasmuch as it knows what is object to itself, and that is itself, as a totality, and is for itself a totality.

Hence the Idea is this totality, and the Idea which knows itself is essentially different from the substantial; the former manifests itself independently, but in such a manner that as such it is considered to be for itself substantial. The subjective Idea is at first only formal, but it is the real possibility of the substantial and of the potentially universal; its end is to realize itself and to identify itself with substance. Through this subjectivity and negative unity, and through this absolute negativity, the ideal becomes no longer our object merely, but object to itself, and this principle has taken effect in the world of Christianity. Thus in the modern point of view the subject is for itself free, man is free as man, and from this comes the idea that because he is Spirit he has from his very nature the eternal quality of being substantial. God becomes known as Spirit which appears to itself as double, yet removes the difference that it may in it be for and at home with itself. The business of the world, taking it as a whole, is to become reconciled with Spirit, recognizing itself therein, and this business is assigned to the Teutonic world.

The first beginning of this undertaking is found in the Religion which is the contemplation of and faith in this principle as in an actual existence before a knowledge of the principle has been arrived at. In the Christian Religion this principle is found more as feeling and idea; in it man as man is destined to everlasting bliss, and is an object of divine grace, pity and interest, which is as much as saying that man has an absolute and infinite value. We find it further in that dogma revealed through Christ to men, of the unity of the divine and human nature, according to which the subjective and the objective Idea—man and God are one. This, in another form, is found in the old story of the Fall, in which the serpent did not delude man, for God said, 'Behold, Adam has become as one of us, to know good and evil'. We have to deal with this unity of subjective principle and of substance; it constitutes the process of Spirit that this individual one or independent existence of subject should put aside its immediate character and bring itself forth as identical with the substantial. Such an aim is pronounced to be the highest end attainable by man. We see from this that religious ideas and speculation are not so far asunder as was at first believed, and I maintain these ideas in order that we may not be ashamed of them, seeing that we still belong to them, and so that if we do get beyond them, we may not be ashamed of our progenitors of the early Christian times, who held these ideas in such high esteem.

The first principle of that Philosophy which has taken its place in Christendom is thus found in the existence of two totalities. This is a reduplication of substance which now, however, is characterized by the fact that the two totalities are no longer external to one another, but are clearly both required through their relation to one another. If formerly Stoicism and Epicureanism, whose negativity was Skepticism, came forth as independent, and if finally the implicitly existent universality of both was established, these moments are now known as separate totalities, and yet in their opposition they have to be thought of as one. We have here the true speculative Idea, the Notion in its determinations, each of which is brought into a totality and clearly relates to the other. We thus have really two Ideas, the subjective Idea as knowledge, and then the substantial and concrete Idea; and the development and perfection of this principle and its coming to the consciousness of Thought, is the subject treated by modern Philosophy. Thus the determinations are in it more concrete than with the ancients. This opposition in which the two sides culminate, grasped in its widest significance, is the opposition between Thought and Being, individuality and substance, so that in the subject himself his freedom stands once more within the bounds of necessity; it is the opposition between subject and object, and between Nature and Spirit, in so far as this last as finite stands in opposition to Nature.

The Greek Philosophy is free from restraint because it does not yet have regard to the opposition between Being and Thought, but proceeds from the unconscious presupposition that Thought is also Being. Certainly certain stages in the Greek Philosophy are laid hold of which seem to stand on the same platform as the Christian philosophies. Thus when we see, for instance, in the Philosophy of the Sophists, the new Academics, and the Skeptics, that they maintain the doctrine that the truth is not capable of being known, they might appear to accord with the later subjective philosophies in asserting that all thought-determinations were only subjective in character, and that hence from these no conclusions could be arrived at as regards what is objective. But there is really a difference. In the case of ancient philosophies, which said that we know only the phenomenal, everything is confined to that; it is as regards practical life that the new Academy and the Skeptics also admitted the possibility of conducting oneself rightly, morally and rationally, when one adopts the phenomenal as one's rule and guide in life. But though it is the phenomenal that lies at the foundation of things, it is not asserted that there is likewise a knowledge of the true and existent, as in the case of the merely subjective idealists of a more modern day. Those last still keep in the background a potentiality, a beyond which cannot be known through thought or through conception. This other knowledge is an immediate knowledge—a faith in, a view of, and a yearning after, the beyond such as was evinced by Jacobi. The ancients have no such yearning: on the contrary, they have perfect satisfaction and rest in the certitude that only that which appears is for Knowledge. Thus it is necessary in this respect to keep strictly to the point of view from which we start, else through the similarity of the results, we come to see in that old Philosophy all the determinate character of modern subjectivity. Since in the simplicity of ancient philosophy the phenomenal was itself the only sphere, doubts as to objective thought were not present to it.

The opposition defined, the two sides of which are in modern times really related to one another as totalities, also has the form of an opposition between reason and faith, between individual perception and the objective truth which must be taken without reason of one's own, and even with a complete disregard for such reason. This is faith as understood by the church, or faith in the modern sense, i.e., a rejection of reason in favour of an inward revelation, called a direct certainty or perception, or an implicit and intuitive feeling. The opposition between this knowledge, which has first of all to develop itself, and that knowledge which has already developed itself inwardly, arouses a peculiar interest. In both cases the unity of thought or subjectivity and of Truth or objectivity is manifested, only in the first form it is said that the natural man knows the Truth since he intuitively believes it, while in the second form the unity of knowledge and Truth is shown, but in such a way that the subject raises itself above the immediate form of sensuous consciousness and reaches the Truth first of all through Thought.

The final end is to think the Absolute as Spirit, as the Universal, that which, when the infinite bounty of the Notion in its reality freely emits its determinations from itself, wholly impresses itself upon and imparts itself to them, so that they may be indifferently outside of or in conflict with one another, but so that these totalities are one only, not alone implicitly, (which would simply be our reflection) but explicitly identical, the determinations of their difference being thus explicitly merely ideal. Hence if the starting-point of the history of Philosophy can be expressed by saying that God is comprehended as the immediate and not yet developed universality, and that its end—the grasping of the Absolute as Spirit through the two and a half thousand years' work of the thus far inert world-spirit—is the end of our time, it makes it easy for us from one determination to go on through the manifestation of its needs, to others. Yet in the course of history this is difficult.

We thus have altogether two philosophies—the Greek and the Teutonic. As regards the latter we must distinguish the time when Philosophy made its formal appearance as Philosophy and the period of formation and of preparation for modern times. We may first begin Teutonic philosophy where it appears in proper form as Philosophy. Between the first period and those more recent, comes, as an intermediate period, that fermentation of a new Philosophy which on the one side keeps within the substantial and real existence and does not arrive at form, while on the other side, it perfects Thought, as the bare form of a pre-supposed truth, until it again knows itself as the free ground and source of Truth. Hence the history of Philosophy falls into three periods—that of the Greek Philosophy, the Philosophy of the Middle Ages and the modern Philosophy. Of these the first is speaking generally, regulated by Thought, the second falls into the opposition between existence and formal reflection, but the third has the Notion as its ground. This must not be taken to mean that the first contains Thought alone; it also has conceptions and ideas, just as the latter begins from abstract thoughts which yet constitute a duality.

First Period—This commences at the time of Thales, about 600 B.C., and goes on to the coming to maturity of the Neo-platonic philosophy with Plotinus in the third century; from thence to its further progress and development with Proclus in the fifth century until the time when all philosophy was extinguished. The Neo-platonic philosophy then made its entrance into Christianity later on, and many philosophies within Christianity have this philosophy as their only groundwork. This is a space of time extending to about 1000 years, the end of which coincides with the migration of the nations and the decline of the Roman Empire.

Second Period—The second period is that of the Middle Ages. The Scholastics are included in it, and Arabians and Jews are also historically to be noticed, but this philosophy mainly falls within the Christian Church. This period is of something over 1000 years' duration.

Third Period—The Philosophy of modern times made its first independent appearance after the Thirty Years' War, with Bacon, Jacob Böhm and Descartes; it begins with the distinction contained in: *cogito ergo sum*. This period is one of a couple of centuries and the philosophy is consequently still somewhat modern.

THE END OF INTRODUCTIONS

'True reality is merely this process of reinstating self-identity, of reflecting into its own self in and from its other, and is not an original and primal unity as such, not an immediate unity as such. It is the process of its own becoming, the circle which presupposes its end as its purpose, and has its end for its beginning; it becomes concrete and actual only by being carried out, and by the end it involves'.

EDITORS' EPILOGUE

THE END OF INTRODUCTIONS

In the Introduction to the *Philosophy of Art*, Hegel spends a great deal of time considering the end or aim of fine art—does art have morality as its aim, or indeed, immorality, or does it aim to purify the passions? As is evident from Chapter 5, Hegel rejects any end attributed to art that lies outside of the domain of art itself. But that is not the point we are trying to make here. The issue being raised is, rather, the numerous alternatives that lie before us in terms of debating the end or aim of an *introduction*.

Introductions, though often self-sufficient, indeed tend to have their end outside of themselves; they tend to serve merely as propaedeutic to the body of a given text. Nevertheless, there are several famous instances where introductions have come to take on a certain life of their own, published and republished independent from the main text which they were originally meant to introduce. The Introduction to Heidegger's *Being and Time* is one such instance, as is Hegel's Introduction to the *Phenomenology of Spirit* as well as his Introduction to the *Philosophy of History*.

One might argue, on the other hand, that introductions cannot fruitfully be considered in isolation from the body of work they introduce, and to attempt to do so would be somewhat tantamount to being presented a cadaver along with the offer to shake its hand—no, a handshake is an opening to deeper acquaintance. From this point of view, it is perverse to present a string of introductions, which, though they provide a wide overview of Hegel's entire system, do not permit the reader to go deeper.

And yet, if one wished to push the point, it could be mentioned that Heidegger's magnum opus, *Being and Time*, could in its entirety be seen as introductory in the sense that it was merely the first part of an unfinished manuscript. Or, if you prefer, Hegel's *Phenomenology of Spirit* was explicitly meant by its author to serve in its entirety as an introduction to his even more capacious *Encyclopaedia*. According to the logic of those opposed to ending with an introduction, then, one may wish to retort that even the entire *Phenomenology* ought not to be read in isolation from the entirety of the *Encyclopaedia*, and Heidegger's *Being and Time* simply ought not to be touched, since it ends abruptly with no hope for a deeper association.

So, one might ask, is the now venerable tradition of publishing certain masterful introductions separate from their main works fruitful, or else is the practice, on the contrary, perverse and unhelpful? In the present volume, we have severed even more of Hegel's introductions from their main bodies than is normally done because we have sought to offer a panoramic introduction to Hegel's works. But it remains open to question, exactly how deep a foray into the writings and thought of G. W. F. Hegel has actually been achieved. This is naturally the question one *should* ask at the end of the introductions.

Now, it is our firm conviction that this collection of introductions is not only a valuable and worthwhile study, but that, to be sure, it is among the best means for any reader to become systematically introduced to this quintessentially systematic thinker. However, we would not go so far as to suggest that the reader has mastered Hegel's thought after having mastered his several introductions. In order to anchor this, we endeavour in this Epilogue to give a glimpse of what lies beyond the horizon of Hegel's introductions.

And in order to provide further direction, after here convincing the reader of his or her need for it, a list of Further Readings follows the Editors' Epilogue.

THE PHENOMENOLOGY OF SPIRIT

As mentioned, Hegel's Preface to *The Phenomenology of Spirit* is routinely read independently from the body of the book insofar as it is in itself a substantial contribution to philosophy. Nevertheless, the Preface, indeed brilliant in itself, is but a foretaste of one of the most brilliant and profound texts ever to have been composed. Sacrificing a summer in order to study Hegel's *Phenomenology* is a widely followed ritual among students of philosophy in universities around the world. This being so, it is difficult for us to maintain that readers are well-enough acquainted with the work by having studied its Preface. Authenticity and the inherent value of Hegel's *magnum opus* demand that one finds the urge to seek out and wrestle with the admittedly capacious and often opaque book.

Of special interest in Hegel's *Phenomenology* are the famous and influential sections on 'Lordship and Bondage', 'The Unhappy Consciousness', and 'Self-estranged Spirit'. The first-mentioned is also popularly referred to as the Master-Slave dialectic, and has been a central theme in continental thought, especially French social and political thought, since the 1930s. The last-mentioned, more commonly known as 'alienated Spirit', was the source of inspiration for Marx's notion of alienated labour, and this seminal idea of Hegel continues to preoccupy social and political thinkers around the world, but perhaps above all the Frankfurt school and the likes of Jürgen Habermas.

Again, the *Phenomenology* was intended by Hegel to serve as the introduction to his entire system of philosophy, and in that respect if one wanted to dive deeper into Hegel after having completed the present collection of his various introductions, the next step would seem to be to move on to the *Phenomenology*. At least, for philosophers. Political scientists, historians, art historians, or those interested in religious studies would rather opt for Hegel's writing relevant to these fields.

THE SCIENCE OF LOGIC

If there is one work of Hegel's that rivals the *Phenomenology* as the natural next step (for philosophers) after having completed the present volume, it is the *Logic*. The *Logic* is regarded as the Bible for Hegelians, and there is scarce a Hegel scholar who would deny that it is the definitive locus for Hegel's ontology and the essence, if you will, of his philosophy as such.

The *Logic* consists of three parts, as Hegel mentions towards the end of his Introduction: the logic of Being; the logic of Essence; and, the logic of the Notion or Concept. Each of these three parts is itself divided into three parts: under the logic of Being come the headings: Quality, Quantity and Measure; under Essence come: Essence as Reflection within Itself, Appearance, and Actuality; under the Notion come: Subjectivity, Objectivity, and the Idea.

Perhaps not surprising to readers becoming ever-more familiar with Hegel's systematic rigor, each of the three headings under each of the three main parts itself consists of three subheadings. For example, under the heading Quality (which is the first of the three headings under the main part, the logic of Being) come Being, Determinate Being, and Being-for-Self. To take another example, in the logic of the Notion, under Subjectivity (the first of its three headings) come the Notion (Concept), the Judgment, and the Syllogism.

Now, the triadic structure does not end there. Under each of these three subheadings (which are under three headings, which in turn are under three parts) come three further divisions or specific topics. For example, under the subheading Being (which is under the heading Quality) falls the tripartite division of Being, Nothing, and Becoming.

So, to put it all together, Hegel's *Logic* is developed on a series of triads which itself illustrates the nature of dialectic, or logic (or, in traditional thinking, the syllogism). We can visualize Hegel's structure through the diagram on the following page (the subdivisions used as examples above are in bold) .

This schema is basically the Table of Contents of the *Science of Logic*; however, it is also much more than that. The fact that the contents are in harmony with the form(s) of logic shows that Hegel's *Logic* can serve as an exemplar for his own demand—mentioned in many of the Introductions in the present volume—that the scientific presentation of a discipline requires identification and exposition of the inherent logic (or dialectic) of that discipline, rather than merely arbitrarily structured expositions.

The contents also show a certain resemblance to the Table of Categories found in Kant's *Critique of Pure Reason*, and indeed Hegel has Kant in mind throughout his study of logic as with all his other writings—the goal is to incorporate Kant's achievements while overcoming the limitations of his sys-

HEGEL'S *SCIENCE OF LOGIC*

MAIN PART	HEADING	SUBHEADING	TOPIC
The Logic of Being	Quality	Being	Being / Nothing / Becoming
		Determinate Being	
		Being-for-self	
	Quantity	Quantity	
		Quantum	
		The Quantitative Relation	
	Measure	Specific Quantity	
		Real Measure	
		The Becoming of Essence	
The Logic of Essence	Essence as Reflection Within Itself	Illusory Being	
		Determinations of Reflection	
		Ground	
	Appearance	Existence	
		Appearance	
		The Essential Relation	
	Actuality	The Absolute	
		Actuality	
		Absolute Relation	
The Logic of Notion	Subjectivity	The Notion	The Universal Notion / The Particular Notion / The Individual
		The Judgement	
		The Syllogism	
	Objectivity	Mechanism	
		Chemism	
		Teleology	
	The Idea	Life	
		The Idea of Cognition	
		The Absolute Idea	

tem. The essential limitation of Kant's critical philosophy, as Hegel understands it, is that for Kant the categories block our access to the absolute even as they constitute our access to the phenomenal world. This is Kant's overturning of Aristotle's categories, for whom the categories were the means of access to being, rather than an insurmountable hindrance to that access.

Hegel returns to the Aristotelian perspective insofar as the categories, that is, the logic, are the means of access to the real, rather than a hindrance to it. Hegel also returns to the Aristotelian perspective insofar as he understands the categories, logic, to be essentially and ineluctably tied up with ontology (and, we might add, language). This is, of course, not explicitly articulated in contemporary formal logic, which is, consistent with its name, merely formal.

Thus we should mention a couple of things about the relationship between Hegel's *Logic* and traditional logic. First, as has already been seen in his Introduction, Hegel rejects that logic should be grounded on the (ultimate) severance of truth and validity. From the traditional logician's point of view, this proclamation would sound just as absurd as Hegel's claim, from the first section of the *Logic*, that Being is non-Being. (To be more accurate, Hegel's point is that all Being is actually becoming, and that Being that is not becoming would be indistinguishable from non-Being.) Hegel does not intend thereby to undermine the basic principles of traditional logic, but rather to harmonize the structure and content of logic with that of all the other fields of knowledge organically related to it. Only if this is possible is the traditional logician's claim that logic is the foundation of all reasoning, and consequently, all the sciences, truly justified.

Second, although Hegel's logic would strike the traditional logician as radically alien, Hegel's intention is not to overthrow traditional logic but to elevate it, or, as Hegelians say, to sublate it. Hegel tries to assimilate traditional logic into his own, much grander, conception of logic, and to this end the third section, the logic of the Notion or Concept, contains within it a series of reflections on the topics of traditional logic, such as the various forms of the syllogism and judgment.

THE PHILOSOPHY OF RIGHT

The Introduction to the *Philosophy of Right* provides a detailed and difficult analysis not only of right, but also of the will and freedom. These are, indeed, the main themes of the book, but the Introduction is free of the specific details, such as laws, or constitutional clauses, as well as the historical surveys which fill the later pages of the work.

The book is, as usual, divided into three parts, the first of which is on Abstract Right, the second on Morality, and the third on Ethical Life. Each of these parts, again as usual, is divided into three sub-parts; for example, Ethical Life is subdivided into :*(i)* the Family, *(ii)* Civil Society, and *(iii)* the State. Then, yet again, these three sub-parts are themselves divided into three divisions. For example, the State (which was the third subdivision of Ethical Life) contains the three sections: *(a)* Constitutional Law, *(b)* International Law, and *(c)* World History.

The work is one of the most influential of Hegel's writings, and Marx has written a substantial critique that is one of his own most important works. Noteworthy is the distinction that Hegel makes between morality and ethical life, as also Hegel's portrait of the progression of ethical life, which permits one to juxtapose his own ideas with that of Aristotle (from the *Politics*) as well as Hobbes, Locke and Rousseau (on the social compact/contract) vis-à-vis the nature of, or indeed the naturalness of, the *polis* or state.

While discussing the triadic structure of the text, World History was mentioned as the third sub-part under the heading 'the State', itself the third subdivision under the heading 'Ethical Life'. What appears as World History in about eight pages in the *Philosophy of Right* is actually a highly condensed version of Hegel's *Philosophy of History*, to which we now turn.

THE PHILOSOPHY OF HISTORY

Truly one of the classics of the philosophy of history, of historiography, and of history itself, Hegel's *Philosophy of History* represents most powerfully and profoundly the optimistic linear-progressive view of history, as opposed to the cyclical view (such as available in Plutarch or Vico), or the pessimistic, non-progressive view (such as that of Spengler or Huntington). The crux of Hegel's argument is present in the Introduction itself, and the body of the work, which is basically a history book, stands more or less as an arrangement of historical details as support of the position already laid out in the Introduction.

The book, as history, is somewhat dated, as there have been innumerable archeological discoveries since the early-to-mid nineteenth century which have forced historians to reconsider the previously-accepted narratives. Nevertheless, in the main, it is still a worthwhile read not least because the reader is presented with a portrait of history wherein the perspective of the historian (his values, presuppositions, prejudices) is abundantly clear rather than hidden and obfuscatory.

Hegel's history consists of three main parts: the first on the Oriental World (covering China, India, Persia, Judaea and Egypt); the second on the Greek World (covering Greece and Rome); and the third on the Germanic World (covering the Arab world, the European middle-ages, the reformation, and Enlightenment up to modern times, which is to say up to Hegel's own day). Hegel's insights into the interrelation of Christian ideas and their secular political incarnation were the building block upon which Max Weber could construct his monumental work *The Protestant Ethic and the Spirit of Capitalism*. There is much to take issue with in both Hegel and Weber, but none can dismiss them without deep thought, reasoned reflection and intensive study.

THE PHILOSOPHY OF FINE ART

Today, among art historians and art critics, as well as philosophers of art and indeed even artists, one hears that a chasm has developed between those favouring *aesthetics* (which prioritizes the sensuous or retinal aspect of art) and those who prefer the approach of the *philosophy of art* (which undermines sensuousness by favouring the contemplative end of artistic experience). It is interesting, then, to recall that the very beginning of Hegel's Introduction to *The Philosophy of Fine Art* consists of remarks related to finding the adequate term to describe the project he has undertaken—is it 'aesthetics', or 'callistics' (from the Greek word *kalos*, meaning fine, noble, beautiful), or must a new word be found or formed? As may be brought to mind, Hegel chose to let the standard term *aesthetics* stand, as he felt that the substance or content of his reflections were far more significant than the name one chose to use to describe those reflections. But more to the point, the supposed chasm that divides contemporary theorists/practitioners of art might well be bridged by means of Hegel's own conception; for, Hegel, by defining art as 'the Idea in sensuous form', had early on already found a workable alternative to the antagonistic dualism between the sensuous and contemplative polarities of art.

The truth is, although Hegel's work contains numerous insights that could be advantageously marshalled to solve contemporary conundrums in our understanding of the nature of art (how to understand art after conceptual art, for example), Hegel's *Philosophy of Fine Art* is probably his least explored and studied work. It is, without a doubt, often obscure and difficult to penetrate, but this can hardly account for its neglect, as so many of Hegel's works are equally challenging. More likely, the cause for the lack of widespread interest in Hegel's view of art originates in his traditionalist prioritization of beauty, or the concept of the *beautiful*. Beauty has been marginalized in art theory since as far back as Impressionism, and seems in no condition now to make any manner of comeback (except in vulgar art, where indeed it has yet to be dislodged from its throne). But if this is the reason, it is a bad one.

Hegel's philosophy of art, far from perseverating on beauty as the ideal of art, is more preoccupied with understanding art in relation to other of man's highest spiritual achievements, such as religion and philosophy—and indeed, these too in relation to the character of the people who have created them. Thus, far more than just a philosophy of art (ordinarily conceived), Hegel's text contains an anthropology, a sociology, a psychology and a phenomenology of art. Thus it is clearly to be recommended as the next step after the present volume for anyone wishing to go further into Hegel who has a compelling interest in art, art history, and art theory.

THE PHILOSOPHY OF RELIGION

Hegel's *Philosophy of Religion* is not merely one of the first of such works; it is arguably one of the most important, and certainly the most comprehensive. Hegel's book does not merely articulate the concept, the essence of (and even the need for) religion as such, it also provides a sketch of the world's religions (organized according to Hegel's own systematic formula, consistent with his other works like the *Philosophy of History*), and then presents and defends the inherent superiority of one of these religions against all the others—protestant Christianity. Now, although Hegel's methods and end would be regarded as terribly politically incorrect, his writing is nevertheless for the selfsame reasons undeniably authentic.

Every canonical work in the philosophy of religion today seems to attempt to equalize all religious traditions (except perhaps primitive nature-religions engaging in human sacrifice or other atrocities which are therefore conveniently denigrated to the lower status of cult) and show us that they are all expressions of our common human nature and that they all seek the same ends. While this is surely a pleasant and most satisfying illusion to rest in, those who espouse this position must nevertheless make at least some effort to justify it (beyond simply labelling the alternatives as colonialist or prejudiced or racist or intolerant), and that ultimately means that current philosophers of religion are required to tackle Hegel's approach head on. We would not dare to suggest that this cannot be done, but instead seek to emphasize that it must be done. There is, however, presently very little serious work in this direction.

Therefore, just as we would suggest that anyone with an abiding interest in art would benefit from a venture into Hegel's *Philosophy of Fine Art*, it is clear that anyone with a serious interest in religious studies, comparative theology and the like would do well to turn to Hegel's *Philosophy of Religion*.

THE HISTORY OF PHILOSOPHY

Hegel's *History of Philosophy* is not only similar to his *Philosophy of History* in name, but also in scope, method and purposiveness. After the fascinating Introduction, which the reader has already encountered, wherein it is shown exactly how and why the history of philosophy is in its essence equivalent to philosophy (properly conceived), Hegel moves on to an intense and profound presentation and critique of the history of philosophy ranging from Thales, through to Aristotle, beyond through to Aquinas, continuing on to Descartes, to Kant, right up to the end: Hegel himself. It is no exaggeration to say that Hegel understood not only the history of philosophy to culminate in his own total, comprehensive, final philosophy, but indeed, he seemed to envision that history itself came to its ultimate fruition at Hegel, the world-historical individual.

It is easy to call Hegel a megalomaniac for thinking this, if indeed he did; it is more difficult, however, to prove him wrong. Why so? Because from the point of view of history and the philosophy of right (including constitutional/international law, the defense of parliamentary democracy as the 'natural' form of government, separation of powers, and so on), global leaders from all 'civilized' nations, and indeed the United Nations itself, espouse and defend nothing beyond the principles that Hegel did, and in perfect imitation of Hegel's thought, sing odes to freedom as the destiny of mankind. It is not mere coincidence that the European Union has chosen Beethoven's *Ninth Symphony* as its anthem: the greatest triumph-of-the-spirit work of Hegel's contemporary and acquaintance which is often referred to as Hegel's *Phenomenology of Spirit* set to music.

From the view of philosophy and its history, one may wish to keep in mind Derrida's dictum that 'the end of philosophy is the end of philosophy', which is to say that it has always been the end or aim of philosophy to solve the most perplexing puzzles that face us, and if these puzzles were indeed solved, then philosophy would have no further function, and would end: the end of philosophy is therefore the end of philosophy. It was Hegel's contention (and if Derrida is correct, it has been most philosophers' contention) that he answered the major, and even many of the minor, questions of philosophy: his encyclopedic system of the philosophical sciences was the compendium of all those answers, and thus if one was struggling with a plaguing philosophical question like What is Being?, for example, then all one had to do was to turn to the section on 'Being' in Hegel's *Logic*, and that was that.

CONCLUSION

We have moved from the end of introductions to the end of philosophy, and have now come to the end of this volume of introductions. Whereas the whole of the book has sought to provide a systematic, comprehensive introduction to the work of G. W. F. Hegel, we have been preoccupied in the Epilogue with highlighting how much more Hegel there is beyond this (series of) introduction(s).

In truth, the present volume, though introductory, does really bring us right in close to the heart of Hegel's thought. One would 'know Hegel' after having worked his or her way to this point. On the other hand, the aim (or end) of this Epilogue has been to maintain the balance, that is, to not allow the reader to be misled into believing that he or she has exhausted either the depth or the breadth of Hegel's work. So, while it is surely not necessary to claim that the reader has only just scratched the surface, it is required to reiterate that, there being so much more under the surface than with most writers, a great body of compelling and brilliant work awaits the reader whose interest in the thought of G. W. F. Hegel has been whetted, not sated, by this book.

FURTHER READINGS

Writings of G. W. F. Hegel in English Translation

Early Theological Writings, trans. T. M. Knox and Richard Kroner, Philadelphia, University of Pennsylvania Press, 1971.
The Difference Between Fichte's and Schelling's System of Philosophy, trans. H. S. Harris and Walter Cerf, Albany, State University of New York Press, 1977.
Phenomenology of Spirit, trans. J. B. Baillie, New York, Macmillan, 1910; *The Phenomenology of Spirit*, trans. A.V. Miller, New York, Oxford, 1977.
Hegel's Science of Logic, trans., W. H. Johnston and L. G. Struthers, London,

George Allen & Unwin, 1929; *Science of Logic*, trans. A.V. Miller, New Jersey, Humanities Press, 1997.

Philosophy of Right, trans. S. W. Dyde, New York, Dover, 2005; *Elements of the Philosophy of Right*, Allen Wood (ed.), trans. H. B. Nisbet, Cambridge, Cambridge University Press, 1996.

The Encyclopaedia Logic, with the Zusätze: Part I of the Encyclopaedia of Philosophical Sciences with the Zusätze, trans. Theodore F. Geraets, W. A. Suchting, and H. S. Harris, Indianapolis, Hackett, 1991.

Philosophy of Nature: Being Part Two of the Encyclopaedia of the Philosophical Sciences, trans. M. J. Petry, 3 vols., London, George Allen & Unwin, 1970.

Philosophy of Spirit: Being Part Three of the Encyclopaedia of the Philosophical Sciences, Together with the Zusätze, M. J. Inwood (ed.), trans. William Wallace and A. V. Miller with revisions and commentary by M. J. Inwood, Oxford, Oxford, 2007.

Philosophy of History, trans. J. Sibree, New York, Dover, 1956.

The Philosophy of Fine Art, trans. F. P. B. Osmaston, 4 vols., London, G. Bell and Sons, 1920; *Aesthetics: Lectures on Fine Art*, trans. T. M. Knox, 2 vols., Oxford, Clarendon Press, 1975.

Lectures on the Philosophy of Religion, trans. E. B. Speirs and J. B. Sanderson, 3 vols., London, Routledge and Kegan Paul, 1895; *Lectures on the Philosophy of Religion*, trans. R.F. Brown, P.C. Hodgson, and J.M. Stewart, 3 vols., Berkeley, University of California Press, 1984.

Lectures on the History of Philosophy, trans. E. S. Haldane and Frances H. Simson, 3 vols., Lincoln, University of Nebraska Press, 1995.

Political Writings, Laurence Dickey and H. B. Nisbet (eds.), trans. H. B. Nisbet, Cambridge, Cambridge, 1999.

Secondary Sources on the Writings of G. W. F. Hegel

Ashton, Paul, Toula Nicolacopoulos and George Vassilacopoulos (eds.), *The Spirit of the Age: Hegel and the Fate of Thinking*, Seddon, re.press, 2008.

Avineri, Shlomo, *Hegel's Theory of the Modern State*, London, Cambridge University Press, 1972.

Beiser, Frederick (ed.), *The Cambridge Companion to Hegel*, New York, Cambridge University Press, 1993.

Beiser, Frederick C., *Hegel*, London, Routledge, 2005.

Dickey, Laurence, *Hegel: Religion, Economics, and the Politics of Spirit, 1770-1807*, Cambridge, Cambridge University Press, 1987.

Ferrarin, Alfredo, *Hegel and Aristotle*, Cambridge, Cambridge University Press, 2001.

Forster, Michael N., *Hegel's Idea of a Phenomenology of Spirit*, Chicago, University of Chicago Press, 1998.

Franco, Paul, *Hegel's Philosophy of Freedom*, New Haven, Yale University Press, 1999.

Gadamer, Hans-Georg, *Hegel's Dialectic: Five Hermeneutical Studies*, trans. P. Christopher Smith., New Haven, Yale University Press, 1976.
Harris, H. S., *Hegel's Development: Toward the Sunlight, 1770-1801*, Oxford, Clarendon Press, 1972.
Harris, H. S., *Hegel's Development: Night Thoughts, 1801-1806*, Oxford, Oxford University Press, 1983.
Harris, H. S., *Hegel's Ladder*, 2 vols., Indianapolis, Hackett, 1997.
Houlgate, Stephen, *An Introduction to Hegel's Philosophy: Freedom, Truth and History*, 2nd ed., Oxford, Blackwell, 2005.
Jaesche, Walter, *Reason in Religion: The Foundations of Hegel's Philosophy of Religion*, trans. J. M. Stewart and Peter Hodgson, Berkeley, University of California Press, 1990.
Kojève, Alexandre, *Introduction to the Reading of Hegel*, trans. James H. Nichols Jr., Ithaca, Cornell University Press, 1980.
Lukács, György, *The Young Hegel: Studies in the Relations Between Dialectics and Economics*, London, Merlin Press, 1975.
Neuhouser, Frederick, *Foundations of Hegel's Social Theory: Actualizing Freedom*, Cambridge, Harvard University Press, 2000.
Nicolacopoulos, Toula and George Vassilacopoulos, *Hegel and the Logical Structure of Love: An Essay on Sexualities, Family and the Law*, Aldershot, Ashgate, 1999.
Pinkard, Terry P., *Hegel's Phenomenology: The Sociality of Reason*, New York, Cambridge University Press, 1996.
Pinkard, Terry P., *Hegel: A Biography*, Cambridge, Cambridge University Press, 2000.
Pippin, Robert B., *Idealism as Modernism: Hegelian Variations*, Cambridge, Cambridge University Press, 1997.
Rosen, Michael, *Hegel's Dialectic and its Criticism*, New York, Cambridge University Press, 1984.
Solomon, Robert C., *In the Spirit of Hegel*, Oxford, Oxford University Press, 1983.
Stern, Robert, *Routledge Philosophy Guidebook to Hegel and the Phenomenology of Spirit*, London, Routledge, 2001.
Taylor, Charles, *Hegel*, Cambridge, Cambridge University Press, 1978.
Toews, John Edward, *Hegelianism: The Path Toward Dialectical Humanism, 1805-1841*, Cambridge, Cambridge University Press, 1980.
Vassilacopoulos, George, *Logic and Utopia: Hegel's Science of Logic and the Order of Ethical Life*, Seddon, re.press, 2009 (forthcoming).
Westphal, Kenneth, *Hegel's Epistemological Realism: A Study of the Aim and Method of Hegel's Phenomenology of Spirit*, Dordrecht, Kluwer Academic Publishers, 1989.
Westphal, Kenneth, *Hegel's Epistemology: A Philosophical Introduction to the Phenomenology of Spirit*, Indianapolis, Hackett, 2003.

Williams, Robert R., *Hegel's Ethics of Recognition*, Berkeley, University of California Press, 1997.
Wood, Allen, *Hegel's Ethical Thought*, Cambridge, Cambridge University Press, 1990.

INDEX

Absolute 4, 5, 6, 7, 8, 9, 10, 11, 12, 15, 16, 17, 18, 19, 27, 29, 30, 31, 33, 34, 36, 41, 43, 44, 72, 78, 82, 92, 95, 96, 97, 98, 99, 103, 104, 105, 106, 107, 108, 117, 118, 122, 123, 124, 126, 130, 131, 132, 133, 137, 138, 139, 140, 142, 170, 171, 186, 194, 196, 197, 198, 199, 202, 203, 206, 207, 208, 209, 211, 212, 213, 214, 217, 228, 235, 237, 239, 242, 243, 253

Absolute knowledge 4, 5, 6, 7, 8, 9, 10, 11, 15, 16, 17, 31, 34, 72

Aesthetics 4, 12, 13, 14, 15, 18, 19, 116, 139, 140, 142, 155, 157, 158, 164, 165, 167, 172, 178, 180, 182, 183, 184, 241, 249, 254, 255, 256, 258

Aristotle 8, 9, 31, 53, 60, 61, 74, 118, 122, 253, 254, 256, 258

Art 4, 12, 13, 14, 15, 18, 19, 116, 139, 140, 142, 155, 157, 158, 164, 165, 167, 172, 178, 180, 182, 183, 184, 241, 249, 254, 255, 256, 258

Beauty 13, 14, 46, 148, 149, 157, 158, 159, 160, 163, 166, 173, 176, 179, 218, 255

Contingency 4, 12, 13, 14, 15, 18, 19, 116, 139, 140, 142, 155, 157, 158, 164, 165, 167, 172, 178, 180, 182, 183, 184, 241, 249, 254, 255, 256, 258

Death 13, 14, 46, 148, 149, 157, 158, 159, 160, 163, 166, 173, 176, 179, 255

Descartes 8, 9, 31, 53, 60, 61, 74, 118, 122, 253, 254, 256, 258

Dialectic 13, 14, 46, 148, 149, 157, 158, 159, 160, 163, 166, 173, 176, 179, 218, 255

Duty 13, 14, 46, 148, 149, 157, 158, 159, 160, 163, 166, 173, 176, 179, 218, 255

Empiricism 13, 14, 46, 148, 149, 157, 158, 159, 160, 163, 166, 173, 176, 179, 218, 255

Encyclopaedia of Philosophical Sciences 5, 94, 249, 258

Enlightenment, the 4, 254

Ethical Life 4, 12, 13, 14, 15, 18, 19, 116, 139, 140, 142, 155, 157, 158, 164, 165, 167, 172, 178, 180, 182, 183, 184, 241, 249, 254, 255, 256, 258

Faith 4, 12, 13, 14, 15, 18, 19, 116, 139, 140, 142, 155, 157, 158, 164, 165, 167, 172, 178, 180, 182, 183, 184, 241, 249, 254, 255, 256, 258

Family 13, 14, 46, 148, 149, 157, 158, 159, 160, 163, 166, 173, 176, 179, 218, 255

Fate 13, 14, 46, 148, 149, 157, 158, 159, 160, 163, 166, 173, 176, 179, 218, 255

Feeling 13, 14, 46, 148, 149, 157, 158, 159, 160, 163, 166, 173, 176, 179, 218, 255

Ficthe 8, 9, 31, 53, 60, 61, 74, 118, 122, 253, 254, 256, 258

Forgiveness 13, 14, 46, 148, 149, 157, 158, 159, 160, 163, 166, 173, 176, 179, 218, 255

For-itself 13, 14, 46, 148, 149, 157, 158, 159, 160, 163, 166, 173, 176, 179,

218, 255
God 4, 12, 13, 14, 15, 18, 19, 116, 139, 140, 142, 155, 157, 158, 164, 165, 167, 172, 178, 180, 182, 183, 184, 241, 249, 254, 255, 256, 258
Goethe 4, 100, 169
Habermas, Jürgen 3, 250
Heidegger, Martin 3, 13, 15, 19, 249
Heraclitus 4, 12, 13, 14, 15, 18, 19, 116, 139, 140, 142, 155, 157, 158, 164, 165, 167, 172, 178, 180, 182, 183, 184, 241, 249, 254, 255, 256, 258
History of Philosophy 4, 17, 19, 221, 223, 225, 229, 232, 239, 240, 256, 258
Husserl, Edmund 3, 13, 15
Idea 4, 12, 13, 14, 15, 18, 19, 116, 139, 140, 142, 155, 157, 158, 164, 165, 167, 172, 178, 180, 182, 183, 184, 241, 249, 254, 255, 256, 258
Idealism 13, 14, 46, 148, 149, 157, 158, 159, 160, 163, 166, 173, 176, 179, 218, 255
in and for-itself 13, 14, 46, 148, 149, 157, 158, 159, 160, 163, 166, 173, 176, 179, 218, 255
Individual[ity] 4, 12, 13, 14, 15, 18, 19, 116, 139, 140, 142, 155, 157, 158, 164, 165, 167, 172, 178, 180, 182, 183, 184, 241, 249, 254, 255, 256, 258
Infinite 4, 12, 13, 14, 15, 18, 19, 116, 139, 140, 142, 155, 157, 158, 164, 165, 167, 172, 178, 180, 182, 183, 184, 241, 249, 254, 255, 256, 258
In-itself 13, 14, 46, 148, 149, 157, 158, 159, 160, 163, 166, 173, 176, 179, 218, 255
Intuition 4, 12, 13, 14, 15, 18, 19, 116, 139, 140, 142, 155, 157, 158, 164, 165, 167, 172, 178, 180, 182, 183, 184, 241, 249, 254, 255, 256, 258
Justice 13, 14, 46, 148, 149, 157, 158, 159, 160, 163, 166, 173, 176, 179, 218, 255
Kant, Immanuel 4, 6, 9, 14, 77, 82, 251, 253
Kantian Philosophy 9, 10, 55, 83, 101, 107
Knowledge 4, 12, 13, 14, 15, 18, 19, 116, 139, 140, 142, 155, 157, 158, 164, 165, 167, 172, 178, 180, 182, 183, 184, 241, 249, 254, 255, 256, 258
Kojève, Alexandre 3, 259
Labour 13, 14, 46, 148, 149, 157, 158, 159, 160, 163, 166, 173, 176, 179, 218, 255
Language 4, 59, 65, 69, 78, 82, 100, 122, 145, 209, 253
Law 4, 12, 13, 14, 15, 18, 19, 116, 139, 140, 142, 155, 157, 158, 164, 165, 167, 172, 178, 180, 182, 183, 184, 241, 249, 254, 255, 256, 258
Leibniz 4, 12, 13, 14, 15, 18, 19, 116, 139, 140, 142, 155, 157, 158, 164, 165, 167, 172, 178, 180, 182, 183, 184, 241, 249, 254, 255, 256, 258
Locke 11, 254
Love 13, 14, 46, 148, 149, 157, 158, 159, 160, 163, 166, 173, 176, 179, 218, 255
Manifestation 13, 14, 46, 148, 149, 157, 158, 159, 160, 163, 166, 173, 176, 179, 218, 255
Marx, Karl 3, 250, 254
Mathematics 13, 39, 40, 41, 60, 65
Metaphysics 4, 12, 13, 14, 15, 18, 19, 116, 139, 140, 142, 155, 157, 158, 164, 165, 167, 172, 178, 180, 182, 183, 184, 241, 249, 254, 255, 256, 258
Morality 4, 12, 13, 14, 15, 18, 19, 116, 139, 140, 142, 155, 157, 158, 164, 165, 167, 172, 178, 180, 182, 183, 184, 241, 249, 254, 255, 256, 258
Nature 13, 14, 46, 148, 149, 157, 158, 159, 160, 163, 166, 173, 176, 179, 218, 255
Necessity 4, 12, 13, 14, 15, 18, 19, 116, 139, 140, 142, 155, 157, 158, 164, 165, 167, 172, 178, 180, 182, 183, 184, 241, 249, 254, 255, 256, 258
Objectivity 4, 12, 13, 14, 15, 18, 19, 116, 139, 140, 142, 155, 157, 158, 164, 165, 167, 172, 178, 180, 182, 183, 184, 241, 249, 254, 255, 256, 258
Organic 4, 12, 13, 14, 15, 18, 19, 116, 139, 140, 142, 155, 157, 158, 164, 165, 167, 172, 178, 180, 182, 183, 184, 241, 249, 254, 255, 256, 258

Parmenides 4, 12, 13, 14, 15, 18, 19, 116, 139, 140, 142, 155, 157, 158, 164, 165, 167, 172, 178, 180, 182, 183, 184, 241, 249, 254, 255, 256, 258
Particular[ity] 4, 12, 13, 14, 15, 18, 19, 116, 139, 140, 142, 155, 157, 158, 164, 165, 167, 172, 178, 180, 182, 183, 184, 241, 249, 254, 255, 256, 258
Phenomenology of Spirit 3, 4, 8, 19, 21, 23, 34, 39, 58, 72, 75, 76, 249, 250, 257, 258, 259
Philosophy of Fine Art 4, 12, 19, 155, 157, 254, 255, 256, 258
Philosophy of History 4, 11, 18, 19, 111, 113, 116, 249, 254, 256, 258
Philosophy of Religion 4, 15, 19, 191, 193, 195, 199, 203, 204, 205, 206, 255, 256, 258, 259
Philosophy of Right 4, 10, 18, 85, 87, 253, 254, 258
Plato 8, 9, 31, 53, 60, 61, 74, 118, 122, 253, 254, 256, 258
Platonic Philosophy 10, 14, 67, 73, 77, 166
Reason 4, 12, 13, 14, 15, 18, 19, 116, 139, 140, 142, 155, 157, 158, 164, 165, 167, 172, 178, 180, 182, 183, 184, 241, 249, 254, 255, 256, 258
Recognition 13, 14, 46, 148, 149, 157, 158, 159, 160, 163, 166, 173, 176, 179, 218, 255
Recollection 4, 12, 13, 14, 15, 18, 19, 116, 139, 140, 142, 155, 157, 158, 164, 165, 167, 172, 178, 180, 182, 183, 184, 241, 249, 254, 255, 256, 258
Revolution 4, 96, 115, 197
Right 4, 12, 13, 14, 15, 18, 19, 116, 139, 140, 142, 155, 157, 158, 164, 165, 167, 172, 178, 180, 182, 183, 184, 241, 249, 254, 255, 256, 258
Rousseau 11, 107, 135, 254
Schelling, F.W.J. 8, 9, 31, 53, 60, 61, 74, 118, 122, 253, 254, 256, 258
Science of Logic 4, 8, 19, 53, 55, 58, 67, 251, 257, 258, 259
Self 13, 14, 46, 148, 149, 157, 158, 159, 160, 163, 166, 173, 176, 179, 218, 255
Soul 13, 14, 46, 148, 149, 157, 158, 159, 160, 163, 166, 173, 176, 179, 218, 255
Space 13, 14, 46, 148, 149, 157, 158, 159, 160, 163, 166, 173, 176, 179, 218, 255
Spinoza 8, 9, 31, 53, 60, 61, 74, 118, 122, 253, 254, 256, 258
Spirit 4, 12, 13, 14, 15, 18, 19, 116, 139, 140, 142, 155, 157, 158, 164, 165, 167, 172, 178, 180, 182, 183, 184, 241, 249, 254, 255, 256, 258
Sprculative 4, 12, 13, 14, 15, 18, 19, 116, 139, 140, 142, 155, 157, 158, 164, 165, 167, 172, 178, 180, 182, 183, 184, 241, 249, 254, 255, 256, 258
State 13, 14, 46, 148, 149, 157, 158, 159, 160, 163, 166, 173, 176, 179, 218, 255
Subject 13, 14, 46, 148, 149, 157, 158, 159, 160, 163, 166, 173, 176, 179, 218, 255
Sublation 13, 14, 46, 148, 149, 157, 158, 159, 160, 163, 166, 173, 176, 179, 218, 255
Substance 13, 14, 46, 148, 149, 157, 158, 159, 160, 163, 166, 173, 176, 179, 218, 255
Syllogism 13, 14, 46, 148, 149, 157, 158, 159, 160, 163, 166, 173, 176, 179, 218, 255
Time 13, 14, 46, 148, 149, 157, 158, 159, 160, 163, 166, 173, 176, 179, 218, 255
Tragedy 13, 14, 46, 148, 149, 157, 158, 159, 160, 163, 166, 173, 176, 179, 218, 255
Truth 13, 14, 46, 148, 149, 157, 158, 159, 160, 163, 166, 173, 176, 179, 218, 255
Understanding, the 13, 14, 46, 148, 149, 157, 158, 159, 160, 163, 166, 173, 176, 179, 218, 255
Unhappy consciousness 13, 14, 46, 148, 149, 157, 158, 159, 160, 163, 166, 173, 176, 179, 218, 255
Universal[ity] 4, 12, 13, 14, 15, 18, 19, 116, 139, 140, 142, 155, 157, 158, 164, 165, 167, 172, 178, 180, 182, 183, 184, 241, 249, 254, 255, 256, 258

www.ingramcontent.com/pod-product-compliance
Lightning Source LLC
Chambersburg PA
CBHW021913180426
43198CB00034B/231